STREET FOOD

STREET FOOD

HAWKERS AND THE
HISTORY OF LONDON

CHARLIE TAVERNER

OXFORD
UNIVERSITY PRESS

OXFORD
UNIVERSITY PRESS

Great Clarendon Street, Oxford, OX2 6DP,
United Kingdom

Oxford University Press is a department of the University of Oxford.
It furthers the University's objective of excellence in research, scholarship,
and education by publishing worldwide. Oxford is a registered trade mark of
Oxford University Press in the UK and in certain other countries

First Edition published in 2023

Impression: 1

Published in the United States of America by Oxford University Press
198 Madison Avenue, New York, NY 10016, United States of America

British Library Cataloguing in Publication Data

Data available

Library of Congress Control Number: 2022942790

ISBN 978-0-19-284694-5

DOI: 10.1093/oso/9780192846945.001.0001

Printed and bound in the UK by
Clays Ltd, Elcograf S.p.A.

Acknowledgements

Street Food is a pandemic book. Its writing started in earnest during the first UK lockdown, so I am grateful to all the library and archive staff who made material accessible online, organized click-and-collect borrowing, and helped make research in person, when restrictions allowed, welcoming and safe. I'm also indebted to everyone who worked on the digital history projects on which I have heavily drawn. These resources have become essential for studying small or incidental subjects like food, and the crisis has only elevated their importance for all historians.

The book's origins lie in my doctoral research at Birkbeck, University of London, a truly special place. From that spell, I particularly need to thank Mike Berlin, Matthew Champion, Vanessa Harding, and above all Brodie Waddell. I was lucky to be one of Brodie's first students and benefit from such a diligent, generous, and inspiring supervisor. Laura Gowing and Mark Jenner were astonishingly kind and encouraging examiners. After my PhD, I made the very short journey across to the Institute of Historical Research. My postdoctoral fellowship, funded by the Economic History Society, allowed me to build my early modern work into a bolder project. The Grace Lawless Lee Benefaction Fund of the History Department at Trinity College Dublin supported the reproduction of images.

There is a long list of people who have shaped what follows, even if they do not know it. I am deeply appreciative of the conversations about street vendors, food, and urban history with Sarah Birt, James Brown, Melissa Calaresu, Aaron Columbus, Anna Cusack, Justin Colson, Evana Downes, Danielle van den Heuvel, Victoria Kelley, Beat Kümin, Anne Murcott, Sara Pennell, Will Tullett, and others. For taking the time to read various chapters, thank you to Esther Brot, Fred Carnegy-Arbuthnott, Susan Flavin, Ben James, Oskar Cox Jensen, Pete Jones, Jonah Miller, Emily Vine, and Jerry White.

Finally, I can never thank my friends and family enough, especially my Mum and Dad. Izzy, my partner in life and lockdown, not only suffered my street food ruminations while sat on the number 38 bus, but read the whole thing with her editor's eye. She helped me see the magic of cities, and led me to this book.

Contents

List of Illustrations

Note to the Reader

All dates in the book, including those before 1751, are based on a calendar year beginning on 1 January. Amounts of currency expressed in pounds (£), shillings (s.), and pence (d.) have not been converted to modern equivalents, but I have endeavoured to provide an impression of their contemporary value. When capitalized, 'City' refers to the area under the jurisdiction of the Corporation of London, what we think of as the Square Mile. 'London', 'metropolis', 'capital', and 'city' refer to the urban area as a whole. Historical quotations have been left in their original spelling, except when differences were potentially confusing.

Note to the Reader

Introduction
Hawkers and the history
of London

A hawker woke early, before most Londoners were up. Her home was a couple of rooms, cramped but with some comforts, in a tangle of narrow and dirty alleys, lanes, and yards tucked off a main drag. Stepping out, the streets were quiet, the light was dim, and the traffic still calm. After the day's first walk, the volume rose as she neared the market, with its creaking carts and bargaining chatter. She picked out what looked good, what was in season, what was priced just right, and loaded a basket or a wheelbarrow. Once more, she took to the streets, lugging the weight until she reached a reliable spot, where she set up shop on the roadside. Or she followed a route, going house to house, pausing only for a sale. Wherever she went, she called a rhythmic, tuneful cry, pitched to rise above the city's rumble and tug the ears of those indoors or passing by. Street work was full of dangers and the risks were acute for a woman alone. Her right to do business was never entirely secure. But her customers, metropolitans of every sort, were not concerned as they peered at her produce, delighted to sample a treat or have food delivered to their door. They were well aware that roadside vendors offering mackerel, cherries, asparagus, and pies helped feed the fast-growing capital.

At its essence, this work changed little from the late sixteenth century, when London's expansion into a sprawling metropolis had begun to accelerate, until the years leading up to the First World War. Throughout this span, street sellers came from a similar swathe of the working poor, trod the streets with similar tools and tactics, and played a similarly vital role in the city's food supply. Hawking would have been a similar experience for Ellen Rigate, who in 1610 sold apples and pears by a tavern between the

Figure 1. An apple seller on Cheapside in the late nineteenth century.

Thames and St Paul's; for Mary Davis and Mary Morson, who one morning in 1744 left their St Giles homes sometime after four, off to Billingsgate to buy fish; for the anonymous 'Coster-lad', interviewed by Henry Mayhew in the 1840s, who during his teens supported his mother by selling greens in the morning and nuts at night.[1] Street characters, drawn in famous series by artists Marcellus Laroon, Francis Wheatley, and Thomas Rowlandson and captured by nineteenth-century photographers, resembled each other. Take the snapshot of a late Victorian fruit seller standing on Cheapside (Figure 1). When you look past the gaslights, multi-storey shops, and railway logos painted on wagons, you realize the portrait could have come from any point in the previous 300 years. The advertising cries of traders like her were tuned by composers into melodies and recorded by folk song collectors for posterity. Street sellers' calls, like their work, seemed part of an ancient, London tradition.

These continuities belie how street trading changed. Who hawkers were shifted, as poor men joined what started as a female business and immigrants found that street work offered a foothold. What they sold changed too, most marvellously in the lengthening menu of foods that were ready to eat, as various as baked potatoes, sausages, and ice cream. Over time, street vendors used different equipment. Hawkers' famous barrows, for example, were not used widely until the end of the seventeenth century, and the donkeys that pulled them were another late arrival. These retailers traded in a transforming city, which they would have felt, in material ways, as they went about their work. London was made up of hundreds of thousands then millions more people, most of them poor, living in districts that were formerly villages and fields. The streets were gradually improved, their surfaces widened, paved, and cleaned, becoming better suited to the quickening traffic, including new types of transport, like the horse-drawn hackney carriage and omnibus. In contrast to her forerunners, the Cheapside apple seller of the photograph was welcomed in the wholesale markets and valued as part of London's food chain. But she faced fiercer competition for customers from more numerous and sophisticated shops, was forced to follow strict orders from police, and would have struggled to make her voice ring out above the escalating din.

This book explores the remarkable endurance of food hawking in London across a period of enormous change. Focusing on the heyday of street selling between 1600 and 1900, it recounts the history of this irregular work, done by poor women, men, girls, and boys, who despite their lowly status were integral to the city's economy and culture. They brought fresh food to neighbourhoods underserved by the slow-moving infrastructure of markets; they were the main carriers of perishable foods such as soft fruit, cheap fish, and milk; and they served snacks and meals for those without the room to cook or who spent the working day far from home. This history asks what the resilience and continued importance of informal retail means and how it challenges our understanding of the city's trajectory, from medieval capital to global metropolis. Food hawking leads us to a distinctive form of urban existence that persisted for several centuries, a street-based experience of working people who scraped, slogged, and hustled to get by. Hawkers help us reconstruct London's story around the basics of metropolitan life: interactions on the street, the exchange of essentials, and the struggle with material conditions, much of which took place outside formal institutions and fixed sites and beyond the grasp of governors and magistrates. In doing so, we find that London—rich, immaculate, twenty-first-century London—also has a deep hawking history, like the cities on every continent still underpinned by extensive informal economies and where the cries of hawkers still resound.

London to this day has street markets, some of which originate in the unauthorized gatherings of hawkers in the late Victorian city.[2] A short walk from my north London flat, vendors spreading out of shops and sheltering under stalls line Dalston's Ridley Road, where the grocery staples and ingredients from across the world are more than a match for the cavernous Sainsbury's and Iceland close by. Heading south, I can quickly reach Chapel Market, a long Islington street with regular traders of food and clothes at one end, and a weekly farmers' market at the other. Down on the fringe of the City, the sedate lunchtime stalls on Whitecross Street are a far cry from the hollering crowds that used to exemplify one of London's foulest slums. Important as they are to residents and nearby workers, the citywide significance of these modern-day markets is minimal. Another difference between them and their semi-legal ancestors? Who can trade and how is decided by a team of market officers from the council, who issue licences, mark out pitches, and clear up when the dealing is done.

In every borough, London remains full of 'street food'. From vans and gazebos, a local or tourist with money to spend can sample stuffed and steamed buns, comforting Thai stir fries, and lovingly tended barbecue, at prices that reflect fine cooking and well-sourced produce. Crowds pack street food markets for entertainment as much as sustenance, and aspirant chefs try out concepts that, for a lucky few, become restaurants. In 2018, the UK's street food industry was worth £1.2 billion and supposedly was growing faster than all sales of fast food.[3] In a symbol of acceptance among British consumers, Walkers Crisps launched two street food flavours.[4] A dining trend spurred on by tourism to Asia and Latin America and food-centric travelogue television, eating on the street has been cultivated into a consumer choice, a source of pleasure pretending to offer authentic insight, via the tastebuds, into exotic cultures. The street food phenomenon of the twenty-first century is very different from the street food of London's past. In earlier centuries, street food was a matter of everyday essentials, not just occasional luxuries. It was the fish, fruit, and vegetables carried in head-baskets and push-barrows to all corners, the morning milk hauled in pails from cowsheds to citizens' doors, and hearty morsels that satisfied the working population.

Historians and hawkers

To those acquainted with London's history, street sellers should be familiar. They have featured prominently in sweeping accounts of the city, as emblems of the grafting, impoverished lower orders and the rowdy street culture that has disappeared in the last hundred years.[5] They are best known through their representation in printed images, ballads, and music, a genre called collectively the Cries of London.[6] Historians of the seventeenth and eighteenth centuries have examined how hawkers were treated as a pressing social problem, akin to vagrants, thieves, and prostitutes, and how hawking was one of the beggarly jobs, like sweeping, cleaning homes, and singing ballads, that the urban poor patched together.[7] The most illuminating research has been done by historians of gender and work, who have shown how wives and widows, many of them working on the street, dominated the retail of fresh produce, even though their movement across the city sparked fears of disorder.[8] For the nineteenth century, we have a better appreciation of how street markets operated and the complex political and cultural significance of street sellers. The hawkers of Victorian London have been characterized as marginal figures who drew ambiguous reactions, 'at the same time fascinating, amusing, useful, pitiful, reprehensible, dangerous'.[9]

For the first time, I put street sellers at the centre of the narrative. I consider their work on its own terms, not as the flipside of more respectable or regulated activities, like the legitimate trading in official marketplaces and the shops that came to dominate the retail landscape. In a more rounded way than previous studies have attempted, I describe the many aspects of hawkers' work, and their position at the core of the city's food system, before establishing their wider cultural importance. By gaining a fuller understanding of irregular retail, we can explore more closely claims mentioned passingly in existing scholarship, such as the need for London's poor to eat outside the home or the importance of itinerant vendors to emerging districts.[10] Taking a long view lets us trace developments that are hard to track in the timespans that metropolitan histories typically cover. We can investigate why women hawkers at first outnumbered men but were overtaken by the nineteenth century, how far back anxieties about unaccompanied women moving through the streets really go, and whether the improvements to the built environment matched the ambitions of reformers.[11] This book is also focused firmly on the less well-off segments of the population. *Street Food* is a long London history, constructed around one part of the heterogeneous metropolitan majority, the working poor, and makes a case for the complexity and profound significance of their labouring lives.[12]

In writing this, I have been inspired by histories of hawkers in other large cities of the past, which have shown there is 'more to street vendors than their poverty and marginality', in the words of Melissa Calaresu and Danielle

van den Heuvel.[13] Their individual research and recent collection of essays
has proven the range of possible disciplinary approaches to the study of
hawking, approaches applied in cities as far apart in time and space as ancient
Rome, the dynamic early modern centres of Naples and the Netherlands,
and a megacity of the present like Kolkata. Even the London Cries are part
of a European tradition. The *Cris de Paris* are the most intensely studied, in
analysis that has brought together the practical aspects of hawking with the
uneasy presence of street folk in urban culture.[14] Historians of other French
cities, such as Lyon and Nantes, have demonstrated how semi-legal retailers
like hawkers were intertwined with the mainstream economy, rendering
distinctions like formal and informal less relevant in the cut and thrust of
daily commerce.[15]

Street vending is still a ubiquitous urban occupation, especially outside
Europe and North America. Current research is mostly engaged with
improving conditions for hawkers and seeks to nudge government policy.
This emphasis dates back to efforts by Western institutions to boost prod-
uctivity in post-colonial Africa in the late sixties and early seventies, when
the term 'informal economy' was coined.[16] Academics and activists have
come together in organizations such as WIEGO (Women in Informal
Employment Globalizing and Organizing), a network that aims to amelior-
ate the circumstances of the three in five workers worldwide with insecure,
unregulated jobs, and New York's Street Vendor Project, a membership
group providing legal support and advocacy for the city's more than 10,000
mostly immigrant outdoor traders. This book cannot give solutions to
hawkers' problems around the world, but it offers a historical perspective on
questions that keep cropping up about how we live with each other at close
quarters in cities.

Exploring the history of London's street sellers also encourages us to see
the capital in comparison with other past cities and those with vast, informal economies today, like Mexico City, Lagos, Bangkok, and Manila. I am
not saying that street selling signifies a primitive stage in metropolitan
development, a backward business cleared away as urban centres march
towards modernity.[17] Instead, I am interested in why the work of street selling was so vigorous in a city like London and how it adapted as that city
transformed. Though London's streets are now largely free of hawkers, cash-
in-hand work, like cleaning, hairdressing, childcare, and labouring, has never
gone away. In the last few years, the internet has fuelled the rise of a gig
economy, encompassing new jobs such as driving cars for Uber and delivering

packages for retailers like Amazon. Without steady earnings and automatic rights, gig workers confront similar hurdles to the street sweepers, cab drivers, and food hawkers of old London.

Medieval capital to metropolis

London on the brink of the twentieth century was a different beast from the city of 1600. We can measure this by population: already home to 200,000 people on James I's accession, the metropolis shrugged off plague, fire, and civil war to more than double in size by the century's end and strike the million mark around 1800. Though other British cities began to expand more quickly, the capital's growth in absolute terms was even more dramatic, hitting 2.7 million in 1851 and more than 6.5 million by the end of Victoria's reign.[18] We can also measure the extending area that could reasonably be called London. At the start of the seventeenth century, London had already breached its medieval bounds and, soon after, the numbers living outside the City, what we call the Square Mile, exceeded those living within. In the following 200 years, London, Westminster, and Southwark formed a single conurbation as the space between them filled with buildings. Smaller settlements in Middlesex, Surrey, and Essex were swallowed by the sprawl, which by 1900 spread even further than the 28 newly founded metropolitan boroughs, limited by Stoke Newington in the north, Lewisham in the south, Hammersmith in the west, and Woolwich in the east.[19] Etched on the city's fabric were the material changes of building and renovation, and technological advancement. The catastrophes of the early modern city, particularly the Great Fire of 1666, catalysed projects of renewal and planning, most impressively in the West End. The revolutions of the nineteenth century, foremost among them industrialization, electrification, and the introduction of railways, laid the foundations for a radically new urban experience. For a resident of this modern city, it might have felt, in the words of one recent chronicler, 'as though the whole living edifice was a creation of the past 100 years'.[20]

Miraculous as this London might have seemed, much of this change was of scale, not of nature. Throughout this period, a large, if not dominant proportion of the city's population could be classed as working poor. While not destitute, they laboured in unstable, ill-defined, and low-skilled jobs. They lived in a street-based city, where domestic and commercial space was at a premium, making the roadways and pavements hubs of conversation, argument, and trade. In 1900, London may no longer have been completely walkable—quickly crossing from one side to the other had probably not been possible for at least 200 years—but remained a city that got around on foot or by horse. The soundscape was still dominated by the same sounds, like church bells, the barks, whinnies, and shrieks of animals, and voices such as street cries, before they were drowned out by the roar of the motor car. In 1836, the capital's first train line started running between London Bridge and Greenwich, though the full effect of the railways on circulation and provisioning took decades more to play out. London's government continued to be fragmented. Since the metropolis had burst from the City's wards, most Londoners fell under the jurisdiction of county justices and parish vestries, some districts like St Martin-in-the-Fields becoming larger than most lesser English cities. Local bodies became increasingly standardized and London-wide authorities with specific responsibilities were eventually established, such as the Metropolitan Police and Metropolitan Board of Works, but until 1889, with the formation of the London County Council, London lacked a single, overarching government.[21]

The history of London is not always told over this duration. Most academic historians study the 'early modern' city, running from the early to mid-sixteenth century to as late as the mid-1700s, or a 'long eighteenth century' sometimes covering almost 200 years, or the 'modern' metropolis of the nineteenth century.[22] Certain histories, to be told at their fullest, are less easily bracketed, like those of food, the working poor, and the street.[23] A further problem with the standard timespans is they make it hard to explain long-term changes. As it grew, London was becoming modern, a term that we generally use to suggest newness, a break from the past with unsettling consequences. In cities, the process of modernization can be traced through a series of interconnected developments, including the renovation of streets and buildings and the rational organization of authorities like police, as well as cultural shifts such as commercialization and a rising sense of alienation. Modernization remains central to the story of London's growth, though we now understand it as a diffuse set of sometimes contradictory changes, rather than a single process.[24] Experts on earlier periods have also blurred the picture, showing that characteristics of modernity, like the worries about women travelling unchaperoned, were present in the Elizabethan city, and how most streets, still unimproved and choked with traffic, were not becoming obviously modern.[25] This history of hawkers offers a ground-level, centuries-long view on London's expansion. Focusing on poor workers and the practicalities of street work reveals that until the last decades of the nineteenth century, many defining features of life in the capital persisted. In this age of astonishing progress, the fundamental changes came late in the day.

Food hawkers came to the City government's attention towards the end of the sixteenth century. The aldermen accused wandering retailers of damaging the integrity of the official markets, where all trading was supposed to take place, and pushing up food prices. Despite such warnings, street sellers carved out a useful role throughout the seventeenth and eighteenth centuries. Though their legal right to do business could always be contested, the aldermen, along with parish vestries and magistrates in the wider metropolis, recognized their importance, giving hawkers leeway to keep trading as long as they caused no trouble. City people of every kind relied on street vendors for basic commodities, such as milk and mackerel, and a panoply of snacks obtainable for pennies. The increasing coverage and coherence of policing, particularly after the formation of the Metropolitan Police in 1829, threatened hawking's delicate position, but most officers were hesitant to disrupt a cornerstone of working class society. From the mid-nineteenth century, hawkers were congregating in street markets, parking their barrows in spots like the New Cut, Petticoat Lane, and Chrisp Street. Hawkers shrugged off repeated attacks—most famously, forcing an amendment to the 1867 Metropolitan Streets Act—and the number of street traders may have actually been rising in the late Victorian period, even faster than London's overall population.[26] But, step by step, police and local authorities became more prescriptive about how these irregular retailers should operate. In the 1920s, the metropolitan boroughs were granted powers to license all street vendors. Just as the appearance of motor cars was reformulating the capital's street culture, this shift in how hawking was regulated was a rupture from what came before.

As much as possible, I use 'hawker', 'street seller', and 'street vendor' to describe women and men who sold food on the streets, not in the shops or markets that made up London's formal or official economy. These terms were not used consistently throughout this period and, when they were employed, they did not just apply to those selling food. But I use them in their more neutral present-day sense, as a way of detaching these workers from the potentially derogatory labels applied to them over the centuries, like the early names 'fishwife' and 'huckster' and the later, catch-all term 'costermonger'. On the streets, Londoners could purchase an array of services and goods, from broom sellers, chimney sweeps, shoeblacks, and countless more vendors, whose experience shared much with their comestible-selling colleagues. Though food hawkers are the focus of this study, much of what we learn applies to other street workers, like porters and coach drivers, and other labourers without regular employment.

Histories of hawkers tend to use the same well-thumbed sources, above all the printed pictures of the Cries and Mayhew's ethnographic journalism in *London Labour and the London Poor*. Early modern scholars have usually examined evidence in which hawkers appear in conflict with authority, like the orders of City aldermen or the records of Bridewell prison. This book employs a more diverse assemblage of material. For the period 1600–1825, I have identified 858 individual street sellers and 443 specific acts of street selling, from a range of archival and printed documents. In some of these sources, such as witness statements at London's church courts and the accounts of criminal trials at the Old Bailey, hawking was unconnected to the matter at hand. In others, street sellers were being regulated, either locally by parish vestries and ward meetings, or by authorities with a wider remit, like the magistrates who doled out summary justice. In both cases, we can mine this evidence for incidental information about who hawkers were, what exactly they sold, and how and where they traded. For interested readers, I discuss these sources at more length in an appendix.[27] By piecing together these scraps, we can build a fine-grained picture of street selling in the older city to compare with what we know about the better-recorded nineteenth-century capital. Moving forward in time, the source base widens considerably. I have drawn on the famous surveys of London poverty by Mayhew and Charles Booth, along with journalism and parliamentary inquiries into topics like housing and markets. I have also used the rapidly proliferating newspapers, not only to provide vibrant details but also for reports of proceedings at London's police courts, which few historians of crime and policing have studied systematically.[28] With many aspects of street sellers' lives leaving few written records behind, I frequently rely on the images and music of the Cries genre, which surfaced at the point this study begins and remained popular in the Victorian city. I read the Cries critically, for what they reveal about how hawkers were perceived, and what they might tell us about the components of street sellers' work.[29] An irregular, loosely defined job like street selling does not produce an institutional archive. Telling the history of hawkers means stitching together very different types of material to gain access to these people and their livelihood.

It also forces us to take multiple approaches. In Chapters 1 and 2, I consider who hawkers were and how they were represented, then how their work was organized and understood—key issues of social and economic history. Drawing on the burgeoning field of food studies, Chapters 3 and 4 deal with the goods that hawkers sold and their dealings in the markets where they procured supplies. The following three chapters embrace cultural histories of the street, as well as the historical geography of the city. I consider how hawkers made the highway a place of petty commerce, where they fitted in the hierarchy of retail, the equipment they used, and the problems of trading among pedestrians and traffic. Having built up an impression of street vendors and their activities, the next two chapters offer a fresh take on well-worn subjects. In the first, I set out hawkers' relationship with the different layers of metropolitan authority, revealing a nuanced story of how street selling was regulated with restraint and pragmatism. The final chapter, informed by studies of music and the senses, concerns hawkers' advertising calls, another part of their trading toolkit, which further embedded these retailers in London culture.

At the end, in light of this long hawking history, I discuss the decline of street food selling in London over the twentieth century, and its recent revival as a culinary craze. The modern trend evokes memories of a previous city, just as hawkers in earlier centuries became vessels for nostalgia. If we want to get beyond these images, we have to listen to street sellers' cries and eavesdrop on their interactions with police. We have to stand by their barrows as they make a sale, sneak a glance at the food inside their baskets, and follow them back to their neighbourhoods and homes. In short, to know why hawkers matter, we first must understand who they were and how they worked. Far from minor characters, street food sellers were bound up in monumental processes of urban expansion and change, and raise difficult, nagging questions about the history of England's capital and cities around the world today.

I

People

According to slum journalists and health inspectors in the nineteenth century, there were tell-tale signs you were near a hawker's home. On entering an unpaved, narrow court, you would spy upended wheelbarrows stacked along a wall. From somewhere out of sight, you might hear a donkey bray: some street sellers shared a room with their equine companion, or several neighbours improvised a row of communal toilets into a stable.[1] Potato peel and cabbage leaves would litter the ground. Depending on the season and the time of day, you might have been splashed by men and women at washtubs scrubbing vegetables, freshening that morning's market haul.[2] Invited indoors, climbing rickety stairs or descending to a cellar, you would find a family squeezed into a room, a mother, a father, their children, perhaps a grandparent, with a single bed between them. They would have some consolations: cups and saucers on the sideboard, a mirror on the mantelpiece, a cat and kitten on the hearth. But there would be drying laundry strung wall-to-wall and a broken window patched with paper. Empty baskets would be piled in one corner; in the other, a full measure of apples would await the next day's business, their fragrance filling the room.[3]

To such observers, the way street sellers lived was typical of the rump of London's poor. Their plight blamed on racial weakness, moral failings, or the inequities of Victorian society, hawkers were emblematic of an underclass of workers, without a recognized trade and trapped in casual labour. For as long as they had walked the streets, hawkers had been reduced to such stereotypes. Writers, artists, and composers created street selling characters symbolic of wider issues. In reality, however, hawkers were hard to pin down. They were a diverse group of Londoners, at different stages in life, from various backgrounds, some much better, some far worse off than others. This wide-ranging experience was indicative of the many-layered working classes of which they were part. Who hawkers were changed across three centuries, but most always suffered a precarious, uneven existence and struggled to find a comfortable home.

Fishwives and costermongers

From the start of the seventeenth century, not long after London's expansion began, depictions of street sellers spread widely through metropolitan culture. Characters who sold food on the go and called out in advertisement were captured in printed images, elite music, and popular songs—part of the burgeoning genre known as the Cries—and sketched by writers in pamphlets and poems. The Cries genre flourished up to the mid-nineteenth century, when journalists of city low-life began to offer readers extensive descriptions of street selling figures. With care, we can study these depictions carefully for evidence of how hawkers worked. But they also present these poor workers as a series of types, revealing as much about the preoccupations of artists, writers, and their audiences as the truth of street sellers' lives.

The earliest of these types was the foul-mouthed, heavy-drinking 'fishwife'. In Donald Lupton's 1632 pamphlet *London and the Country Carbonadoed*, which satirizes a host of English characters, this seafood seller stands in for every kind of hawker:

> These Crying, Wandring, and Travailing Creatures carry their shops on their heads, and their Store-house is ordinarily Bilingsgate or the Bridgefoote, and their habitation Turnagaine-lane…when they have done theire Faire, they meet in mirth, singing, dancing, & in the middle as a Parenthesis, they use scolding, but they doe use to take & put up words, & end not till either their money or wit, or credit bee cleane spent out. Well, when in an evening they are not merry in an drinking-house, it is suspected they have had bad returne, or else have payd some old score, or else they are banke-rupts: they are creatures soone up, & soone downe.[4]

This fishwife subverts a slew of social norms. Rather than stick to a shop or marketplace, she roams the city, basket aloft. Supposedly married, she works and socializes away from her husband and associates with those selling sex ('Turnagaine-lane' evokes Turnmill Street in Clerkenwell, long linked to prostitution).[5] Her boozing and arguing are rejections of feminine decorum. On the whole, the fishwife is not a sexualized figure. A few decades later, the narrator of Ned Ward's *London Spy*, a literary ramble through London, compares a gathering of women fish sellers to a 'Litter of Squab Elephants'.[6]

Four for Six pence Mackrell
Maquereux quatre pour Six Sols
Quatre Sgembrij sii Soldi

Mauron delin: *P.Tempest exc:*
                                   Cum Privilegio

Figure 2. The mackerel seller from Marcellus Laroon's landmark series of printed images, *The Cryes of the City of London Drawne After the Life.*

Instead, the fishwife is an essentially comic creation, whose behaviour poked and prodded the conventions of early modern society. The stereotype certainly influenced Marcellus Laroon's drawing of a mackerel seller (Figure 2), from his 1687 suite of printed images, *The Cryes of the City of London*. In a patched costume and creased hat, the old woman seems to be winking. From her hand, bizarrely, swings a lone fish.

This strange character was the product of a specific moment in metropolitan culture. Running against expectations of gender and sexuality, the fishwife embodied the anxieties of a strongly patriarchal society about women working and moving through the city independently.[7] She appeared in print, songs, and ballads from the 1590s, a fraught decade in London history, when the population was surging and prices were rising, leading to heightened attention on marginal groups, such as the poor, vagrants, and women retailers. Around this time, the City aldermen first tried to force street sellers to take out licences, as a way of capping their numbers and regulating their behaviour. In this context, the character of the fishwife was the paradigmatic unruly trader, a foil to more orderly, male-dominated commerce.[8] Even divorced from her origins, the fishwife endured as a London type. Billingsgate, the waterside market where these women stocked up, remained slang for coarse language until well after 1800.[9]

As the genre of Cries developed, the cast of street selling characters grew. Boisterous fishwives were joined by erotic oyster sellers, bucolic milkmaids, rosy-cheeked women selling new season strawberries, and Jewish men in long coats with baskets of oranges. At the same time, the depictions diverged in style and tone. Visual artists pursued two loose traditions: building on Laroon's landmark prints, artists like Jacopo Amigoni and Francis Wheatley presented hawkers as a succession of idealized types, posing in pleasant, picturesque scenes with overtones of sentimentality; in reaction, William Hogarth, Paul Sandby, and Thomas Rowlandson took a more playful approach to these well-worn characters, creating Cries images that were 'naturalist rather than sentimental, comic rather than serious, and satiric rather than congratulatory'. Rather than suggesting a more peaceful urban past, these latter artists used street sellers to demonstrate the rough and raucous actuality of London's present.[10] This meant that, in some eighteenth-century prints, women milk sellers were shown benevolently doling out cupfuls to cherubic youths. Or they appear dancing and dressed up on May Day, with crowns of metalware and ribbons on their heads, a custom that recalled a simpler, rustic lifestyle.[11] Meanwhile, Sandby's milkmaid (Figure 3) is in the heat of work, serving an older woman. The hawker wears heavy, practical clothes and her attention is focused on a tally stick, emphasizing the commerciality of her labours. The drabness is reminiscent of the 'sallow Milk-maid' in John Gay's 1716 poem *Trivia*, who glumly chalks her bills on the doors of customers, and is compared unfavourably to the healthy, vivacious 'Milk-maid of the Plains'.[12]

Figure 3. A milk seller marking an account at a customer's door.

If the Cries reflected divergent opinions about how London was changing, in the nineteenth century depictions of street sellers focused overwhelmingly on their poverty and low status. The dominant stereotype became the 'costermonger'. Though the term has a long history associated with the selling of fruit, this character was fleshed out most fully in Henry Mayhew's *London Labour*, a journalistic survey of the city's poorest sorts, which started as a series of newspaper articles in 1849, continued as a

standalone periodical, and was published as a multi-volume book.[13] Mayhew
described street sellers as a class apart. As well as possessing a culture distinct
from more respectable workers, these 'nomad tribes' were a separate race,
which gave them high cheekbones, strong jaws, an indecipherable dialect,
and a distaste of religion.[14] Though later writers did not always apply the
same racialized thinking, they still presented hawkers as members of the
intransigent, unreformable poor. This characterization was influenced by
both the damaging impacts of economic growth, and middle class and
educated prejudices. Street traders were part of the mass of casual labour
produced by the particular structures and lop-sided growth of London's
economy, which became a creeping source of concern as the Victorian era
progressed. Mayhew's investigations anticipated the hand-wringing over the
health and housing of the working classes of the 1880s, which revealed the
existence of a chronically poor 'residuum' living in filthy neighbourhoods.[15]

   This Victorian costermonger typically sold fish, fruit, or vegetables, which
he carried through the streets on a barrow pulled by a donkey (costermongers were mainly men, though their wives could assist or keep a stall). That
is just how he appears in one of the images accompanying Mayhew's text,
from a daguerreotype by Richard Beard (Figure 4). Wearing a long jacket,
waistcoat, and cap, the hawker stands atop his cart, holding the harness of his
donkey in one hand and a whip or stick in the other. The caption below
tells us he is crying, in a heavy accent, 'Here Pertaters! Kearots and Turnups!
Fine Brockello-o-o!'[16] This figure featured frequently in popular entertainments, like at the music hall, where famous performers played street selling
characters and sang wise-cracking songs.[17] On the stage and in the street, art
and reality blurred. An April 1892 news report about a case of hawkers causing an obstruction made the link between the music hall and the street
market. The article began: 'The characteristic delineator and poet laureate of
the London coster, Mr Albert Chevalier, of "Knocked 'em in the Old Kent-
road" fame, might have found the text for a fresh song at the City Summons
court on Saturday.'[18] Increasingly divorced from its origins on the street, the
costermonger character eventually underpinned later archetypes of London
working class culture, like cockneys and pearly kings and queens.[19]

   These stereotypes were not merely the product of the imaginations of
artists, performers, and their audiences. Details from the street and aspects
of real-life hawkers of course fed into the content of the Cries. Collectors of
early prints, like the diarist Samuel Pepys, marked up their copies with notes
on real people the figures resembled.[20] The journalism of Mayhew and

THE LONDON COSTERMONGER.

" Here Pertaters ! Kearots and Turnups ! Fine Brockello-o-o !"

[*From a Daguerreotype by* BEARD.]

Figure 4. A stereotypical London costermonger, as pictured alongside Henry Mayhew's descriptions in *London Labour and the London Poor.*

those who came after him not only allowed the stories and voices of hawkers to come to the fore, but was the result of interactions between investigators and interviewees.[21] Even so, genres like the Cries and the low-life surveys of the nineteenth century boiled down the complexity of the street trades into recognizable types and tropes. This allowed hawkers to become powerful symbols. But for exploring the history of street selling, these characters obscure as much as they reveal.

All sorts of Londoners

When we consider the 858 hawkers identified between 1600 and 1825, alongside the voluminous surveys and journalism produced from the mid-nineteenth century, it soon becomes clear that street sellers' lives were not easily summed up. Very different people took up baskets and pushed barrows. The subtle shifts in who did so and why were connected to some of the major transformations in the capital's history.

Over the course of three centuries, selling food in the street went from a business dominated by women to one where men were at the forefront. Among the several hundred street selling individuals, the proportion of women fell from 82 per cent up to 1675, to 68 per cent over the next 75 years, to 61 per cent over the final third of the period. In the 1851 census, the number of women among those London residents who can be categorized as 'street sellers, pedlars, and hawkers'—many of those were not just selling food—was 38 per cent. By 1901, this had fallen to 27 per cent.[22] On the surface, it seems the seventeenth century of the fishwife gave way to the nineteenth century of the costermonger.

Those apparently convincing figures should be handled with care: the pre-1825 numbers derive from multiple sources and are unevenly spread over time, while the snapshots offered by the census are not as transparent as they appear.[23] Rather than precise measures, they propose more general, if still meaningful patterns. The first is that women continued to earn a living selling food on the street throughout London's history. The male costermonger may have become the standard representation of a hawker, but he always had a female counterpart. If anything, many more women, especially those who were married, were hawking food in Victorian London than statistical surveys like the census, which underestimated part-time, intermittent, or seasonal work, could count.[24] Anecdotal evidence also suggests this was the case. Testifying to a parliamentary committee in 1839, a Covent Garden wholesaler claimed that more women than men sold fruit from wheelbarrows and street stalls across the capital.[25] Women described as 'costermongers' were regularly summoned to the nineteenth-century police courts. Among them were Margaret Larey, the infamous 'terror of Whitecross

Street', and Sarah Hughes, who by 1882 had faced charges before magistrates more than sixty times.[26]

If most London hawkers were initially women, they were gradually joined by more men. Those men never took over the street trade entirely, but at an early stage ascended to the upper tiers of its more lucrative sectors, such as the milk business. This encroachment connects to long-term changes in the status and range of women's work, processes that continue to be debated among historians. In their classic studies, Alice Clark and Ivy Pinchbeck argued that developing capitalism in the seventeenth century pushed women out of skilled industries, before the industrial revolution further diminished the home-based production and commerce to which women had been integral.[27] Since then, historians have honed in on the late eighteenth and early nineteenth centuries as a critical period, when the models emerged of separate spheres, in which women were restricted to the private realm, and of the male breadwinner supporting his family.[28] These narratives have been well contested and we know that middle and working class women kept working in a multitude of occupations and most labouring households would have failed to get by without a woman's contributions.[29] We also know that, since at least the late medieval period, a patriarchal culture and economy thrust the majority of women into work that was 'part-time, unskilled or semi-skilled, and poorly paid'.[30] For London women, the story was one of continuity. Between the late sixteenth and early twentieth centuries, most remained in the same collection of jobs: domestic service, needlework, laundry, and branches of retail.[31] The transition that took place involved more and more metropolitan men resorting to similar employment that was low status and insecure.

The stereotype of the fishwife contained an element of truth. During the seventeenth and eighteenth centuries, when the character featured prominently in the Cries, street selling was one of the most common jobs for women who were married.[32] Within the sample of individuals, women street sellers had husbands who were labourers, porters, coalheavers, bricklayers, sailors, servants, painters, butchers, gardeners, pewterers, silk-weavers, hairdressers, and tailors. Several of their spouses were food hawkers too. The job may have been even more important to married women than we can judge: the legal doctrine of coverture, in which a woman's legal status was subsumed by her husband, hid much of wives' independent labour.[33] Because selling small amounts of food could be done from time to time, married women could fit such extra activities around their domestic duties. Yet the trade also attracted widows and the city's many singletons.[34]

Street sellers were Londoners at every stage in life. Within the individual hawkers identified up to 1825, the median age was 22, with the women on average slightly older than the men.[35] Clearly many street sellers were in their physical prime. This was still true in the 1890s, when 70 per cent of London men giving their occupation as 'coster' or 'street seller' were between 20 and 54.[36] Hawking was never just a job for those with no alternative.

Done in different ways, it suited those of all ages and abilities. Before the nineteenth century, the two youngest hawkers I have found were aged just 10.[37] Street sellers in their early teens could help out parents, like brother and sister John and Ann Bowers who staffed their mother's stall near Blackfriars Bridge, or they traded on their own, like John M'Namara, a cooper's son who 'used to go about the streets with a jack-ass selling greens and things'.[38] After 1800, despite the passing of laws that limited child labour and extended formal education, young people still took to the streets, usually those from the poorest families.[39] In December 1895, a woman who kept a stall in Roman Road was summoned to Worship Street police court, accused of putting an underage girl to work selling celery and watercress for several hours a day. The 10-year-old's father, hobbling on a stick and visibly unable to support his daughter, was presented to the court. 'I only employed her out of charity,' the stall keeper said.[40]

There had always been far older women and men hawking food. Towards the end of the nineteenth century, Charles Booth's survey of London's working classes noted a 'more than the normal' share of elderly, those in their late fifties and beyond, among those who toiled as street sellers.[41] The oldest of the hawkers before 1825 was John Irish, who at 70 had spent two decades 'going about to sell Fish and Fowl, both in London and in the Country'. In a past career, he had been a tenant farmer in Sussex, near Chichester, until his landlord threw him off.[42] Other senior vendors sat down with their stock or stood at regular pitches, maybe glad at their age no longer to be on the move.[43]

Because it was flexible and the bar to entry was low, hawking suited people from a range of backgrounds. Throughout this period, London's booming population was fuelled by migration, with thousands of arrivals pouring into the capital each year, many of them youthful women and men hoping to work as servants or take up training as apprentices.[44] A large proportion, most likely those without contacts or a steady position lined up in advance, wound up in casual labour, in jobs like hawking. We should not assume that most street sellers were immigrants. Modern studies have found that food hawkers, wherever in the world they work, tend to be long-standing residents, the business benefiting from local knowledge.[45] In London, the situation would have been no different. Even those born in the metropolis would have found the city's flux unsettling, and to make a good return a street seller would have to know which were the best markets, the ins and outs of their rules and customs, and the most likely locations to make a sale.

However, many street sellers were first-generation Londoners. An unusual but rich source for street sellers' lives in the eighteenth century is the *Ordinary of Newgate's Account*, a serial publication that reported the biographies, confessions, and final words of those condemned to death, as recounted by the prison chaplain.[46] The dozens of hawkers included in its pages are those whose experience of the city culminated in disaster, but their stories also reveal the winding road many incomers followed to the street. Born in Yarmouth and brought up by her uncle in Hertfordshire, Mary Knight came to London in her late teens, where she served an apprenticeship with a 'Fishwoman' at Billingsgate.[47] In comparison, Thomas Hartshorn's route was Odyssean. Raised in Worcester, he briefly went to school in Gloucester, before finding work winding quills for weavers. Moving to London at just 12, he waited in taverns and jumped on ships to the Caribbean and back, until a Hatton Garden lawyer took him on as a footman. In his twenties, after a failed marriage and another stretch at sea, Hartshorn took up various manual jobs, one of which was driving a wheelbarrow filled with greens and fruit.[48] Other street vendors originated further afield, like a Spitalfields milkman who had moved over from Hanover and Mary Hobbins, a fish seller's servant, who was Dutch.[49]

Certain immigrant groups were linked to parts of the street trade. Welshmen and women, chiefly from the far west counties of Cardiganshire and Carmarthenshire, came to work in the intensifying dairy industry that ringed the capital.[50] Drawing on a rural upbringing, they kept cows, milked, and carried pails door to door. The Welsh connection lasted through the nineteenth century, even as the railways and the rise of dairy firms allowed the milk business to expand significantly.[51] Despite working among compatriots, many young arrivals had a rocky experience. When Margaret Griffiths, a milkman's servant, was charged with theft, she pleaded for leniency. 'My family are decent, prudent hard working people in Wales,' Griffiths said. 'I have hardly any acquaintance in town, nor a friend near me that I can call to my character.'[52]

The poor Italians who reached London were tightly knit. There had long been a small community in the capital, but in the nineteenth century they congregated north of Holborn in the courts and alleys around Hatton Garden and Saffron Hill.[53] From the mid-Victorian era, rising numbers of so-called Neapolitans (more accurately, most were from villages in the Liri Valley between Rome and Naples) travelled to London, either for the summer season or for good, where many of them subsisted by making and selling ice cream. The 1881 census counted forty-six ice cream vendors across London, all but one born in Italy, all but a handful living close together in the district of Clerkenwell. In a sign of how the community matured, twenty years later more than 700 Italian ice cream sellers were scattered across the city.[54] To the English, for a long time their presence seemed a novelty. An 1889 newspaper report about 'Italian costermongers' blocking the streets took the time to explain how their ice cream operations worked. The sellers of cool treats were not the only problem: apparently the gaggles of young customers gawping at their barrows would not move when police constables asked.[55]

For centuries, Irish immigrants had been settling in London, where many worked in physically demanding jobs, as labourers, chairmen, porters, and coalheavers, or in lesser trades, like weaving and shoemaking.[56] So it is unsurprising that many also hawked food. After 1815, emigration to England gathered momentum, with London home to more than 100,000 Irish-born by mid-century, roughly 4–5 per cent of the metropolitan population, making them by far the largest minority.[57] According to Mayhew, there were by this time several thousand Irish street sellers, mostly dealing oranges and nuts.[58] This link may go back further than is immediately obvious. Several of the street seller biographies in the Ordinary's *Account* commence in Ireland.[59] Before they were associated with fruit, the Irish were important to the dairy trade. By looking for typical surnames, one technique available to historians of immigration, we can find other early examples of street sellers possibly of Irish heritage, such as Mrs Kennady, a 'Milk Woman' who lived off the Strand in the 1740s.[60] The presence of Irish hawkers may have contributed to the hardening of the costermonger stereotype and its racialized tinge.[61]

The other great street selling minority were Jews. After being tacitly granted permission to resettle during the Interregnum, a few dozen families grew to a London community of 7,000 to 8,000 by the mid-eighteenth century. By that point, the Sephardim from Spain, Portugal, and North Africa who defined early Anglo-Jewry were outnumbered by a factor of three by Ashkenazim, originally from Central and Eastern Europe. Many of the latter were poor with no formal skills and turned to irregular retail, peddling in the country, dealing old clothes, and selling food on the streets.[62] From the 1790s, Jewish men and boys were common sights hawking oranges in the City, at busy spots like outside the Royal Exchange.[63] As the community grew more slowly in the early nineteenth century, Jews' standing in the citrus trade reflected their improving fortunes. Members of a rising middle class graduated into wholesale, supplying oranges and lemons from their warehouses on the City's north-east fringe to new retailing recruits, like the Irish. When the final wave of mass Jewish immigration made it to London from the 1870s, fewer tried their hand at food hawking, with more employed in small workshops and vending manufactured goods like clothes and metalware.[64] A number maintained the historical tie to street food. In 1891, when Russian sweet seller Abraham Abunovitch was charged with obstructing the highway, he could not understand the evidence in court. An alderman was able to interpret, discovering that Abunovitch had been in London just five weeks and still could not speak English.[65]

Examples like this do not only highlight the mix of people who sold food on the streets. They reveal the diversity of experience within London's labouring classes. Just as it is wrong to speak of a typical hawker, reduced to a clichéd fishwife or costermonger, we should be careful speaking simply of 'poor' or 'working' London.

The status of street sellers

Many street sellers lived in desperate situations. When asked to estimate her wealth at one of London's church courts, Shadwell butter seller Mary Risebrook said she was 'not worth anything', the same answer that a quarter to a third of London women gave to that question in the late seventeenth and early eighteenth centuries.[66] In records like these witness statements, in which we have a suggestion of the deponent's voice, women and men often described themselves in the language of poverty. Someone who had known Mary Shepard since she was a child said that she 'used to sell water cresses, and go out begging with her mother'.[67] Another street seller explained herself: 'I am a poor woman, I sell fruit in the street.'[68] Others gave their circumstances away through their actions. One oyster seller was brought to court by her landlady, having stolen a bed, blanket, and coverlet from the next-door room. The hawker had taken the lodging unfurnished and at first planned to sleep on the bare boards.[69] Like the Ordinary's *Account*, the surviving examination records of those trying to claim poor relief include numerous accounts of street sellers' lives that give an unusual amount of detail about their parentage, background, and work history. But those interviews make a wider point too: many street sellers could not sustain themselves through hawking.[70]

From the mid-nineteenth century, the street trades became the object of charity as well as investigation. At the centre of James Greenwood's well-known *Telegraph* report on Whitecross Street market was the Costermongers' Mission House, run by Reverend J. Orsman. From this tall building looming over its crowded neighbourhood, Orsman dished up meals and ran improving schemes for the thousands of poor, hungry residents.[71] The Earl of Shaftesbury, the philanthropist peer, patronized several such efforts, like the Watercress and Flower Girls' Christian Mission. A fundraising pamphlet related how in 1871 the founder, John Groom, arranged for 300 young women, accustomed to the smog and bustle of inner London, to one day catch the train to Hampton Court for a picnic in the fresh air.[72]

This is not to say that all hawkers were struggling. Some had always earned a steady living, built up sizeable businesses, and purchased belongings that allowed them to live in relative ease. We can quantify their success in terms of wealth. Answering the same question as Mary Risebrook, only earlier in the seventeenth century, Elizabeth Charter stated that her husband was worth £5, placing this fruit and herb seller above the accepted threshold of reasonable substance at the time.[73] We can also look at what they owned. Among the possessions stolen from street sellers' homes were silver watches (one in a tortoiseshell case) and silver-plate candlesticks, in addition to stashes of money.[74] Those involved in selling milk, the street trade with the most potential profit, had the best chance to enjoy the expanding world of consumption and leave something behind for the next generation. After milkman Nicholas Spincser died in 1694, his household goods were itemized in an inventory. The list suggests that his kitchen and sleeping area were well-furnished and he also owned a looking glass, a silver spoon, and a bible, his goods altogether appraised at more than £31.[75]

Until the nineteenth century, evidence for what street sellers earned is almost non-existent. I have only come across a single reference: in 1782, Abraham Cohen said he made 8s. to 10s. a week by selling lemons and old clothes, not far off what a labourer in an industry like construction was taking home a few decades before.[76] By smoothing out the ups and downs of the year and accounting for breaks in business, Mayhew worked out that a costermonger working regularly could make 14s. 6d. a week. Including those who traded from time to time, his average dropped to 10s.[77] In the 1840s, this was just less than the wage of an unskilled labourer in a working class East End district and well below the 20s. mean for that part of London.[78] Fifty years on, Booth's survey pegged weekly returns for a hawker of fish or fruit between 20s. and 60s.[79] Classifying metropolitan society by income and living conditions, Booth divided the working classes into lettered categories. In East London and Hackney, two-thirds of the area's street sellers were slotted into brackets B, C, and D, above the loafers and semi-criminals but with casual, intermittent, or low wages that made them either 'poor' or 'very poor'. Another quarter were in category E, with a regular income that put them on the right side of the poverty line, where they did not fight continually to make ends meet.[80] In a trade like street selling, such averages can only ever be indicative. Some did the job part-time or for a couple of months each year. There were always those whose profit far exceeded the average and those making little at all. Potential returns varied week to week and by the season, as produce came into and out of supply (January, February, and March were known to be lean).[81] Then there were other uncertainties, even harder to account for, like bad weather and the shock of injury or illness.

The difficulty of placing street sellers precisely is partly explained by how London's population was changing. During these centuries of expansion, metropolitan society was becoming more stratified. In the social structure of the Elizabethan capital, those who had to work for a living were crudely split into merchants, craftsmen, and labourers, but a middling sort was also emerging, peopled by more prosperous tradesmen, shopkeepers, and manufacturers, which eventually coalesced into a distinct middle class.[82] Below this successful minority was the mass of working Londoners. By the later eighteenth century, around half of the adult male population was working in semi-skilled or unskilled occupations, a large proportion of those lacking a secure job or a consistent income. In his study of 'Outcast London' in the late Victorian period, Gareth Stedman Jones included street sellers in the 400,000 working people, about 10 per cent of the city's population, that he estimated were locked into casual labour.[83] Rich and poor were increasingly polarized. Not only were those of means pulling away from labourers and servants, but within the middling and working classes fine gradations of wealth and status developed.[84]

Because of this, it is sensible to talk about street sellers' status in broad terms. Some hawkers were just scraping by, falling in and out of penury. But many sat above the truly destitute, traded continuously, and managed a reasonable living, at least in the context of labouring London.[85] A few were as well off as the upper ranks of working men and women, those trained in a craft or with a substantial shop in a reputable part of town.

In most aspects of their lives and work, hawkers are tough to describe succinctly. This goes too for the basic question of how many street sellers there were. In 1590, the City aldermen planned to issue 160 licences to 'Fyshwyves', allowing them to carry food about the streets. At a stage when London's population was around 200,000, there were likely hundreds more who did not meet the Corporation's criteria or did not wish to pay for a badge.[86] Dissatisfied with the paltry official estimates, Mayhew counted more than 13,000 street vendors of food, out of approximately 2 million metropolitan residents, based on the numbers stocking up at Billingsgate and Covent Garden, stalls dotted across the metropolis, and attendance at the street markets.[87] This was still a best guess. Booth's later survey used a total of almost 12,000 from the 1891 census. But that included those with vague or non-food related titles, such as 'booth keeper', 'horse slaughterer', and 'moth eradicator'.[88] Whatever the real numbers were, street sellers were entrenched in the city and its neighbourhoods.

Hawkers at home

Street sellers lived in the poorest quarters of working London. Mayhew explained that most resided near the street markets where they gathered, listing the 'costermonger districts' in order of importance, with the areas around the New Cut in Lambeth, Whitecross Street in St Luke's, and Leather Lane in Holborn at the head.[89] The 1851 census suggests that many also lived in a wider range of localities long dominated by the labouring classes, such as Southwark, Whitechapel, and St Giles.[90] Though London's sprawl opened up areas distant from the centre—fifty years later, Kensington, Wandsworth, Islington, and Camberwell joined the list of typical residences— the main areas in which street sellers lived had changed little since the seventeenth century.[91] Mapping the parishes that hawkers called home before 1825 (Figure 5) makes this pattern evident. Street sellers were concentrated on the immediate fringes of the City, to the west, north, and east in particular. Their enduring presence in other areas, such as Westminster, is also explained by the historical character of those districts. A nucleus of politics, law, and fashion, Westminster possessed service and entertainment sectors large even by London standards, which demanded a constant flow of food and drink.[92]

These street selling neighbourhoods started off as suburbs. So precocious was the capital's growth that, a few decades into the seventeenth century, the metropolitan population outside the City's twenty-six wards surpassed those living in the centre.[93] Small houses densely packed in rows typified the less salubrious parts of these early suburbs. Labourers and immigrants were attracted by the cheaper rents, which were lowest of all to the east along the river.[94] Over the next 200 years, those districts were themselves encircled, at first by the development of the West End after the Restoration and the flight of middle class households to what had been semi-rural villages, like Hackney and Chelsea. Eventually, all of these were taken in by the immense outer belt of Victorian London, leaving the old suburbs, such as St Giles, to become inner-city slums.[95] Over the course of the nineteenth century, the continued rebuilding of the City and Westminster, along with house-building that never kept pace with demand, squeezed central London's working classes into restricted, ever more crowded neighbourhoods, zones of chronic under-employment, sweated labour, and crime that were the focus of Booth's survey. The East End districts of Bethnal Green, St George in the East, and Stepney, and southern parishes that hugged the Thames were particularly troubling.[96]

Within these areas, the way hawkers lived became symbolic of endemic poverty. Districts inhabited by street sellers were evocative subjects for journalists of late Victorian slum life. From the roof of the Costermongers' Mission House near Whitecross Street, James Greenwood recalled gazing into the ' "slummiest" of slums', with its 'intricate network of zig-zag cracks, chinks, and crevices, which really are courts and alleys threading among homes teeming with busy life'.[97] In his 1883 pamphlet *The Bitter Cry of*

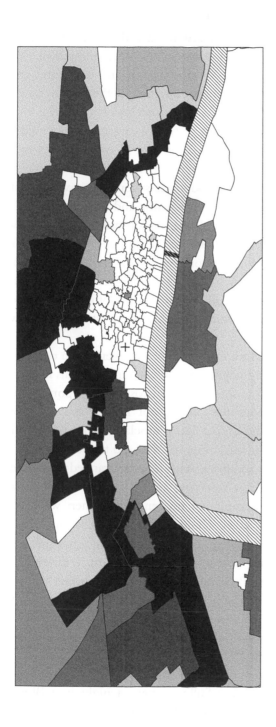

+ St Paul's Cathedral   ▨ London Bridge   ▨ River Thames

0   0.5   1 mi

Figure 5. Map of London parishes where individual street sellers in the 1600–1825 sample were resident, based on mid-eighteenth-century boundaries. The darker the shading, the more street sellers were resident in that parish. Given the sample size and the variety of sources, the general pattern is more important than the exact numbers.

Outcast London, which brought public attention to the combined crises of housing and poverty, Reverend Andrew Mearns described the parlous state of enclaves like Collier's Rents in Bermondsey, where more than 3,250 costermongers, bird catchers, street singers, thieves, and prostitutes crammed into 123 homes. Entering tenement rooms, most of them no more than 8 ft square with blackened walls, broken furniture, and beds of rags and straw, Mearns smelled the 'fragrance of stale fish or vegetables, not sold on the previous day, and kept in the room overnight'.[98] Such reports prompted public scrutiny, including the appointment of parliamentary committees and a Royal Commission into working class housing, at which witnesses testified to the dramatic examples of squalor and incivility in the places where street sellers lived. Before a House of Commons inquiry in 1881, the medical officer of Clerkenwell recounted the former condition of Turnmill Street, home to 'colonies of costermongers' before a rebuilding scheme tore down the vilest dwellings. Branching off the street were narrow courts, with no drainage and waste piled up in the gutter. The officer concluded, 'The houses were known all over London as being the most wretched hovels on the face of the earth.'[99]

Not that these problems were all new. In the seventeenth century, much of the artisan and labouring population already rented rooms in subdivided houses or, at worst, stayed in sheds and lean-tos. The Corporation and the Crown were anxious about the division of homes and overcrowding, launching investigations and issuing fretful proclamations on the subject. In a process accelerated by the Great Fire of 1666, old timber-framed London was being rebuilt in stone and brick, with houses arranged in more orderly terraces, but there remained a worrying gulf in quality and thousands still resorted to cramped and crumbling residences.[100] When we have more detailed addresses for the street selling individuals I have identified, they tended to be living in courts, lanes, and alleys, the tighter passages off major streets, in which inhabitants were more likely worse off.[101] Hawkers' homes could be very basic indeed: Benjamin Walker, a self-described 'milk carrier', slept in the hayloft of a cattle barn.[102] For those dealing dairy and fruit, cellar dwellings may have been common, doubling as a home and a shopfront.[103] Some rented cheaper ground floor rooms, while a fortunate few took breezier, lighter apartments up two flights of stairs.[104]

Many street sellers lived in temporary arrangements, close to people they did not necessarily know. Mary Sullivan spent a night in a Bloomsbury lodging house, a kind of rough-and-ready short-term abode typical of poor districts, where rooms or spaces on the floor were rented by the day or week. Sullivan's house hosted as many as ten other guests, one of whom had to pass through the muffin seller's room to get to their own and used the opportunity to steal her clothes.[105] Lodging like this or renting a room from a householder was normal for the poorer part of the population, at all stages in life.[106] Perhaps glad to have the extra money, a few hawkers took in lodgers themselves, a further reminder of how widely the experiences of street sellers could vary.[107]

When initiatives to improve workers' housing eventually arrived, street sellers could not always take advantage. Retailers without shops, hawkers used their lodgings and the street outside for storing equipment, animals, and stock and for preparing food for sale. In the 1880s, describing slum districts like St Luke's, journalist George Sims noticed donkeys led through corridors, even upstairs, to be 'stabled' in dirty rooms. One anecdote recorded a marital dispute ignited by a donkey sleeping under a bed. At day's end, street sellers piled up their barrows in any available open space, sometimes taking off a wheel to ward off thieves. Unsold cabbages turned limp when piled up in rooms overnight, having to be revived with water in the morning. Before being baked and sold to hungry workers, potatoes were scrubbed in the shared tubs where neighbours washed cups and plates. The food waste left behind each day, Sims warned his readers, 'would have cured such among you as are fond of a bargain at the door from ever patronising a barrow again'.[108] These extraordinary snippets were not just indications of depravity. They were solutions to practical problems. Where else could these poor, self-employed retailers prepare for the day? According to health officials in several districts, street sellers would not move into model dwellings, the purpose-built blocks and terraced houses erected by development companies, because the new constructions did not suit hawkers' work and way of life. Strict rules about residents' behaviour and regularly collected rents were also prohibitive.[109] Other witnesses at parliamentary inquiries claimed that such buildings occasionally offered dedicated facilities—a Peabody Trust scheme in Whitechapel promised storage for barrows on the ground level of each block, next to the bathroom—but that hawkers rarely availed themselves of these provisions.[110]

At the start of the twentieth century, conditions were improving. Just as slums were being cleared and housing blocks constructed, many hawkers moved out to the new working class suburbs, made more accessible by the omnibuses, trams, and railways and where rents might be cheaper. But for

street sellers it would have been a wrench to leave. Areas like Camberwell
and Walthamstow were distant from the wholesale markets still located in
London's centre. The new suburbs also did not offer the sheer density of
customers that hawkers, with their low-cost produce, required to make a
return. For other working Londoners, the presence of street sellers was itself
a reason not to leave. These retailers provided affordable food to the communities of which they were part. As a Westminster silver-plater who lived
surrounded by hawkers put it bluntly, 'The costermonger is quite as necessary a class as almost any other working class of society.'[111]

Like the questions of who street sellers were and how poorly they lived,
the matter of where hawkers resided suggests that London was changing
profoundly, but deep-rooted patterns and problems persisted. As the chapters that follow will keep showing, street sellers are proof of the dual nature
of London's growth and modernization, even late in the nineteenth century.
In their lives and work, they were evidence of an intractable, old London
and a fast-moving, modern metropolis seemingly in existence side by side.

2

Workers

Hawkers had a hierarchy, at least among themselves. In the nineteenth century, 'regular or "thorough-bred" costermongers', those dealing day in and day out with their iconic barrows and donkeys, were supposed to look down on the women who sold oranges or nuts from a basket or tray. Similarly shunned were the Jews who sold coconuts, and the hawkers of on-street edibles, like cakes, sweets, and pea soup, concoctions not purchased at the wholesale markets. Below them all was a miserable tier of broken-down artisans and labourers, driven to street selling when there was no work in their trade. 'Some of these poor fellows lose every penny,' one hawker told Henry Mayhew, bemoaning their incompetence at haggling and selecting stock. 'We pity them. We say, "Poor fellows! They'll find out it out by-and-bye." '[1] Such distinctions existed in previous centuries, though the ranking was more subtle. Given the chance to explain their livelihood, some hawkers said they sold food alongside other lowly jobs—Mary Risebrook wound silk, washed linen, and nursed children, but also sold butter and eggs—while others suggested that hawking was not a proper trade at all. 'I do not follow any business', Judith Donnevan told a courtroom in 1784. 'Only sometimes I sell fruit.'[2] Meanwhile, the most successful vendors had a better defined, more reputable identity. On making his last will and testament, Benjamin Wilkinson assigned himself the pithy title, 'milkman'.[3] Eventually, selling milk became so large-scale and organized that it was no longer considered, by those who surveyed the poor, part of the street trades at all.

Because hawking contained such multitudes, it is hard to sum up as work. Sometimes, street selling was a badly paid, draining job, with irregular hours and carried out in and around other employment. In other cases, hawkers spent all their working lives selling in the street, building up a good custom and taking on assistants, trading in a way that had much in common with the operations of respectable retailers like fishmongers and greengrocers. But for most hawkers, for most of this stretch of London history, their work was not seen as a genuine occupation. Theirs was not a decent way of making a living, with a standard set of practices and a recognizable title, a shorthand to be scrawled beside their name in a marriage register, a petition, or a census return, a process of classification that became more important over time. In this, once again, hawking was typical of much of the metropolitan economy. Street sellers were left to prove their identity through the way that they worked.

Gutter merchants

For a long time, London produced and relied on insecure workers like street sellers. Compared to other English cities, the capital had an unusually large service sector, owing to its roles as a port and hub of government and social life. At the lowest level of services, below recognized occupations like cutting hair and keeping a tavern, was a range of flexible, low-skilled jobs. Work like domestic service, carrying loads at the docks, doing laundry, cleaning houses, and hawking food required little investment or formal training, just a willingness to take on manual tasks. London's particular economic characteristics were apparent by the eighteenth century, if not before.[4] The capital did have some manufacturing, even after the Industrial Revolution, but in the inner city where most street sellers lived it generally centred on turning out higher-value finished goods, such as clothing, and was based in small workshops and homes, rather than factories. Like the humbler services, this industry drew on a pool of casual workers, taken on by manufacturers and warehouse owners for days, weeks, and months, before being released in downturns and seasonal slumps. The perils of casual labour were decried in the later nineteenth century, but were hardly novel.[5] Working Londoners were used to taking on short-term or menial jobs to get by.

Those who turned to hawking frequently described how they had fallen out of steadier engagements. Greenwich-born Susan Perry completed an apprenticeship with a gownmaker, but 'not being able to find Work in that Calling for her Maintenance' briefly lived with a seamstress, before selling 'sometimes News-Papers and other times Fruit'.[6] Other hawkers blamed dips in trade for pushing them onto the streets. One said he only sold muffins because work was 'slack' during the American wars from the 1770s.[7]

A cigar manufacturer took up a costermonger's barrow in the last decade of the nineteenth century, when the country was enduring another episode of economic distress. 'I cannot see my children starve for bread in a great city like this,' he explained to a police court.[8] Demobbed soldiers and sailors, used to hard work but lacking marketable skills, turned to street selling too.[9]

For the truly desperate, selling food on the street could be a last resort. Illness and injury lay in many hawkers' backgrounds. Houndsditch cake seller Hannah Marks supported four children and a husband, a former pastry cook who had become blind.[10] Mayhew's interviews are replete with accounts of misfortune. In a standard tale, a shellfish seller recounted how in his former career as a boot closer, which involved stitching the upper parts of a shoe, he had earned as much as 40s. a week. 'I had an attack of rheumatic fever, and lost the use of my hands for my trade,' the vendor told Mayhew. 'The streets hadn't any great name, as far as I knew, then, but as I couldn't work, it was just a choice between street-selling and starving, so I didn't prefer the last.'[11] Miserable as such stories are, it is notable that in all these examples hawking is not rock bottom. It was a way to stay above water, a rung above destitution. Similar jobs included cleaning houses, selling cheap print, scavenging waste, sweeping the street, chopping wood, and wearing a sign as a 'sandwich-man'.[12]

Local officials recognized that hawking could keep the badly off in some employment and stop them adding to the rising burden of poor relief. In the 1830s, the head of the Whitechapel Poor Law Union noted that some struggling men and women in his district, hoping to avoid the workhouse, asked to be handed a few shillings. With the cash, the recipients bought baskets and stocks of fish or fruit to sell.[13] Made at the discretion of officials and not systematically recorded, such provisions were probably used more widely than we can ever know. Scraping together a few coins for stock money, from whatever source, was normal for those who sold food intermittently or were first starting out. Some borrowed money from friends or a nearby publican. One St Giles woman pawned her husband's breeches to buy a basket and some seafood.[14]

However close to the breadline they were, hawkers could sell food alongside other work. Among the 858 street selling individuals I have identified up to 1825, there were men who worked primarily as labourers, porters, glass grinders, gunsmiths, painters, glaziers, and chocolate makers. Boys ran errands and shined shoes. Women cleaned, nursed, told fortunes, and ran early versions of corner shops, in addition to the unavoidable housework that was rarely mentioned as proper labour. Some hawked other goods such as pamphlets and second-hand clothes. By-employments were extremely common in the seventeenth and eighteenth centuries, at all levels of the social scale. With flexible hours and no formal commitment, street selling was just the kind of job that could be carried out in the downtime from other activity, though such extra tasks were hidden in records which list a single occupational title or a marital status in the case of women.[15] In the nineteenth century, new means of surveying labour like the census, which required people to reduce their complex lives into what fitted into a box on a form on the day the census was taken, solidified the impression that workers were becoming more specialized. But huge numbers of men and women, particularly in the poor neighbourhoods of inner London, still combined more than one job.[16]

Changing work throughout the year was also unremarkable. Some hawkers switched jobs with the seasons. In the eighteenth century, Bridget Lewis sold apples in summer and washed laundry in winter; James Blundell went from labouring in the brickfields to hawking muffins.[17] Later on, the street selling ranks were thought to swell from late spring when the fruit and vegetable markets started bulging with produce. Come autumn, those traders returned to graft on the docks or sweep chimneys. Hawkers' working opportunities were connected to the rhythms of the London economy. Demand for certain services peaked during the London Season, when the West End swelled with wealthy families in spring and early summer; the docks were at their busiest between May and October; outdoor work such as building was thinner on the ground and more arduous in winter.[18] Food hawkers could even switch occupations from one day to the next, sometimes within a few hours. A whelk seller told the journalist Adolphe Smith that seafood 'don't pay more than a poor living'. From time to time, he left his wife with the barrow and took odd jobs, such as beating carpets and cleaning windows.[19] Street trading's flexibility allowed hawkers to jump at whatever means of earning a crust came along, but it also made it seem as if selling food on the kerbside was scarcely real employment.

Aristocracy of the kerb

The idea of hawking as an almost-occupation is not the whole story. Many street sellers traded constantly at their stalls or out on rounds, earning an income that dragged them above the poverty line and, for a few, let them live reasonably well. Like more reputable jobs, this was work that could support a household. Married men maintained their wives and children by selling herbs, fish, and vegetables.[20] Husbands and wives both worked on the street, either separately by selling different foods or by trading together, sharing the load as they hauled milk into the city or dealing side by side at a pitch.[21] In such cases, there may have been a division of tasks. One vendor told Mayhew that his wife manned a stall, while he and their 10-year-old daughter went off hawking.[22] Even in households with just one street seller, strengths and skills may have been shared. Margaret Hart's spouse was a gardener, who might have sourced supplies for her herb selling. In turn, Hart could have shared experience of the streets and markets, and specialist knowledge of her stock and how it sold.[23]

Unrelated hawkers formed partnerships of their own. For the most part, it is hard be sure what these relationships entailed. Joseph Taylor vaguely explained how he and Richard Challenger traded in tandem, selling greens in the morning and fish at night. 'We were partners,' Taylor said. 'He was the first that let me into the Business.'[24] At the wholesale markets where they purchased supplies, street sellers joined more temporary alliances. When Elizabeth Barley was grilled about her familiarity with Dorothy Lloyd, a woman on trial for theft, Barley confirmed she had known Lloyd for years and 'shared fish with her at the Gate'. This meant 'putting our money together to buy fish', Barley followed up. The 'Gate', of course, was Billingsgate.[25] Clubbing together was a way for hawkers to buy in bulk or pick up costlier produce that would not have been affordable alone.[26] For single women, arriving to a city with few existing ties, partnerships may have acted as a 'virtual family', offering social support on top of financial benefits.[27]

Those needing more regular assistance took on help. In some cases, families who did not work in street selling at all employed servants whose duties included hawking food. Elizabeth Draper's mistress went to Billingsgate herself to buy oysters for the servant to sell in the evening.[28] London was teeming with domestic servants. Their numbers shot up in the seventeenth century and by 1750 they were equivalent to almost one in ten inhabitants. Most were young women, under the age of 30, and many were employed in the homes of artisans, tradespeople, and retailers, not just the well-to-do.[29] For less wealthy households, sending out a servant with a basket helped bring in additional income. This may have become less common in the nineteenth century, as the servant population remained enormous but was more restricted to middle and upper class families.[30] More ad hoc arrangements developed. Male street sellers occasionally hired boys called 'chirpers', who cried out their master's produce in an unbroken voice and pulled or pushed the barrow. Such lads were paid in meals or earned a few pennies a day.[31]

Hawkers who built up considerable businesses employed dedicated servants. In the early seventeenth century, the governors of Bridewell hospital, the house of correction near Blackfriars, tried to clamp down on the practice. Street sellers' servants, almost all of them young women, were dragged before the governors' court, some of them multiple times, and their bosses were prosecuted too.[32] At this early point, hawking fish was a big enough trade to encourage established retailers to take on staff. But Bridewell's attention also tells us that City leaders were uncomfortable with these women roaming the streets. We cannot be certain what their employment involved, whether the women received wages and lodgings or were engaged on looser terms. Some appointments were certainly more formal. In the mid-eighteenth century, Margaret Edwards took on Jane Shoen, dispatching her into the streets with fish in winter and fruit in summer. For her year of work, Shoen stayed with her mistress and earned 52s. This fits the model of live-in domestic service and Shoen's pay was not far off the average rate most London servants took home.[33] But 'servant' was a baggy term and, in practice, lengths of contract, expectations for boarding, and servants' and employers' responsibilities varied.[34] Because of the vagaries of the street trade, mistresses and masters may have used this flexibility to their advantage.

Some took on apprentices, usually at the request of local authorities. In 1657, Bridewell's governors ordered that Mary Kirby, 'a poore Girle being helplesse & freindless' should be bound as an apprentice to a milk seller. Kirby was given a petticoat, waistcoat, stockings, shoes, two smocks, and an apron.[35] Such apprenticeships were not the formal craft training regulated by the City's livery companies that offered a route to full citizenship. These were pauper apprenticeships. To help poor families and discipline the young, magistrates and parish officials placed boys and girls, some as young as 7, with households in crafts and trades of every type. The practice spread widely from the late seventeenth century and remained important, especially for young women, until the New Poor Law of 1834 brought most pauper children into workhouses.[36]

We do not know exactly what a hawker's apprentice might have expected to learn. Like service, pauper apprenticeship was not strictly defined and, in fact, the two institutions blurred into each other. The unluckiest apprentices were exploited as cheap labour; others gained valuable skills, while boarding in a stable home.[37] However diverse the experience could be, the involvement of street sellers in such training is revealing. It shows that some food hawkers were seen by prominent members of the parish or London government as upstanding employers, who could take youths into their care and direct their education. These apprenticeships also imply that selling food on the street was a trade or a craft, though a lesser one, an occupation that could be learned and passed on. Some hawking trainees stayed with their mistresses for long terms, sometimes six or seven years.[38] Officeholders and parents had expectations of how children would be taught and treated. In 1696, Frances Hall petitioned the Middlesex justices because her daughter Sarah had not received 'such necessarys as are fitting for an Apprentice'. She had also been beaten and abused by her fish seller mistress.[39] Children and teens like Sarah might have learned how to shuck oysters and clean fish, how to select the choicest wares at market as the seasons shifted, and how to price their goods to make a profit. Milk sellers had to build relations with a cowkeeper and maintain repeat customers. All hawkers, to do well, had to keep perishable produce intact, find a moneymaking round or pitch, and use their voice to draw in buyers. At the side of their employer, they also acquired resilience for surviving long hours of exhausting, outdoor work. One street seller told James Greenwood what intangible rewards the chirper who worked by his side was receiving. 'It's as good as being bound 'prentice being along o' me,' the man said. 'He learns how to buy, and he learns how to sell, and gets to make nothing of early risin', summer or winter, which is the pivot everything turns on.'[40]

Milk sellers were most likely to take on staff, including many adults, a sign of the business's scale and sophistication.[41] Over the course of the eighteenth century, some dairy hawkers described themselves as 'carriers' for other milkmen and women.[42] It is unclear initially whether carriers were paid regularly or just committed to buy milk from a hawker with a cowkeeping connection. By the later nineteenth century, as the industry became increasingly sophisticated, carriers were more often than not on the payroll of a dairy firm and earned commission on their sales. Those who drove a cart took home more than those who pushed a 'pram', a two or three-wheeled barrow that could carry several churns. Above them were managers and foremen.[43]

Selling milk was always the most complex part of the street trade. From at least the eighteenth century, individual hawkers laid claim to a number of streets or houses, which they supplied daily or a few times a week, allowing their customers to rack up a bill. They called this their 'milk walk'.[44] The right to a milk walk was customary. Like most agreements typical of informal economies, there was no paper record, as rival milk sellers and their customers shared an understanding of who held what patch. This did not mean that milk walks were worthless. Hawkers discussed buying and selling them, and some fetched as much as £100 in the early nineteenth century, but most changed hands for single or double figures.[45] On her death in 1787, Mary Wordsworth left to her children the 'two Milk Walks which I die possessed of', with the 'Scores remaining unsettled' to be sold off to pay creditors.[46] Making such bequests was another way for street sellers to raise themselves above the genuinely poor.

Atop the hawking hierarchy, certain milk sellers pulled away. Wills like Mary Wordsworth's are one way to track their rising status, even early in London's expansion. Up to 1750, I have found twenty-three wills of men from London parishes who used the title, 'milkman', registered in different probate jurisdictions. From the evidence of their bequests, some clearly had a modest business. As well as his clothes and watch, Benjamin Wilkinson was able to leave £10 each to his niece and his executor's daughter, and several guineas to siblings and friends.[47] That fifteen of these milkmen had their wills registered at the Prerogative Court of Canterbury, which dealt with the largest and most complicated estates, points to the size of their operations.[48] William Smallwood passed on land, buildings, and gardens in Hertford, a long way from his Hungerford Market address. Having split his 'Milk Trade or Business' between his two sons, John Lester left behind £500 in annuities, £40 in cash, and two gold rings, each worth a guinea.[49] Such legacies placed these milkmen in the upper echelon of artisans and tradesmen, closer to many professional Londoners in terms of wealth.[50] On this plane, they probably stopped lugging milk themselves, instead hiring carriers and servants, running a shop or cellar, or even keeping some cows. For this reason, we have to be careful with the title of 'milkman'. Those who used it were not necessarily hawkers.[51] In wills, the title of 'milkwoman' only appears later, though we know the term had a longer history and women dairy sellers had always been prominent.[52] This disparity is indicative of how men jumped to the head of the developing dairy industry and assumed a recognizable title for their work. Most street sellers did not have that option.

The costermonger class

For most of London's history, elite and popular culture reinforced the idea that street selling was not a respectable or coherent form of work. In Donald Lupton's satirical pamphlet of 1632, the 'Crying, Wandring, and Travailing' fishwives are mocked for how they 'set up every morning their Trade afresh'. Lupton teased that, besides running through their small stock, the women 'change every day almost, for Shee that was this day for Fish, may bee tomorrow for Fruit; next day for Hearbs, another for Roots'.[53] Because they were not specialists, hawkers lacked a solid occupation. Street sellers' fluidity was a recurring theme from the outset of the Cries genre. Among the first examples were large, single-sheet prints, showing dozens of hawkers. In one of these (Figure 6), thirty-seven street characters are arranged in four rows. With the space for each character limited we cannot tell, from the image, what they are selling. The men and women are anonymous, apart from the short line below each figure which gives their call, such as 'Mackerel', 'Lettuce', and 'Buy any milk'. Without a proper job, they are simply defined by what

Figure 6. An early example of the Cries genre, a large, single sheet of street characters arranged in rows.

they cry. In musical representations, this lack of identity was captured in sound. A seventeenth-century ballad called 'Jolly Jack of All Trades' explains the many ways the titular narrator gets by, dressed up in the saucy double-entendres for which these songs were known. Jack asks listeners, 'Come will ye buy my Flounder? | my Gudgin, or my Roach?', having already mentioned singing birds, pins, and mouse-traps and recalling that he had worked, on occasion, as a tinker and tapster. The ballad was sung to 'A-Begging We Will Go', a tune used in many songs about comic vagabonds and salesmen, other mobile ne'er-do-wells.[54]

These representations were anchored in reality. As we have seen, many hawkers had multiple jobs or switched employment through the year. They also changed what they sold. This was central to street selling, hawkers' adaptability being one of their points of difference as retailers. As a biography of street seller Joseph Laycock in the *Ordinary of Newgate's Account* put it neatly: 'He sometimes was a Considerable Gainer, at other Times he was a broken Merchant, though his little Shop not requiring a very large Stock, was soon furnished again; when Oranges were not in season, he sold Fish, and by such Methods, picked up a Livelyhood.'[55] Mayhew believed street sellers had a seasonal cycle, which began the calendar year with fish, before berries, currants, and cherries arrived in early summer and were followed, in autumn, by other fruit and vegetables.[56] The rhythms most hawkers worked to were less rigid, as vendors reacted to a glut or a moment when the going rate in the market would let them make a margin. In a city full of casual workers, hawkers' changeability may not have been unusual, but it diminished the clarity of their occupation.

For women street sellers, this problem was compounded. Historians of work and gender have been fascinated by the question of occupational identity, the sense of self-worth and social status forged through the way people make a living. In the past as much as today, occupational identities matter not just for how individuals feel about themselves, but are a way of communicating the value of workers within the economy. Titles like 'butcher' and 'fishmonger' conveyed what their holders did, along with the notion that their trade was distinctive and productive. Women were less often assigned these titles in official documentation and, even when they were, such labels were poor indications of the various tasks they actually did, inside or outside the home.[57] Over the seventeenth and eighteenth centuries, English culture placed greater weight on these identities, with what people did becoming more important than what they were worth in monetary terms. Those shorthand titles became more meaningful.[58] So women street sellers were caught in a double bind: their work hawking food was not always recognized as a proper job and, when titles like 'milkman' and 'costermonger' emerged, they were mostly applied to men.[59]

The few identities available to women's street sellers were turned into characters in the Cries with negative associations. 'Fishwife', the early catch-all term for a female hawker, had connotations of rudeness, insobriety, and social conventions being flipped on their head. The label and its variants were used widely in records of regulation, when hawkers were being policed. 'Huckster', a word used across the country for women who sold food, chiefly referred in London to someone breaking the rules of the capital's marketplaces.[60] Though 'milkwoman' was less pejorative, young women dairy sellers were identified as 'milkmaids'. In ballads and poetry, the metropolitan milkmaid was cast as a rustic naif, a single woman at risk of corruption in the big city.

Faced with these challenges, hawkers were forced to describe, in greater detail, how they worked. The formulaic preamble to a statement Mary Knapp gave to one of London's church courts in 1695 only lists her as a widow. But when asked how she maintained herself, Knapp said she 'gets her livelyhood by selling Fish and fruit & the like'.[61] Avoiding the more suggestive labels of fishwife or huckster, Knapp explained her specific activities, just like a mounting proportion of London women around the same time. In this situation, only a tiny number of women claimed a formal occupational title.[62] Poor men without a trade did the same. In a petition to the Middlesex justices, begging for reprieve from conviction, John Castle called himself a 'poor labourious Person', who supported himself 'by selling Herbs & Fish'.[63]

Hawkers drew on standard phrases like these, stating that they 'sold' or 'cried' certain foods, or 'carried them about the streets'.[64] Using these words, hawkers expressed a working identity, one less concise and discrete than most others but significant nonetheless. This identity articulated their low position, but it also referred to hawkers as sellers. Because retailers were middlemen who took a cut of final prices, they were traditionally an awk-ward presence in the urban economy. In this period, re-sellers were slowly accepted and their reputation improved, with economic commentators extolling their usefulness.[65] Street vendors were part of this broader group of traders who made buying to sell again their business.

The distinctive identity of the 'costermonger' took longer to emerge. The term itself dates to the sixteenth century if not before, referring originally to someone who sold apples or other fruit, from a shop, market stall, or on the street.[66] This was still the case in 1618, when 'Coastardmonger' Adam Harrison was accused of blocking Fleet Street with baskets of fresh produce.[67] By the last decade of the eighteenth century, the word was gaining broader connotations. Two hawkers, Richard Peers and Joseph Hewitson, described themselves as costermongers: one sold vegetables from a cart, while the other used a donkey to carry his stock.[68] This was closer to the term's meaning in Mayhew's *London Labour*, in which a typical costermonger was a man selling fish, fruit, or greens with a donkey and barrow.

The costermonger stereotype may have become a symbol of poverty, but street sellers seem to have embraced the title. Whether or not they agreed with Mayhew's characterization, the costermonger became an identity for food hawkers to rally around. In the course of his investigations, the journalist himself chaired a meeting of more than a thousand hawkers at the National Hall in Holborn in July 1850. The street sellers agreed to form a 'Friendly Association of London Costermongers', which would make payments to those that were ill, struggling, or in old age, alongside other functions.[69] This anticipated the numerous groups that street sellers established on their own initiative to bolster their collective interests and lobby the government and police, on issues such as the disastrous impact of the 1867 Metropolitan Streets Act and the clearance of Sunday morning street markets.[70] In 1901, one of the more substantial bodies, the 'Costermongers' Federation', printed a short book of rules as part of its official registration. On the cover is a picture of a street seller, his hand resting on a donkey. According to the Federation's first rule, its objects were 'to uphold the rights of Male and Female Costermongers, to provide a sum at Death, and to combine and improve in every direction the general position and status of the Street Vendor, and secure unity of action amongst its members and regulate relations between them'. Those members were organized in branches and paid regular fees.[71] By the turn of the twentieth century, most street sellers in the capital were associated with an organization such as this, proof that they were perfectly able to show solidarity, despite their perception as selfish individualists.[72] Solicitors acting on behalf of hawking societies defended those appearing at the capital's police courts.[73] Bundled among the records of the Metropolitan Police are letters from the general secretaries of street sellers' unions, sometimes written on impressive, headed note paper, vocalizing hawkers' points of view and negotiating compromises with the authorities to keep on trading.[74]

Street sellers also strengthened their identity through a shared culture, which expressed itself in sad as well as happy times.[75] One journalist related how, when a coster died, his colleagues arranged a 'brick' or 'friendly lead', a collection involving drinking and singing that would cover the costs of the funeral.[76] The send-offs could be grand. In January 1884, the *Standard* reported the demise of an 'eccentric old lady named Healy', who kept a fruit stall. Attracted by the flowing beer and intrigued by the lavish instructions the late hawker had left, 'crowds of spectators lined the road from Camden Town to Finchley Cemetery, and hundreds of costermongers joined the procession'.[77] There were moments of lighter relief. The Costermongers' Federation held a sports day at Kensal Rise in September, which by the start of the twentieth century became an annual event. One newspaper described how thousands of street sellers and their families rolled up in painted carts to compete in events that ran on until nightfall:

> The one-mile scratch race was won by W. Anderson, in 5mins 22secs . . . There was a race for coster ladies, won amid great enthusiasm by Miss N. Ferguson, and there were 3- and 5-mile bicycle races, [a] sack race, three-legged race, pail of water race, bare-back donkey race, and donkey and barrow race, all of which were watched with the greatest excitement and interest.[78]

For readers, the culture of these costermongers was presented as a curiosity and their entertainments had a fair-like appeal. A photograph of such festivities shows several street sellers racing with toppling piles of baskets on their heads.[79] These activities contributed to the idea that this slice of working London was cut off from the rest of metropolitan society. But they also suggest that street sellers, even if they worked alone, could feel part of a bigger whole.

Donkey races and political campaigns should not be seen as the endpoint of a centuries-long accretion of street sellers' collective identity. It is true that the growing number of hawkers as London expanded and the heightening legitimacy of street markets as retail locations clarified food hawking as a recognizable occupation by the late Victorian period. But there are signs, as far back as the early seventeenth century, that some street sellers organized and acted as a group. Hawkers variously described as the 'poore woemen selling milke', 'pore woman Fruterers' and 'ancient poore Fishwifes' petitioned the City aldermen, defending their right to carry food through the streets.[80] In the 1660s, during a back-and-forth debate about the right of street vendors to stock up at Billingsgate, the 'poore women' selling fish petitioned the Corporation again. Ruling that these hawkers had as much of a claim on the market supplies as the fishmongers, the aldermen ordered the women to pay for copies of the relevant by-law to be printed and published.[81] They must have had the resources to do so.

In the records of London government, like most evidence of street selling in the past, the words of street sellers are mediated by a clerk or scribe, who would have summarized and reached for stereotypical labels. This means we cannot tell whether women hawkers used such phrases themselves. But by the very acts of petitioning and making demands of London's rulers, these street sellers proved they had a conception of who they were and the work that they did. The women, men, girls, and boys who hawked apricots, cabbages, sprats, and gingerbread did not need a title to give them a sense of self-worth. They found identity in the distinctive way they traded, their coming together in the streets and at the markets, and their accumulated knowledge of the foods that they sold.

3

Street food

In the early hours, London's food chain cranked into motion. Strong-armed men and women marched to the fields and barns that fringed the built-up city where, by moon and candlelight, they milked the waiting cows, with heavy udders and bellies stuffed with grains and hay. At Billingsgate dock, in the heart of the City, fishermen unloaded boats at speed, conscious that their catches would not keep. More boats raced up the river behind them, from fisheries in the North Sea, the Channel, the Thames estuary, and off the coasts of Kent and Essex. From the opposite direction came barges, low in the water from the weight of produce of thousands of acres of gardens stretched along the north and south banks. Their destinations were the stairs and wharves of London's waterside, from which porters heaved the fruit and vegetables uphill to the markets. The rest of the day the roads thronged with carts, wagons, and carriers, jostling with the cattle, sheep, and poultry driven on the hoof from distant counties.

The way London fed itself was a marvel. In an 1854 book on the subject, the journalist George Dodd was thrilled by the recent innovations, the revolutionary impact of steam-powered ships and the 'immense' railway service that had started to convey fresh food swiftly, cheaply, and in good condition from faraway parts of Britain and beyond.[1] But this food chain had been extraordinary well before the mid-nineteenth century. Since the start of London's take-off, its provisioning system was not only more extensive than those of other urban centres. It was adaptable and progressive, quick to embrace new technology and fashions, and offered a choice of foods not available elsewhere. This unique set of advantages comes plainly into view when we think about what street sellers sold.

Some dealt in staples. Throughout these centuries, meat and bread were the cornerstones of city people's diet, the main sources of energy that demanded the largest chunk of household budgets.[2] But, for these foods, hawkers tended to stick to selling stale bread or cheaper cuts of meat, like offal, rather than the prime goods whose trade was tightly controlled and in the hands of sanctioned retailers.[3] Instead, most street sellers concentrated on a different selection: fish, fruit, vegetables, milk, and cooked foods to be taken home or wolfed down on the spot.[4] These early street foods—notice that many were raw ingredients, unlike the street food of modern-day London—had a number of common characteristics. Until the late Victorian period, most were produced within the city, its immediate periphery, or the wider region. The majority were perishable, with supplies that swung considerably by the day, week, and season, making the fast and flexible distribution of hawkers essential. And their production, cultivation, and consumption shifted markedly over time. Carried across the city by hawkers, these foods helped form a distinctive metropolitan diet.

Garden city

Much of the fruit eaten in early Tudor London was imported from the Low Countries and France, but from the mid-sixteenth century home production increased in scale. Pioneering growers planted orchards in the counties that ringed the capital, employing varieties and know-how from the continent. Kent quickly secured the first place. From the fruit belt nestled between the North Downs and the coast, Kentish apples and cherries were carted or shipped the short journey to the metropolis.[5] One indication of success was the explosion of new varieties. According to one contemporary estimate, by the 1650s English orchards cultivated more than 500 kinds of pear, some grown for early ripening, others for taste, beauty, size, longevity, or making perry.[6] In 1715, a London hawker described selling 'Codlings', a small, green apple. This was one of dozens of apple cultivars, the most popular being the pearmain and the costard, the latter the root of the street selling moniker, costermonger.[7] Another street seller dealt specifically in 'duke Cherries', a hybrid variety that took its place alongside carnations, morellas, and egriots.[8]

Fruit and vegetables were also grown far closer to the city. Dutch and Flemish gardeners who settled in Kent and East Anglia in the sixteenth century started sending celery, peas, carrots, and cabbages up to London, before some of their descendants dug plots on the Surrey bank of the Thames.[9] Their arrival kickstarted a boom in suburban market gardening.

From a few pockets in Southwark and north and east of the City, the capital was soon surrounded by commercial growing. John Rocque's 1746 map shows gardens spreading west into Chelsea, reaching around the City's limits into Mile End, Bethnal Green, and eastwards into Stepney, and the circuit completed by vast acreages to the south.[10] By the turn of the nineteenth century, about 10,000 acres around London were under cultivation, equivalent to fifteen times the footprint of the Square Mile. This included an intensively farmed inner zone, worked with spades and producing delicate crops like asparagus, broccoli, and lettuces, and an extensive outer circle, pushing further into Middlesex, Surrey, and Essex, where ploughs were used to break the ground for hardier greens and roots.[11]

With hungry Londoners on their doorstep, market gardeners were encouraged to invest in cutting edge methods and technology. In a sheltered spot in what is now Pimlico, the Neat Houses were probably the capital's longest lasting and most sophisticated gardens. The gardeners enriched the alluvial soils with dung, which they also fermented in hotbeds, the heat produced warming the soil and accelerating growth. They spent heavily on glass, to retain warmth and protect their crops.[12] These advancements allowed growers to lengthen the seasons for in-demand vegetables. Wandering some London gardens in February 1748, the Swedish botanist Peter Kalm noted large bell-glasses under each of which several cauliflowers were growing. Forced under glass frames, mats, and straw, the asparagus was 'one inch high, and considerably thick', despite the chilly weather.[13] These gardens relied on an army of labourers. In his 1798 survey of Middlesex agriculture, John Middleton totted up all those engaged in working the soil, planting, pruning, picking, carrying the harvest to market, and hawking it through the streets. He reckoned that 30,000 men, women, and children were supported by London's fruit gardens alone.[14]

The mutually beneficial relationship between the capital and its gardens was also based on muck. Gardens, orchards, and dairy farms produced food that nourished London; in turn, the manure created by the tens of thousands of horses, cattle, and sheep that lived in or passed through the city was used to fertilize vegetable plots and pasture. The geographer Peter Atkins has proposed that we think of Greater London during this time as a 'manured region', an integrated agricultural territory limited by the distance at which the cost of carting this bulky waste or floating it downriver on barges became unviable. In the early 1800s, this was usually five to ten miles, as many as twenty if the roads were good. Farmers and gardeners made deals with stable owners or received cartloads from the laystalls, the great heaps of manure in Bloomsbury, Hyde Park Gardens, Lincoln's Inn Fields, and else- where.[15] Hawkers would have been aware of these ties between town and country, some more materially than others. Edward Fennell worked on a dung cart for a Hammersmith farmer, but previously 'used to go out with greens upon an ass'.[16] According to Atkins, the weight of manure generated by the metropolis multiplied more than fivefold over the nineteenth cen- tury, becoming by the 1890s too much for the nearby farms and gardens to take.[17]

By that point, market gardening on London's borders was in decline. Its end was hastened by a combination of outside forces, including pressure on land for building homes, competition from new greenhouses using industrially made glass in the Lea Valley, a shortage of the low-cost, seasonal labour required for spadework, and shrinking numbers of horses after the First World War. The most significant factor was the introduction of the railways.[18] From the mid-nineteenth century, special vans attached to trains brought greater amounts of apples, pears, cherries, strawberries, and rasp- berries from Kent, which shored up its status as a leading fruit-growing region. The railways also put districts further away within reach, like Essex, Bedfordshire, and Worcestershire's Vale of Evesham. Early potatoes, toma- toes, and salads arrived from as far off as the Channel Islands.[19] As the price of long-haul transport dropped, the high costs of suburban gardening were harder to justify.[20] Hawkers were not made redundant overnight. The old trading centres where they stocked up, Covent Garden, Borough, and Spitalfields, remained pre-eminent and street sellers attended new markets, like the potato depot at the King's Cross rail terminus, where wagons of spuds rolled in from the east and north of England.[21] By extending the ten- drils of the capital's food supply, the railways dimmed the brilliance of the London farming region.

Perishing commodities

Of all the foods sold by hawkers, milk was the most dramatically affected by the railways. In 1845, rail shipments of milk started from Essex to London and, the following year, a Romford farmer signed a contract to supply St Thomas's Hospital, at a cheaper rate than the hospital's long-time, neigh- bourhood dairyman. By the 1870s, the railways were the single biggest source of London's milk. By 1914, they delivered almost all of it. In just over half a century, the city's 'milkshed', the radius of farming areas that could feasibly supply the capital with fresh dairy, grew from ten to 200 miles.[22] The transition was given a jolt by successive outbreaks of cattle plague in the cramped barns and cellars scattered across the metropolis, the last and most brutal wave striking in 1865–6. As urban customers became more used to their milk coming from further afield, railway companies and dairy firms developed ways to cool milk with water, giving distant suppliers an extra edge.[23] Railways and refrigeration overcame a core challenge: fresh milk, once taken from the cow, goes off very fast.

For centuries before the railways, London's dairy industry tackled the problem of perishability with an intensive system of local production. In his 1598 *Survey of London*, John Stow recalled, in his youth, collecting milk 'hote from the Kine', from a farm owned by the abbey known as the Minories, near Tower Hill.[24] From the seventeenth century, more and more farmers kept herds in fields just beyond the sprawl or in barns within the city itself. Numerous inventories of goods belonging to these 'cowkeepers' survive. They ran farms of 7 cows in Hoxton, 10 in St Giles in the Fields, 22 in St Giles Cripplegate, 33 in St Martin-in-the-Fields, and 66 cows in Islington. In 1694, Richard Gray's St Pancras dairy had 69 cows and a bull, along with 16 horses, 120 loads of hay, grain carts, milking tubs, and pails.[25] In time, most of London's herds were located in an arc that spanned the north side of the city, from Marylebone in the west to Hackney and Bethnal Green in the east. In his recent history of animals in the Georgian capital, Thomas Almeroth-Williams used the presence of all these cows to argue that, counter-intuitively, urban growth increased interactions between humans and livestock.[26] The total number of cattle may have peaked as late as the 1860s, when about 20,000 were kept within the County of London. Two decades later, despite stiffer competition for space and tougher sanitary rules for how cows should be accommodated, there were still just under a thousand registered cowkeepers in the metropolitan area.[27]

Like the market gardens, London's suburban dairies were among the most sizeable and forward-thinking in England. The average herd contained several dozen cows. At the top end, Richard Laycock kept as many as 700 head across 500 acres in Islington and the next-door parishes in the early nineteenth century. Today this would be in the largest 2 per cent of the country's herds.[28] Worked harder than in many dairy regions, London cows were typically kept inside half the year or longer, with those closer to the centre housed throughout the seasons. Their diet was enhanced with protein-rich brewers' grains (the by-product of another London industry) and fodder like hay and turnips.[29] Hay-growers and cowkeepers also profited from the prodigious piles of town manure, which they liberally spread on their fields. These advances meant that metropolitan herds could yield 3,000–4,000 litres of milk per cow each year. This was how much a standard English dairy farm achieved as recently as the 1970s.[30]

Tending the animals and carrying their milk, dairy workers were divided into specialized roles. The occupational titles of cowkeeper and milkman, to judge by their appearance in probate documents, both seemed to have emerged in the seventeenth century.[31] The former denoted someone more involved in husbandry, while the latter suggested a person engaged in distribution and retail, though as we have seen the responsibilities sometimes overlapped.[32] Whatever they called themselves, the men and women who sold milk on the streets tramped out to the barns and fields, milked the cows, and carried the sloshing pails back into the city. Cowkeepers and milk sellers built lasting, commercial ties. Hawkers could buy from the same farmer for years and several described keeping 'cowkeeper's money', presumably a pot of cash owed to their suppliers for milk.[33] This division of labour gave carriers independence, even later on when they were employed by dairy firms. But this relative freedom could be open to abuse. In 1888, a milk carrier appeared at Bow Street police court, charged by his boss for conspiring with a customer, a coffee-stall man, to rob him 'in a systematic manner'. This was hardly a high-stakes scheme: detectives spotted the carrier pouring out multiple cups of milk and swapping them with the stallkeeper for a slice of bread and butter.[34]

This division of labour was another solution to the perishability problem. Milk, like fish and soft fruit, had to be sold and consumed quickly. Not tied to particular routes and hours, hawkers found a market for these foods by bringing them directly to customers. In this way, they were an asset to London's farmers, fishermen, and gardeners, as well as the broader population, which the capital's government recognized. In 1619, a committee of City aldermen argued that fruit sellers should be allowed to stand in the streets on market days from morning until sunset, their goods 'being a perishinge Comoditie, [which] requireth a quicke utterance and sale'.[35] In the eighteenth century, vendors of milk and mackerel enjoyed a partial exemption from restrictions on Sunday trading, because those foods would not keep an extra day.[36] Walked into town by hawkers, milk produced at three or four in the morning was on Londoners' tables by breakfast. In summer, gluts of strawberries and raspberries could be picked and sold the same day. Within hours of its landing at Billingsgate, fish was proffered at citizens' doors. Until the Victorian era, when steam power enabled faster transport, and cooling systems and packing with ice kept food fresh for the journey, these industries had to stay within easy reach of London. Even then, shipped-in fruit, heavy catches of fish, and churnfuls of milk would not keep long. Street sellers remained indispensable.

Cumulative improvements in production, retail, and distribution separated milk from the rest of the street trade over the nineteenth century. In his journalism, Henry Mayhew did not equate dairy sellers with the majority of costermongers and stallkeepers. He claimed there were just twenty men engaged in the trade, vending milk as a pleasurable drink at the wholesale markets and on green spaces, like Clapham Common and Hampstead Heath.[37] By then, those serving London homes were part of a more organized industry. Though the door-to-door trade persisted, customers could find milk in the expanding network of dairy shops, many of them branches of chains. By 1900, the ten largest dairies controlled more than two-fifths of the city's stores.[38] The epoch of the cowkeeper and the independent, mobile milk seller had not yet ended, but it was certainly on the wane.

As regular as the weather permits

In the seventeenth and eighteenth centuries, fish was already brought to the capital from an enormous catchment: salmon was shipped down from Scotland via Berwick and Newcastle; herring began their season in the North Sea, before passing through the Channel; pilchards and mackerel were taken off the south coast, especially off Cornwall; sprats were netted all over. The Thames and its estuary also offered a host of fish and shellfish, such as flounders, oysters, and shrimp, as did the waterways of Essex and Kent.[39] These were almost word for word the same sources listed by Dodd and other commentators in the mid-nineteenth century.[40] Though there was some costly overland transport involving horse-drawn carriages racing from coastal ports, most seafood continued to reach the metropolis by water. In the 1830s, according to one salesman's estimate, waterborne volumes still exceeded those coming by land by three times or more. They still dominated a couple of decades on, benefiting from the introduction of 'well vessels' in which fish could be kept alive and the more general use of ice for preservation.[41] Eventually, steam trawlers and railways opened up more fisheries as far away as Iceland and the White Sea, while increasing supplies from established areas like East Anglia came on dedicated rail lines.[42] The point of arrival in the city was another fixture. Despite a number of short-lived challengers, Billingsgate remained London's fish selling centre.[43]

From the stunning diversity landed at the wharf-cum-mart, hawkers stuck to certain varieties. Most of the time, they left the privileged fishmongers to the expensive fresh cod, turbot, and lobster, and focused their energies on options more affordable for the public at large.[44] The foremost street sellers' fish were mackerel, herring, sole, whiting, and plaice. Sprats were another mass-market favourite. One young hawker called them 'God's blessing for the poor'.[45] Street vendors also were important sellers of shellfish, such as whelks, mussels, and oysters. Londoners were discerning about their origins, with oyster varieties named for specific towns, such as Queenborough, Faversham, Milton, and Colchester, around which bivalves with specific qualities were harvested. Early on, street sellers were chiefly associated, at least in music, literature, and art, with one variety in particular. 'Wallfleet' was more than a punning term tying hawkers to a notorious London district, to the west of the City, near Bridewell prison. No coastal town called Wallfleet exists, but these mysterious oysters probably came from an island in the River Crouch, across from the Essex parish of Burnham, in the brackish waters around what is now the nature reserve of Wallasea. The location supposedly grew some of the country's tastiest oysters, small with a greenish tint.[46]

All this seafood did not flow into Billingsgate in a steady stream. The popular notion that oysters are only safe to eat in months containing an 'R' derives from the traditional season for English natives. In the mid-sixteenth century, the borough of Colchester banned the harvesting of oysters between Easter and Holy Rood Day (14 September), to allow the shellfish to breed in warmer waters and the young spat to establish.[47] By the nineteenth century, this old seasonality was rendered less relevant by the farming of immature oysters in nurseries in the Thames and along the south coast, and the opening up of new beds in the Channel, as well as illicit practices like dredging and harvesting too soon.[48] Most street-sold fish had their seasons and, within those, supplies came in surges. Giving evidence to a parliamentary inquiry in 1833, several Billingsgate buyers described the mackerel rush that started each June. One day, 100,000 fish might be unloaded from boats docking one after the other; the next day might bring just 5,000. Conditions overhead added a further wrinkle, affecting how much time boats could spend at sea. Asked whether London's supply was regular, salesman John Tyler answered dryly: 'Quite as regular as the weather will permit.'[49] This uncertainty had an impact on what those fish could fetch, sometimes by the hour. The same was true for other seasonal foods like fruit. A Kentish gardener explained how the first cherries he sent to Covent Garden at the beginning of July made 6d. a pound. The cherries were still sold by hawkers, but only the upper classes could afford them, until prices dropped to a penny or lower when the season hit full stride.[50]

Street sellers followed these rhythms as they changed their stock throughout the year. Mayhew laid out for his readers the street sellers' fish season, which began with the influx of herring in October and finished with the last mackerel in July, and a fruit and vegetable season, starting with the soft fruit of high summer, passing through apples and pears from early autumn, with greens like kale and cabbage lasting over winter.[51] Cycles of production, on land or at sea, translated into the appearance of different foods sold on the street. Most of the specific incidents of street selling I have identified before 1825 can be tied to a particular month. The eleven references to selling strawberries, cherries, apricots, and peaches all occurred between June and August. All but one of the seventy-two incidents of oyster selling took place from August through to April, the classic English season. Most fish varieties are not named individually, but the half-dozen times sprats were mentioned all fell in December and January.

This culinary calendar influenced how hawkers and other food sellers marked time. In 1671, giving evidence about an argument between vendors at Newgate market, Catherine Pitts could not remember the date of the dispute. She only knew that it took place 'in the latter end of last summer, viz. when Wall Nutts came just in season, and black Cherrys were going out'. Other market traders referred to parts of summer as 'damson time' and 'Lamb time'.[52] These were not just euphemisms for vague stretches of the year. To make a living, hawkers had to pay close attention to what was arriving at the markets. Elizabeth Rigby hurried down to Billingsgate on 1 August 1789, 'the very first day of oysters coming in', while Mary Bryant, whose husband was a hawker, sent their servant to Spitalfields the first week of July 1825, 'to see if cherries were come in'.[53] Just as watches and clocks were becoming more prevalent, attending to these comings and goings was not confirmation of street sellers' backwardness. These rhythms of nature and

agriculture were crucial to hawkers, and through them these senses of time
continued to resonate in the metropolis.[54] They still did in the nineteenth
century. Lord Mayor's Day, then 9 November, was known by some hawkers
as 'sprat day', the date around which the small fish so vital to their winter
fortunes began to flood in. Crowds rushed down to the Thames, jumping
onto boats and scrambling up the rigging, desperate not to miss a moment
of the season.[55]

For foods with fluctuating supplies, street sellers clung on to their position as essential retailers the longest. After the launch of special railway lines
in the 1840s, such as the 'fish-train' that set off from Lowestoft for the capital
every evening, the late Victorian period saw an expansion in the variety and
volume of fish available in London. Seafood became a more routine feature
of working class diets.[56] Amid all this improvement, old characteristics of the
London fish trade endured, as the Royal Commission investigating Britain's
markets discovered in the 1880s. The City Corporation initially resisted the
introduction of refrigeration facilities at Billingsgate, concerned that keeping stocks overnight would manipulate prices that were supposed to be
driven by supply and demand on a given day, a remnant of the medieval
economic thinking that still shaped market management in the capital. And
street sellers remained key distributors of fish that would not keep. 'I should
say that the costermongers were really the best customers to Billingsgate
Market,' the secretary of the London Fish Trade Association told the
inquiry.[57] By then, the waterside setting would have looked quite different.
A renovated Billingsgate opened in time for oyster season in August 1852,
the site's first permanent buildings constructed of red brick in Italian style,
with gas lights to illuminate early morning trade, a market devoted to shellfish on the lower storey, and a system of mechanical ventilation that cun-
ningly expelled air through the central clock tower.[58] But the fish selling
business, with hawkers at its centre, remained fundamentally the same.

Movable feasts

Most of what we know about on-the-go food in the seventeenth and
eighteenth centuries comes from unusual evidence. While descriptions of
snacking or eating outdoors are few and far between, we can draw on
alternative sources like music and images that represented hawkers and the
dishes they sold. In a piece for voices and strings that evokes the cries of

street sellers, the composer Orlando Gibbons mentions eleven kinds of fruit, ten vegetables, and ten fish, but also six different cakes and pies.[59] In his prints of street selling characters, Marcellus Laroon included vendors shouting 'Hot Bak'd Wardens Hott' (a variety of pear suited to cooking), 'Colly Molly Puffe' (some kind of pastry), and 'Buy My Dutch Biscuits' (by the looks of the picture, a flat, round baked treat).[60] A ballad, 'The Cries of London', lists a smorgasbord comprising dumplings, nuts, pies, tarts, oysters, plum pudding, 'hot-spice gingerbread', and 'Yorkshire muffins', along with drinks like rice milk and salop, the latter a spiced and thickened beverage originating in the Ottoman Empire.[61]

Because these pictures and songs were produced primarily to delight an audience, they should be approached with scepticism. See, for example, the view of Covent Garden painted in the early eighteenth century by Flemish-born Pieter Angillis (Figure 7). In the bottom left of the image, a woman sits behind a hotplate, cooking what seem to be pancakes for a pair of young children. To her side is a tub, filled with what could be batter. Pleasing as it

Figure 7. A view of Covent Garden market in full flight in the early eighteenth century.

is, this street food portrait should make us wary. The particular choice of Shrovetide delicacy fits snugly into the carnivalesque scene Angillis has conjured. And the pancake seller bears a more than passing resemblance to one sketched by an earlier Low Countries artist, Rembrandt van Rijn.[62] Wherever possible, these creative sources need to be weighed against other material, such as descriptions of street selling in court reports, government records, and journalism. These sources do not turn up any pancakes but do show that London's seventeenth- and eighteenth-century hawkers indeed served up, in addition to abundant fruit, oysters, and shrimp, an assortment of baked goods, such as cakes, pies, gingerbread, and muffins. A few sold cooked meat, including baked sheep's heads and sausages, like the heavily spiced polonia pudding. The unusual street drinks mentioned in the Cries of London ballad, rice milk and salop, were also on offer.[63]

Sometimes these foods were prepared in small-time, family operations. Teenager Thomas Smith walked the streets with sausages made by his mother, while William Rose's mother baked cakes for her son to take out.[64] But it is likely that many bought supplies from specialist tradesmen, like makers of muffins and gingerbread.[65] Baking and cooking foods like sausages required laying out money for ingredients, not to mention room and equipment for preparation and storage. In her 1664 recipe book, Hannah Woolley instructed cooks making polonia pudding to mix pounded meat with salt, pepper, cloves, mace, ginger, nutmeg, cinnamon, aniseed, caraway, and coriander, and let the mixture soak in salted water and then wine for several days. Finally, the stuffed sausage should be smoked overnight in a chimney.[66] For most hawkers, making such long-winded dishes at home was impossible. The same limitations on household space and amenities that made Londoners rely on street sellers also pushed street sellers themselves to rely on professional cooks and bakers.[67]

Major changes in the culture and economy of food were reflected in what hawkers carried in their baskets. From the late seventeenth century, Britain experienced what food historian Sara Pennell has called a 'baking bonanza'. Sugar and milled flour became more widely available, as did portable ovens made of earthenware and metal that fitted into smaller homes.[68] Sweet treats like gingerbread would have been altered by these developments. Hannah Woolley provided a recipe for 'fine' gingerbread, which involved taking spiced and sweetened breadcrumbs and boiling with wine to make a stiff paste. The result would have been a claggy dough.[69] A century later, another cookbook writer, Hannah Glasse, published a recipe for

'Ginger-Bread Cakes' that would be more recognizable today. She called for flour and sugar to be rubbed into butter, then flavoured with nutmeg and ginger, before moistening with warm treacle and cream. The dough was to be cut into cakes and baked 'in a slack oven'.[70] Of course, these books do not tell us what contemporary cooks actually turned out, but the product of Glasse's recipe would have been closer to the flat, spiced biscuits we know were sold warm on London's streets. Lighter and sweeter, these gingerbreads were also connected to the leap in sugar consumption that followed the establishment of English plantations in the Caribbean. These cheap, tasty snacks were the final stage of a chain, reaching thousands of miles across the Atlantic, linking hawkers to the forced labour of African slaves.[71]

Sugar was far from the only import to find its way to the street. Hawkers gained from the growing appetite for citrus fruit imported from Spain and Portugal. The volume of oranges and lemons shipped to London trebled over the second half of the seventeenth century.[72] In a newsletter of 1700, part of a series on the topics of food and agriculture, John Houghton claimed the fruits' popularity in the capital was due to their distribution by hawkers. 'For since they are carried in the eye of all about the streets,' Houghton wrote, 'we see they are very much consumed by ordinary people.'[73] Later arrivals included coconuts, like oranges frequently sold by young Jewish men, and pineapples, which were pushed around in barrows decked with special flags.[74] Able to switch their stock as tastes and fashions changed, hawkers may have introduced many Londoners to these exotics. These novelties continued to excite and, perhaps, confuse. In 1897, a costermonger called Henry Nathan appeared at Thames police court, the sanitary inspector of Poplar having found bananas 'bad and unfit for food' on his barrow. Nathan pleaded that the inspector 'might be a judge of meat, but was not of bananas', because the outsides turning black did not mean the fruit was rotten.[75] To be fair to the officer, bananas were not a common sight until the early twentieth century. Hawkers like Nathan were at the forefront of a trend.[76]

In the nineteenth century, the range of ready-to-eat street foods exploded. In *London Labour*, Mayhew split his lengthy list into those substantial enough for a cheap meal (such as hot eels, pickled whelks, sheep's trotters, pea soup, ham sandwiches, and boiled meat puddings), sweet indulgences (tarts of rhubarb, currants, and gooseberries, mince pies, plum cake, Chelsea buns, and crumpets), and drinks (as run-of-the-mill as tea, coffee, and cocoa, as surprising as ginger beer, 'Persian sherbet', and peppermint water).

Some of these trades were of 'great antiquity', like the vending of hot green peas, while others, like the sale of baked potatoes, were recent inventions.[77] However strong this upswell in street foods actually was, the factors that made eating out so important in earlier centuries—the premium on domestic space, lack of cooking facilities, and need for sustaining meals for those working away from home—continued to exert themselves and with even more force. We should also read Mayhew with care. Though his information was based on extensive interviews, he was versed in the tradition of the Cries and the genre's nostalgia rippled through his reporting. From his 1850s perch, Mayhew lamented the decline in street sellers of 'Eatables and Drinkables' that had taken place in the previous decades, blaming a slump in labourers' wages and the spread of petty shops stocking the same low-cost luxuries.[78] He was correct that some foods lost their hawking association. One of these was fried fish. This may have started as a street trade: in back alleys where neighbours were less inclined to complain about the stink, vendors battered and fried flatfish, haddock, and whiting, which were carried around on trays or offered at stalls. At some point, this somehow combined with the frying of potatoes—the moment of revelation is lost to history—creating the fish and chip shops ubiquitous in the capital and the industrial cities of the north.[79]

New street foods continued to appear, with fresh generations of hawkers bringing their own specialities. Londoners had sampled ice cream before the poor Italian community settled in the metropolis in the second half of the nineteenth century. But armed with first-hand experience of cold treats back home and taking advantage of commercial ice production, the immigrants brought ice cream to the masses.[80] Early in the morning, Italian men purchased ice from shops dotted around Hatton Garden and Saffron Hill. They churned it with sugar and flavourings, adding eggs and milk if they were making a richer 'cream ice'. Their earnings depended on the season and the temperature, rising as high as several pounds profit a week in a hot spell.[81] To be served, the ice cream was scooped from the hawker's barrow into small returnable glasses. Alternatively, some sold what the English called 'Hokey Pokey', stripes of stiffened ice cream wrapped in paper, the name a possible corruption of the Italian cry, 'Ecco un poco' ('Here's a little bit').[82] This new treat was not universally welcomed. Investigations into the insanitary conditions where the Italians lived and kept their ingredients were succeeded by a flurry of claims from newspapers that the vendors were trying to poison children. In 1885, thirty people fell ill and some were admitted to hospital, having bought ice cream from an Italian stallkeeper in Lambeth Walk. Apparently, a metallic substance was found in the cream.[83] Such accusations were laced with xenophobia, but they also reveal London writers, readers, and consumers attempting to make sense of one more addition to the capital's larder.

The metropolitan diet

The foods hawkers sold were not the foundations of what Londoners ate. This probably explains why fish, fruit, vegetables, and milk have received less attention from historians, compared with energy-rich bread, meat, and beer and the imported sugar, tea, and coffee that became increasingly common-place between the sixteenth and twentieth centuries.[84] But that did not make these early street foods unimportant. In large part thanks to hawkers, these foods were more accessible in the capital than anywhere else.

Street sellers helped city people participate in a fruit and vegetable revo-lution. In early Tudor England, turnips, carrots, parsnips, and cabbages were seen as the unrefined foods of poor peasants, until harvest failures and soar-ing grain prices in the last decades of the sixteenth century prompted a re-evaluation. Governors and local justices began to encourage their culti-vation, writers proposed recipes, and dietary theorists recommended them as healthy for all sections of society. This coincided with the rise of market gardening, which allowed fashionable leafy greens, such as lettuce and asparagus, to appear more often on the plates of those who could afford them.[85] Fruit underwent a similar makeover. Renaissance physicians were cagey about the benefits of fruit, though in practice it had long been enjoyed by the wealthy. But by the start of this period fruit eating had shrugged off its ambiguous reputation and became a way for the members of the emer-ging middling sort to ape their betters and distinguish themselves from the labouring majority.[86] From the seventeenth century, hawkers played an important role, delivering vegetables that wound up on the tables of rich and poor, and offering small portions of fruit that became a quick, easy snack for much of the population. In 1618, a Venetian visitor described how the English did not take fruit at dinner or supper, but 'between meals one sees men, women and children always munching through the streets, like so many goats, and yet more in the places of public amusement'.[87] Because it ranged from inexpensive apples to fancy strawberries, and prices swung from season to season and throughout the year, even London's lower classes, with just a few pence to spare, could enjoy some fruit once in a while. This was obvious by the nineteenth century. A committee of MPs convened to investigate the fruit trade argued that it was important to balance the protection of British growers from imports with the 'adequate supply of the Public, and more especially of the middle and poorer classes of the Metropolis, in an important article of domestic consumption'.[88]

Hawkers' distribution also allowed London to be awash with milk. Since the medieval period, drinking fresh dairy or using it to cook was only possible in places where cows were kept close by, which most of the time meant the countryside.[89] London shrugged off this restriction by developing its intensive, suburban dairy industry, reliant on the labour of street sellers. In 1695, John Houghton estimated that, on average, each home in the capital purchased a gallon of milk a week, if businesses like chocolate and coffee houses were included.[90] How much each household actually consumed was determined by wealth and status. In the seventeenth and eighteenth centuries, trendy drinkers quaffed glasses of milk and tasted creamy dishes like syllabubs while visiting the city's parks.[91] London milk was known to be 'extremely dear', the price related to the high-cost system of production, though we know it was still on the menu in less rarefied venues, such as workhouses.[92] Despite all the technological improvements of the nineteenth century, the labouring classes still consumed much less milk than their social superiors, with rates of adulteration and watering-down higher in the East End where money was tight.[93] Milk sellers did most of their business at the homes of the best-paid workers and the middle class.

Up to now, food historians have argued that fish was rarely eaten by working people before the late Victorian period, the usual explanation being the few calories it provides for the price.[94] But London may have been an exception. Archaeological remains suggest that, as far back as the Middle Ages, the city's inhabitants ate plenty of seafood, especially herring, cod, whiting, and eel.[95] Even after the Reformation, the state and church set aside several days each week, along with periods such as Lent, when no meat was meant to be eaten, with fish consumed instead.[96] While these mandates lost their force over the seventeenth century, fresh and preserved fish was still eaten in places, like London, where supplies were ample and organized. Even institutions for relieving the poor included fish in their regimes. A weekly bill of fare for a Quaker workhouse at Clerkenwell in the early eighteenth century included the note that 'when peas, beans, mackerel, herring, salt fish &c. are in season' the steward should add these extras to the inmates' diet.[97] With gluts driving down prices, labouring Londoners could occasionally afford fish, even before the impact of steam shipping and refrigeration. In 1833, the chief officer of Billingsgate and one of the market's salesmen both told MPs that, when mackerel, herrings, plaice, and soles became cheap, the poor ate a 'great deal' of fish.[98] Speedy dissemination by hawkers made sure that, when fish was well priced, it found its way into the frying pans of all sorts of city folk.

The importance of these street-sold foods is hard to quantify. In the typical sources used to study what people ate in the past, such as the household budgets collected by social investigators, the likes of fish, milk, fruit, and vegetables were a minor element. In the 1840s, a skilled workman supporting a wife and three children on 30s. a week might spend 8s. on bread and 3s. 6d. on meat, but just 9d. on herrings and 6d. on greens, turnips, and onions. In straitened moments, such add-ons would be struck out altogether.[99] At the start of the twentieth century, similar budgets show labouring families able to spend more on meat than bread, with the better off able to buy slightly more fruit, vegetables, and fish, as Londoners gained from the improving living standards of the late Victorian period. Food costs fell due to rising imports, more efficient rail and water transport, and the wider uptake of intensive farming. But in budgetary terms, fish, greens, potatoes, and milk from street sellers' barrows were still not priorities for working class housewives.[100]

Such evidence does not give the full picture. Hawkers sold meaningful supplements to workers' humdrum diets. Affordable seafood in its seasons, the odd piece of fruit picked up on a whim, fresh milk swilled down or used for soups and porridges when wages allowed, even cooked dishes like fried fish, sausages, and pies—these were nutritious and likely satisfying accompaniments to the staples of meat and bread.[101] Over several decades, historians have debated whether industrialization improved or worsened conditions for working people. More recently, some scholars have argued for using more qualitative evidence that can shine a light on the complexities of labourers' lives.[102] Considering street food adds another layer to the story. In London, thanks to specialized food production and the presence of street sellers, the majority of the population, every so often, could eat with more variety and interest.

This variety was possible in the capital earlier than anywhere else in England. From the late sixteenth and early seventeenth centuries, London was growing much faster than other cities, and was able to support intensive market gardening and dairy farming, and provide a ready market for nearby fishermen. The essentials, meat and grain, were available all over, but the options available to Londoners outstripped those in other large centres.[103] Hawkers carried milk, fish, and poultry to the people of York, but suburban farming was slower to expand around the northern city and the seafood offering was more limited. Middling men in provincial centres like Canterbury could pick up street snacks like cherries, oysters, and sweets, but these luxuries were out of reach for most inhabitants. Bristol's merchants brought back exotics from across the Atlantic world, but the port did not form the productive bonds with its rural hinterland that London developed. Only the industrial cities of the North, like Manchester and Sheffield from the late eighteenth century, supplied their working population with such affordable diversity, as they benefited from the improved transport technologies of turnpike roads, canals, and eventually railways.[104] Nowhere else but London, from such an early stage, possessed this confluence of advantages that shaped the diets of people a long way down the social scale. And nowhere else were street sellers so important. We cannot put a number to hawkers' significance, but it is clear that their impact on London's food culture and economy was profound.

4

Markets

On the page, nineteenth-century writers captured the pulsing energy of London's markets. The morning scenes typical of novels, sketches, and journalism were most often set at one of the great old trading centres, like Billingsgate or Covent Garden. The time was a few hours after the start of business, when the bustle and bargaining were at their height. As if the market were the city's beating heart, traffic flowed in and out in all directions, carts and horses packing the streets on every side. Through the air shot barks of haggling, enquiry, instruction, and complaint, and the whinnies and snorts of animals. A fine author, attentive to their senses, would put into words the pervasive stench of fish, the intense sweetness of just-ripe fruit, and the feeling of cabbage leaves squelched by innumerable footsteps. Buyers, salesmen, and porters squeezed between rows of stalls and shops, beside the fishermen and gardeners who still came to market directly. Among the crowd, in the middle of the action, were street sellers. Depending on the market, the day, the season, the potential profits to be made, there could be hundreds, if not thousands of hawkers. They inspected stock, filled up baskets, and ordered carriers to take their purchases to the donkeys and barrows that waited outside.[1]

In more official views of London's economy, the place of hawkers was quite different. Since the sixteenth century if not before, the capital's governors had cast street sellers as marginal characters, trading on the edges of the legitimate buying and selling carried out in the main markets and shops. Food hawkers were emblematic of what we now call the informal economy, the semi-legal flipside of respectable work and business.[2] In an 1893 report, a London County Council committee described the 'informal markets, established by the costermonger in the public streets, which, as is well known, are quite unauthorised'.[3] Without this authorization, hawkers traded outside the approved structures of economic life. But that never stopped them stocking up in the markets and hauling fish, fruit, and vegetables to wherever their customers wanted.

Taking a long view, we can see how this tension played out. At first, hawkers were clearly at odds with the ideals of exchange. But as the city expanded and the market system struggled to adapt, their usefulness as retailers was recognized. Unauthorized they may have stayed, street sellers proved themselves essential to meeting the everyday needs of Londoners. If we look at the economy from the pavement, the division between formal and informal blurs into irrelevance.

Liberty of the markets

In the market system inherited from medieval London, street sellers were outliers. Between the sixteenth and eighteenth centuries, the ruling principle of the city's food trade was the notion of the open market. As liberal as this sounds, it actually meant that all food arriving in the metropolis, from grain to cattle to vegetables, should be brought immediately to one of the sanctioned marketplaces. With all buying and selling supposed to take place in public view, there could be no hiding of produce or manipulation of supplies, ensuring that the prices achieved were just and fair. Cloaked in the language of God and community, the rule of the open market was a core component of a moralized economic culture.[4] Across the City were a number of markets, where on certain days, between set hours, trading was allowed to take place. Some of these sites were more specialized, like the fish market Billingsgate or the livestock centre Smithfield, while others were more general, such as Cheapside, historically the main shopping street, divided into sections where different foods could be found.[5]

This traditional system, based on country farmers coming to sell their surplus to urban residents, was complicated by the demands of the growing capital. For sourcing food from the provinces and then distributing those supplies on arrival, London had long relied on middlemen, such as grain merchants who shipped corn from distant counties, and citizen retailers like fishmongers and fruiterers who kept their own shops and stalls. But re-selling goods bought at the market, if done without the Corporation's permission, was illegal. This was called 'regrating', defined in a 1552 act of Parliament as buying goods at a market or fair in order to 'sell the same again'.[6] A ban on regrating was one of London's seven *Lawes of the Market*, as listed in a pamphlet published repeatedly by the City aldermen.[7] In the early seventeenth century, regrators were among the 'evill disposed persons' accused of abusing the market system and pushing up prices for ordinary inhabitants.[8]

Some of these rule-breakers were street sellers. Regrating was the most commonly mentioned trading offence in a book of fines paid into the Corporation's coffers. The culprits were on the whole small-scale buyers and several were women, the kind of people likely to take that produce to the streets.[9] Billingsgate particularly concerned the City authorities. The aldermen and the officers of the Fishmongers' Company, the guild of retailers with a seafood monopoly since at least the fourteenth century, issued intermittent orders to keep regrating street sellers at the market in check.[10] In 1618, the aldermen ordered a cucking stool to be erected at the dock 'for punishment of Wenches yonge girles fish wives hearbe wives and such like that repaire thither for fish oysters and other victuals'.[11] This was a chair to which women deemed to be troublesome were strapped and then dunked in the water. A few decades later, when the markets were being re-established after the Fire of 1666, the Fishmongers tried to bar the hawkers from Billingsgate. The company members petitioned the aldermen, complaining that the right of women to buy and sell fish at the wharf had no basis in law and threatened the 'Lib[er]ty of Marketts' that was the Fishmongers' privilege.[12]

If their presence was so undesirable, then why did street sellers continue to come? The answer seems to be that the City government was flexible in pursuing the open market ideal. Though technically regrators, hawkers were broadly accepted, their activity raising alarm only from time to time, usually whenever the citizen retailers kicked up a fuss. Between 1590 and 1628, the City's chamberlain only received ninety-one fines for regrating, most of them coming in bursts. These low numbers indicate that punishment was, at most, irregular.[13] The pivotal street selling by-law of this early period, the 1612 licensing act, permitted some hawkers to do business, so it follows that they could purchase supplies to begin with. A rare depiction of London's streets, Hugh Alley's 1598 plan for the City's markets known as his *Caveat*, shows that re-sellers were envisioned among the ranks of buyers. The drawing of 'Newe Fish Street' shows a line of shops and stalls, with a number of carriers walking down the highway, one with a basket on her head probably a hawker. A central pillar is labelled 'Regraters', a hint that these middlemen and women should be given somewhere to stand.[14]

Their right to stock up was firmed up after the 1660s, a decade that saw furious arguments between Fishmongers and street sellers about accessing Billingsgate. A committee of aldermen was assembled to hear the worries of the women fish sellers, who claimed that the privileged retailers were swallowing up all incoming shipments and creating a monopoly—an argument to which the Corporation was sympathetic. To satisfy both sides, the aldermen told the hawkers to hold off for the first hour of trading each day and to stick to a corner of the market.[15] An act of Parliament passed in 1699 went further and prompted yet more outrage. Under new rules that confirmed Billingsgate as a 'free and open Market', the hour of grace was cast aside and the monopolizing Fishmongers were restricted even more.[16] Anyone, including hawkers, could come to buy.

This battle over Billingsgate was a flashpoint in the wider story of how London's markets were changing. From the mid-seventeenth century, limits on trading days and hours were loosened, with markets allowed to run throughout the week, apart from Sundays. In a process sped up by the Fire, markets that had formerly taken place in the streets, distinguished only by lined-up carts, temporary stalls, and piles of baskets, moved into dedicated spaces, out of the way of traffic. Some markets relocated and new ones were founded, overseen by the Corporation within the City boundaries and by private owners in the suburbs. Later on, market authorities constructed permanent, covered buildings with numbered shops, offices, running water, and ventilation.[17] Covent Garden exemplifies these developments. Part of an initial wave of market foundation when its charter was granted in 1670, the market hosted sellers of fruit, vegetables, herbs, and flowers daily, not on a few set days, and across an open piazza, rather than a street crossed by traffic. Even as business blossomed, the gardeners and salesmen still worked in a mishmash of wooden shacks and stalls, until the Bedford estate got together the money to build a market hall, designed by architect Charles Fowler in neoclassical style, completed in 1830, and still the linchpin of the market today.[18]

Covent Garden was an example of another trend. Eventually, many long-standing markets became focused on wholesale, serving retailers rather than shoppers. The number of predominantly wholesale markets across London trebled from seven in 1660 to twenty-one in 1800. Building on existing specialties, Billingsgate was the place for seafood, Leadenhall and Newgate were hubs for poultry and meat, and Covent Garden, Spitalfields, and Borough were known for garden produce.[19] This shift proves that worries about regrating were easing and that re-sellers, from shopkeepers down to hawkers, were encouraged.

In the nineteenth century, street vendors were welcomed. Henry Mayhew claimed that a busy Saturday at Covent Garden saw 2,000 men turning up with barrows and donkeys and 3,000 women arriving on foot to fill up their baskets. At the cheaper markets, like Borough and Spitalfields, hawkers may have dominated.[20] They became so ordinary a sight that, when the Royal Commission on Market Rights and Tolls was gathering evidence in the 1880s, seven costermongers were invited to testify. The men were asked for their opinions about how London's markets should be run. Henry Cosgrove, a street seller of thirty years' standing, described a normal day at Billingsgate:

> Q. At what time in the morning do you go? A. Sometimes I get there at five, sometimes at half past five, and sometimes at eight o'clock.
>
> Q. When is the time when you begin to buy fish? A. As soon as I get there, as soon as the market starts at six o'clock.
>
> Q. You begin at once? A. No, I walk round the market to see the cheapest I can get.
>
> Q. Are you kept waiting until the shopkeepers are served? A. No, if you like to top them you can top them if you think it is cheap enough for you to get a living out of it.
>
> Q. You are not interfered with if you do that? A. No.

Like other street sellers, Cosgrove was free to use the market as he wished. When he made a purchase, he went on to explain, he even paid a porter to take the fish to his cart ('Four pence a package, if it is just outside the market, and if it goes to Tower Hill it is 6d.').[21]

By the mid-Victorian era, the presence of street sellers in the markets was not questioned. But as long as hawkers had taken to the streets, they had batted off the criticism of City governors and guild members, and joined the market crowds. This fits into the bigger story about the rise of retailing across England, the chronology of which continues to be debated by historians. Scholars were once split between those who argued that distribution remained 'fairly basic' until the second half of the nineteenth century, when glitzy department stores and chains with branches joined the fray, and those that made the case that the market-centred medieval economy was already becoming multifaceted from the late eighteenth century, with the expansion of cleverly designed, efficiently run shops.[22] More recently, historians of earlier centuries have revealed how shopkeepers in towns and villages across the country had long been skilled, innovative, and responsive to their customers' demands and new fashions.[23]

The extended story of London's markets—and the enduring presence of hawkers—offers a different perspective. From the late Elizabethan period, the aldermen, whose prime concern was keeping citizens fed, were already willing to apply the old, moralized rules of the open market with pragmatism. Throughout the seventeenth century, London relied on a diverse set of retailers, including shopkeepers and street sellers, who worked alongside a market system that was slowly transforming and specializing to meet the population's needs. And the late Victorian developments did not suddenly do away with what came before, as timeworn features of food marketing persisted. Covent Garden gained an impressive market hall enclosed in glass and iron, but was still mocked in *Punch* throughout the 1880s as 'Mud Salad Market', due to its messy passageways, congestion in the nearby streets, and shoddy management.[24] Over three centuries, whether they worked on the kerbside, at market stalls, or behind the counter of a shop, London retailers adjusted to how their city and its commercial opportunities were evolving.

This did not make the markets easy places to work. In the trading scenes typical of nineteenth-century literature, visitors were met with a sensory barrage, which street sellers faced every day. Sketching a London morning, Charles Dickens described Covent Garden and its environs, where 'men are shouting, carts backing, horses neighing, boys fighting, basket-women talking, piemen expatiating on the excellence of their pastry, and donkeys braying'.[25] In previous centuries, when the official markets were held in the streets, the commotion would have been equally powerful. During the period in which it was the capital's main general market, Cheapside was also a thoroughfare, and the aldermen had to balance the competing interests of country and City-based traders, customers, residents on either side, and walkers and passengers just trying to sneak through.[26] To buy what they needed for the day, hawkers would have had to watch their step.

Doing business in the markets was also challenging. Over the centuries, street sellers were far from the only buyers. Apart from the Fishmongers and other retailing guilds clinging on to their privileges, there was a rising number of salesmen, working as agents for gardeners and fishermen or receiving shipments on consignment and taking a cut of eventual sales.[27] Another rival, from the nineteenth century, was the 'higgler' or 'bummarree'. Arriving at market early, these speculators bought up large lots as soon as they came in, parcelling them up to sell on to retailers who turned up later. This annoyed both hawkers and shopkeepers, who believed the practice inflated prices.[28] Street sellers were also vulnerable to deception. Many appeared in

London's police courts as victims, having found themselves landed with tainted or rotting produce. On 7 May 1868, a Vauxhall hawker named John Burke was called in front of a Lambeth magistrate to give evidence. The morning before, he had bought a box of fish from a Billingsgate salesman, who had only let the street seller see a sample. When Burke got home, he discovered that 'only a few of the mackerel were sound, the others being in a putrid state'. The magistrate inspected the fish ('an unpleasant task', one newspaper said), then summoned the salesman and decried the 'atrocious fraud'.[29] With London's legal officers now acting in his interests, Burke was an ordinary marketgoer who had been duped.

In defence of hawkers

More than grudgingly accepted, hawkers were thought to be helpful. Speaking to the Royal Commission on markets, the owner of Spitalfields was effusive in his praise. He had built special lanes for the hawkers to bring their barrows into the centre of the market. 'The costermongers are a very useful people in clearing the market,' the owner said. 'They clear out fish and green stuff.'[30] One of the testifying street sellers, John Denton, explained what 'clearing' meant. At Spitalfields, the greengrocers made their purchases hastily in order to return to their shops. Hawkers like him waited until about nine, when the main portion of trading was done and the growers and their agents tried to sell off the leftovers. 'When the market is over, we buy much cheaper,' Denton added.[31] This practice was not restricted to the late nineteenth century. In 1798, agriculturalist and surveyor John Middleton wrote that London's market gardeners were similarly grateful for street sellers. Superior retailers with shops and stands only bought the choicest vegetables, but both farmers and consumers were indebted to the 'jack-ass drivers, barrow-women, and other itinerant dealers', who hawked the rest of the greens at a 'moderate price'.[32]

Connected to this role was the widespread belief that hawkers merely sold inexpensive food. In his testimony, Denton went on to describe how he ran a high-volume outfit: 'We have to buy cheap, because if we did not buy cheap we could not sell cheap, and if we could not sell cheap we could not sell a quantity, and if we did not a sell a quantity it would not pay us.'[33] James Greenwood argued that street sellers' approach of 'small profits and quick returns' was valuable for keeping food prices down. He reported that everywhere in Whitecross Street plaice sold for 2d. a pound, but if the hawkers were turned out the fishmongers' shops would demand twice as much.[34] Earlier on, it is hard to ascertain how much street sellers actually charged. In his eighteenth-century guide, John Trusler advised London newcomers that they could buy mackerel from hawkers for a third of the price that other retailers asked.[35] The actual rates of course would have fluctuated, but there are many reasons why street food may have been affordable. Hawkers followed the seasons, took advantage of abundant supplies, seldom sold top-grade produce, and mostly dealt with working and lower middle class customers whose spending was limited. Their trading costs were also low. In comparison to shopkeepers and market stallholders, fewer street sellers employed staff or paid rent for a spot to sell.

Emphasizing cheapness, however, risks diminishing the nuances of the street trade. Even standardized produce varied in price. How much hawkers paid cowkeepers for milk depended on the farm's distance from the city (that is, how far they had to walk there and back), though the only differences consumers likely saw were determined by how much water the retailers added, an unexceptional form of adulteration.[36] Nor were the varieties of fruit, greens, and seafood all worth the same. In the winter of 1800–1, Elizabeth Dunn was running an 'oyster ware-house' in Long Acre, a basic shop a rung above a street stall. That season she carried at least three options: 'best oysters', 'common ones', and some mussels. Her best sort, reserved for 'country' customers, were Whitstable natives.[37] Many street sellers also targeted wealthier clientele, particularly at the start of a certain food's season, when prices were higher.[38]

According to some commentators, street sellers benefited the overall economy by boosting consumption. In one of his eighteenth-century newsletters, under the title 'A defence of hawkers', John Houghton challenged these traders' critics to consider 'what would become of our milk and mackerel, our other fish, oranges, and lemons, &c. if no body could buy a single penny-worth, unless they went to a market or a shop for them'.[39] The anonymous author of a 1759 pamphlet, *The London Fishery Laid Open*, believed that street sellers could break the stranglehold of the largest seafood buyers at Billingsgate:

> Now, if the market was fairly supplied with all the fish that was really caught, and it was brought up directly from catching, without stop, and sold at the market without fraud, there would then be an end of forestalling or monopolizing of fish, and of all kinds there would be such plenty, as in general it must, and would be, afforded at reasonable rates; and the hawker then would be able

to bring to your own door every kind of fish, as good, both in freshness and quality, as the greatest fishmonger in town.[40]

Both arguments depart from the traditional principle that a town's inhabitants were best served by an amply stocked marketplace where no middlemen were allowed to influence prices. Competition within that marketplace, and the regulation of who could trade, had been the way to check the emergence of monopolies. But increasingly the market was not imagined as a specific, physical location. The market became the whole metropolis, wherever customers could be found.[41]

Putting a figure on street sellers' economic significance is difficult, a typical issue of studying informal activity in the past as well as the present.[42] One stumbling block is the size of their transactions. In descriptions of hawkers' sales, they handed over a 'half-penny' of codlings, 'two penny-worth' of pears, and 'sixpence' of oranges. Customers bought a 'pottle' of strawberries, 'five apricots' for a shilling, and a single cabbage. Sarah Metyard, a widow, had a quart of milk delivered 'every other morning, sometimes every day, sometimes two quarts a day'.[43] Such minor purchases would not always have been listed separately in a customer's written record of their spending, if they kept one at all. In towns and cities, fixed trading sites like markets and shops have left behind the few institutional records of food selling we possess, in books of accounts, rents, tolls, and customs. At the least organized end of the street trade, even measures were not consistent. In an article on watercress sellers in the 1880s, Greenwood described the haggling at Farringdon market around dawn. Hawkers paid a shilling for thirteen thumb-to-fingertip measures and a customary bonus called a 'blessing'. The only negotiation was over how much watercress that 'fair blessing' amounted to.[44]

In *London Labour*, Mayhew calculated how much food arrived at the capital's markets every year and what share of the total street sellers sold. He reckoned hawkers at Billingsgate bought the majority of the plaice, mackerel, fresh herrings, sprats, flounders, dabs, mussels, cockles, periwinkles, and whelks. At the green markets, they purchased more than half of the apples, pears, cherries, redcurrants, strawberries, and hazelnuts. They bought fewer vegetables, their largest shares being a third of the cabbages, turnip tops, marrows, and onions and half of the peas. Because of the immensity of the food supply, even in goods for which hawkers were not the biggest buyers, the quantities were still notable. Street sellers supposedly sold a quarter of the 496 million oysters that Londoners swallowed each year.[45] We should not place too much faith in the exact volumes, but take from them the fact that nineteenth-century hawkers accounted for a substantial proportion of the sales of foods in which they specialized. They had done so for a while. Before the advent of railway milk, almost all of London's supply was carried by hawkers from suburban farms. In the mid-seventeenth century, the aldermen pointed out that it was the custom for street sellers to buy at market the 'middle & worse sort of fish'.[46] 'Middle' and 'worse' could mean low-quality catches or varieties in less demand, but these would still have been a great part of what fishermen delivered to the Thameside. Just because hawkers' contributions were not easily counted did not make them measly.

Friends of the poor

Instead of quantifying their business, we can think about the ways that street sellers proved themselves indispensable to London residents. We know that their customers were scattered across the metropolis. Of the incidents of street selling identified up to 1825, it is possible to link 340 to the parish in which they took place (Figure 8). Almost nowhere was unknown to hawkers. Some sold in the centre of the City, like the fruit sellers who gathered outside the gates of the Royal Exchange. Others traded at London's limits, selling shrimps out in Kensington or pickled salmon on Mile End Road.[47] They worked in both the stylish West End, serving the middle classes, professionals, and politicians drinking and socializing, and downmarket neighbourhoods, like Houndsditch and Whitechapel, where the poor eked out their existence.

This dispersal matches the spread of street markets, the frequent congregations of hawkers in the second half of the nineteenth century. Greenwood explained that 'the busiest and most flourishing of London markets and market-places are situate midst of an extremely poor population'.[48] In 1893, the thirteen largest were located within the ring of impoverished districts in which most hawkers lived: King Street (Hammersmith), Berwick Street, Leather Lane, Chapel Street, Hoxton Street, Whitecross Street, Wentworth Street, Watney Street (Shadwell), Brick Lane, Chrisp Street, Lambeth Marsh, East Street (Walworth), and Southwark Park Road. But there were a hundred more sites, smaller in scale and distributed right across the capital.[49] Then there were the countless single stalls and roving hawkers, unplottable on a map but extending north, east, south, and west into London's furthest reaches.

The range of hawkers' customers has been obscured by their Victorian association with downtrodden districts. Mayhew bears some blame

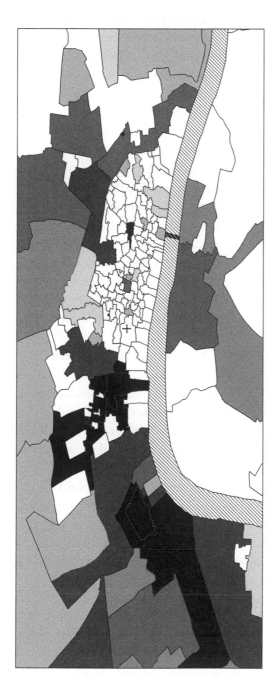

Figure 8. Map of London parishes where street selling incidents in the 1600–1825 sample took place, based on mid-eighteenth-century boundaries. The darker the shading, the more incidents took place in that parish. Once again, the general pattern is more important than the exact numbers.

0	0.5	1 mi

('the pedlar or hawker is the purveyor in general to the poor') but his own interviewees undermined such simplification. A mobile vendor pushed his vegetables around the airier suburbs, where his best customers lived in 'detached villas'; an oyster seller called her patrons 'gentlemen'.[50] Many of the earlier descriptions of street selling provide a sense of the customers' status. Most of them came from many-layered working London too. They included sailors and soldiers hungry for oysters while off duty; a gold chain-maker's apprentice who fancied some late-night gingerbread; singletons and married women walking the city alone; clerks, book-keepers, servants, and men labelled simply as 'labourer'; some were hawkers themselves.[51] A few were called 'gentle', hinting at a loftier standing. Street sellers supplied some splendid addresses. Daniel M'Carthy sold as much as 3s. of fruit a day to the Marylebone house of Lady Isabel Dashwood, whose husband had a 'position' in South Africa.[52] The middling and professional classes were no strangers to street sellers either. In his Restoration-era diary, naval adminis-trator Samuel Pepys mentioned buying three eels from a crier passing his Tower Hill home one Saturday morning in 1660. On another occasion, Pepys slipped down 'two pennorth of Oysters, opened for me by a woman in the Strand'.[53]

For these different customers, hawkers played distinct roles. Until the late nineteenth century, street sellers were the main way most Londoners bought milk and cheaper sorts of fish and fruit in their seasons. Before the railways and improved refrigeration, gardeners, cowkeepers, and fishermen relied on street sellers to find a market for their perishable products. Through these essential functions, street sellers became ingrained in metropolitan life. It was why the Corporation upheld their right to buy fish at Billingsgate, and why they found support among commentators like John Houghton.

Street sellers also carried food to underserved areas. From the early seven-teenth century, the proliferation of the city's official marketplaces did not keep pace with London's growth. Despite the population of the wider con-urbation quickly outstripping those living in the old centre, the western suburbs had just four markets by mid-century and the east had none. The City, meanwhile, was served by fifteen. As many as 40,000 residents of Hackney and Stepney had to walk several miles to buy food.[54] The rush of market building that followed the Fire of 1666 filled some of the holes, but the East End and south of the river remained patchily provisioned into the nineteenth century.[55] For these neighbourhoods, hawkers and small shops were crucial.

At the same time, the official markets stopped being places for ordinary shoppers, as they concentrated on wholesale business. According to estimates by historian Colin Smith, those markets' share of the retail food trade peaked in the mid-eighteenth century, before dropping to less than a fifth in 1840.[56] Later, the 1893 London County Council report made the stunning claim that the capital 'differs in one very striking particular from perhaps every other important city, in the fact that it has no general retail markets'. The nearest alternatives were the places where hawkers parked their barrows on a regular basis.[57] As Charles Booth's survey put it, street sellers' significance had 'no parallel in any other city'.[58] By the late nineteenth century, the flaws of London's food system and the benefits of hawkers were obvious.

The slimness of retail options hit workers and the poor hardest. The middle and upper classes had servants to do their shopping, and their homes were better served by the growing numbers of shops. Itinerant hawkers, roadside stalls, and street sellers' unauthorized markets became the chief ways for London's working population to buy food. Specifically, the necessity of the street markets was appreciated. In 1888, the managing clerk of Spitalfields told the Royal Commission: 'I conceive the secret of the market question to be the costermonger. He is really the great friend of the poor in the shape of cheap supplies.'[59] As we have seen, the affordable food offered by hawkers was one of the reasons why it pained many workers to leave the crowded inner city.[60]

Londoners of every class used street sellers for occasional treats. We have more information about eating on the go in the nineteenth century.[61] But we also know that for centuries the streets had been filled with oysters, fruit, nuts, and cakes, snacks that might cost as little as a few pence. To drinking houses, hawkers brought olives, anchovies, pickles, pies, and seafood. Historians of retail and fashion have written about 'small luxuries'. As part of a burgeoning consumer culture, middling and working people could treat themselves to ribbons, lace, buttons, books, toys, and other trinkets. The foods most discussed within this bracket have been the exotic imports, tea, coffee, and sugar.[62] The morsels available on London's streets should also be considered petty pleasures. They were momentary delights in reach of most of the population. And they pleased the upper orders too. On a visit to the city in 1786, German writer Sophie von la Roche was desperate to sample 'really fresh English oysters', so settled down at a Billingsgate inn and had a hawker bring over a selection.[63] A niche branch of the milk business involved keeping cows in the grand parks of West London. Visitors to the likes of Green Park could stop at a kiosk or stall, where they could glug down bowls of milk, fresh as could be, from a small herd of cows grazing a few steps away.[64]

Street food was not just a leisure activity. Since the Middle Ages, eating out had been a routine metropolitan experience. Household space was restricted for most of the population, for whom, until the nineteenth century, cooking facilities typically amounted to little more than a hearth and some utensils. That was why manufacturers and retailers of processed food, such as bakers and brewers, had historically been prominent.[65] Even with the eventual uptake of ranges, boilers, and gas ovens, housewives still relied heavily on specialized food sellers, as they balanced their domestic duties with the need to earn money. Most of the Lambeth housewives surveyed by Maud Pember Reeves in the early twentieth century lacked cupboards to store fresh food away from rodents, and were keenly aware of the cost of coal and gas for cooking, maybe preparing a hot, home-cooked dinner just once a week on Sundays.[66] As a result, working class areas were littered with stalls selling smoked and cured fish, sausages, and pies, and the first fish and chip shops.[67] With the city sprawling further and further, and workplaces often a long way from home, Londoners became used to eating out to sustain themselves through the day.[68] Historians have not always listed street sellers in the hierarchy of dining venues in English cities of the past, from cookshops, ordinaries, and alehouses, up to taverns, inns, and latterly restaurants and hotels. But buying from a hawker was one of the many ways to eat out in London.[69]

Today, as in the past, dining out straddles the line between luxury and necessity. Certainly, having supper at a restaurant or enjoying a spontaneous snack can be deeply gratifying. But we have to eat to survive and meals outside the home are part of our sustenance.[70] Most of the time, the street food of twenty-first-century London is an indulgence. Its burgers, tacos, and noodles are the offerings of a diverse, high-quality catering industry, serving customers spending disposable income in pursuit of pleasure as much as grub. The street foods of London's history were no doubt a source of satisfaction, a handful of fruit brightening an otherwise drab diet or a salty oyster well matched to beer or wine. But many of these foods were essential as well. Taking to the highway, stock piled high in baskets and wheelbarrows, hawkers brought working people, with little choice but to eat on the go, the food they needed to fuel their everyday lives.

5

Retailers

Leaving the hubbub of the markets behind, hawkers set off in search of customers. Some marched regular rounds, crying out as they went door to door. Some headed for taverns and pubs that overflowed with drinkers. Others planted themselves where walkers were guaranteed to pass, standing on the roadside or behind a portable stall. They had tools to assist them: baskets wielded with dexterity, wheelbarrows stacked with produce, donkeys that bore the load. But working in the midst of the thoroughfare was not easy. London's roads and lanes were unforgiving places, packed with pedestrians, horses, coaches, and carts, where conditions underfoot and overhead never stayed the same for long. Hawkers were caught in rain and muddied by dirt, threatened by strangers and knocked down by traffic. They had to be natives of the street environment, open to its opportunities, alert to its dangers.

The next three chapters reconstruct food hawkers' experiences doing business in the capital's streets. They unpick, in turn, how and where hawkers traded, the technology they carried with them, and the difficulties of being a worker who walked. And together they examine a number of bigger questions, about how we should think about the street.

Streets are one of the building blocks of city architecture, though their form and function has differed throughout human history.[1] In London, the three centuries after 1600 witnessed the emergence of a notion of the street that still holds, for the most part, in much of the world today. The streets of medieval and Renaissance Europe were profoundly public spaces, where rulers and religious elites displayed power and order through processions, feats of construction, and capital punishment, and where neighbours and acquaintances gathered to gossip and squabble, share in rituals, and haggle in markets.[2] In a process that started in earnest from the seventeenth century,

London's roads were straightened and widened, more properly cleansed and policed, and more comprehensively lighted and paved. Though the old, communal functions were never entirely abandoned, these developments privileged the free flow of people, traffic, and goods, an ideal that was embraced by nineteenth-century architects who moulded the streets into channels for unrestricted movement. Cleared of material obstructions and community ties, the street became somewhere to wander, dream, and consume the delights and commodities of the modern metropolis.[3] If any part of London was modern, it was the West End. Regent Street, the sweeping, stucco-lined boulevard designed by John Nash, was finished in 1825. As the century progressed, the surrounding area became the capital's 'pleasure district', where the wealthy and middle classes could browse in glittering arcades and grand department stores, goggle in theatres, music halls, and cinemas, and indulge at clubs, bars, and restaurants.[4]

This is not the only story we can tell about the street. Supposedly 'modern' features of street life, such as anxieties about women travelling alone or the regulation of traffic to stop annoying and costly blockages, were well established by the early seventeenth century, if not before.[5] What we think of as 'pre-modern' activities, such as buying and selling, never fully went away. In the nineteenth century, even the widened streets of Westminster and the City were choked with walkers, vehicles, and animals. Away from the West End's shimmering shopfronts and dazzling lamps, much of London remained dimly lit, its muddled houses made of crumbling wood and plaster, its narrow roadways muddy and rutted. Nash's Regent Street was a dramatic intervention, but London was not renewed in a totalizing scheme similar to what Baron Haussmann achieved in Paris. The improvement of the streets was incomplete.[6]

Taking to the streets throughout this period, hawkers experienced the contradictions of metropolitan modernity first hand. They gauged the progress of improvement by the sureness of their grip on the pavement and by how much they could see after dark. On the lookout for speeding vehicles and ill-intentioned citizens, they walked mindful that London's arteries were not truly safe for travel and work. And as retailers criss-crossing the city in pursuit of a sale, they knew how the streets merged with the city all around. Hawkers ensured the streets were never just a passageway, but remained a place of petty commerce, where everyday essentials and occasional treats were bought and sold.

About the streets

Hawkers' work was not limited to the highway. Each of the 443 incidents of street selling identified up to 1825 can be linked to a type of location, most of which continued to be popular with food hawkers during the nineteenth century. They reveal that street sellers traded in a variety of spaces that fringed the main current of walkers and traffic, spaces that confused the distinctions between public and private, open and closed, indoors and out. But they also tell us about their tactics as retailers, placing themselves at sites that they knew would be bustling or bringing food to where would-be customers lived.

Some street sellers who worked door to door were allowed inside Londoners' homes. Around two in the afternoon on 1 January 1807, Jane Metcalfe stepped down 'as usual' into the Shoreditch kitchen of Sarah Mitchell and delivered a pennyworth of milk.[7] Other residents mentioned leaving their 'street door' or 'back door' open, which hawkers took as an invitation to enter.[8] For much of London's history, public and private spaces were not sharply delineated. Inside homes, manufacturing and retail mingled with domestic functions, and temporary, wooden walls divided buildings between tenants. With the ground area at a premium, upper storeys jutted out over the street. Passers-by dealt with shopkeepers through open, unglazed windows. Larger dwellings had separate entries for servants and tradespeople to come and go.[9]

From the mid-seventeenth century, the interior–exterior divide became starker, with brick replacing timber and plaster in many buildings, and glass, doorsteps, and iron railings solidifying the borders of domesticity. This may actually have enhanced the role of the doorway as the 'archetypal liminal boundary'.[10] Most hawkers worked across this threshold. In one of his *Cries of London* prints from 1799 (Figure 9), the artist Thomas Rowlandson depicts a poultry vendor pushing a limp goose towards customers waiting on their doorstep. Through his choice of backdrop, Rowlandson makes a series of comic contrasts: the ruddy-faced, rotund hawker and his skinny, pale customers; ornate Westminster residences and outdoor labour; the comfortable middle classes and coarse working London. Amusing as the artist made it seem, crossing this divide was dangerous. House-to-house sellers were accused of using their business as a cover for theft. In 1729, Ann Parsons was charged

Figure 9. A poultry seller offers some geese to a pair of wealthy residents. Note the several comic contrasts set up by the artist, Thomas Rowlandson.

with stealing silver cutlery. The Old Bailey trial report stated that the hawker came to the prosecutor's house to sell oysters, but 'took an Opportunity to take the Spoons'.[11]

Drinking houses posed a different mix of risks and rewards. Hawkers were attracted to the alehouses, inns, taverns, and coffeehouses of the seventeenth

and eighteenth centuries, and continued to work in and around the
thousands of pubs in the Victorian city. Some were invited inside the more
public rooms to sell, while others pitched up outside. By the mid-1620s,
Hester Lacke had been selling oysters at the door of the White Horse tavern
in Friday Street 'for the space of thirtye years past'.[12] Shellfish remained
strong sellers. One vendor told the journalist Adolphe Smith, 'Oysters,
whelks, and liquor go together inwariable.'[13] More than half of the forty-six
descriptions of hawking at drinking places before 1825 involved oysters.
Street sellers also carried in fruit, gingerbread, pies, and shrimps, all snacks
that could be picked at while imbibing. Hawkers supplemented the food
offering that drinkers could expect at these venues, from the bread, cheese,
and cakes of the Tudor and Stuart alehouse to the pork pies and sandwiches
of the nineteenth-century pub.[14] But they also brought with them foods for
the household, such as cabbages, cauliflowers, fish, and milk. Not just for
entertainment, London's watering holes were alternative trading centres,
around which illicit markets were organized when dealing was supposed to
be restricted to certain settings.[15]

Most establishments served a broad clientele of working and middling
London. Only in the late nineteenth century did the more respectable parts
of the middle class start to abandon the pubs, partly due to temperance
movements and the appearance of new venues like cafés, teahouses, and
restaurants.[16] Despite the old belief that drinking houses were male-
dominated spaces, we now know that women were always among the
crowd. Women drank and socialized, ran their own venues, were hired by
publicans, and stepped in from the street to offer food and other services.[17]
Operating up and down the crude hierarchy of locales, hawkers traded in
venues that varied wildly in decency, from an elegant coffeehouse near
Whitehall to rougher spots frequented by the sailors and porters of East
Smithfield.[18] Hawkers found themselves in uncomfortable situations. A fried
fish vendor told Henry Mayhew how landlords welcomed him into the
different compartments of the public houses, earning him the nickname
'Fishy'. But more than once he had suffered his tray being 'kicked over
for a lark...and a scramble for my fish', on one occasion winding up in
hospital.[19] In previous centuries, hawkers were thrown around by rowdy
drinkers and had their pie tins knocked to the floor, while women retailers
were accused of selling sex.[20]

The hunt for customers even took street sellers to church. With religion
more central to metropolitan life than today, churches were conspicuous in
the cityscape. Before the Fire of 1666, there were more than a hundred

parishes within the City alone. Drawn by the stream of churchgoers, especially at the time of Sunday service, hawkers set up around church porches, in churchyards, or in the lanes nearby. Throughout the seventeenth and eighteenth centuries, the vestries of several parishes repeatedly ordered their constables and beadles to remove fruit and herb sellers from churches and their surrounds.[21] Parish authorities were fighting a losing battle. In the congested City, churchyards were appropriated for secular purposes. Some were used as cut-throughs, for hanging laundry, keeping poultry, and industrial tasks like cloth-stretching and brick-making. For a moment, the churchyard of St Paul's was the City's main herb market.[22] Among these many activities, the presence of hawkers was more often than not accepted and sometimes explicitly sanctioned. In 1654, the churchwardens of St Dunstan in the West received 15s. a year from 'the Applewoeman that sitteth at thee West end of the Church yard'. She was joined by John Smith, a fishmonger, who paid more than twice as much for a standing described only as a 'Board'.[23]

Street sellers placed themselves outside similar locations where Londoners were constantly coming and going for work or leisure. Offering oranges and oysters, vendors clustered by the doors of the Covent Garden playhouse on Drury Lane, which first opened after the Restoration and was rebuilt several times.[24] Outside the theatres for high and low tastes that popped up across nineteenth-century London, audiences could find ham sandwiches, baked potatoes, and whelks once the curtain had dropped.[25] Hawkers also had stalls by the gates of gardens and parks, where strollers could pause for a cup of milk or a handful of fruit.[26]

The most enduring prime pitch was outside the Royal Exchange. Opened by Sir Thomas Gresham in 1571, the institution hosted merchants from across the world who clinched deals each day in the ground floor courtyard, while fashion-seekers purchased luxuries like hats, jewellery, and fabric in the shops around the edge and on the balcony above. After being destroyed by the Fire, the Exchange was reconstructed and opened again just three years later.[27] Either side of this upheaval, hawkers gathered by the entrances, which throughout the seventeenth century drew the ire of local householders. In 1611, those who 'sell apples and other frutes at the Exchange' were blamed for blocking the street with baskets, which meant 'Coches and carts cannot well pass'.[28] Not long after reopening, an unnamed fruit seller was permitted to trade on the north side, if they paid £4 a year for the privilege.[29] Street vendors continued to line the passages leading into the Exchange

into the first decades of the nineteenth century. Among them were many
Jews offering oranges and lemons. The centre of Jewish London, around
Aldgate and Whitechapel, was just a short walk to the east.[30]

Churchyards, theatres, and commercial hubs were places of heavy footfall,
where hawkers hoped to pick up passing trade. Another tactic was to head
to pinch-points, such as bridges, where pedestrians were pressed together.
Until the opening of Westminster Bridge in 1750 and Blackfriars Bridge the
following decade, London Bridge was the capital's only Thames crossing.
Before it was demolished and replaced in the nineteenth century, the medieval structure was lined with shops and houses that loomed above a narrow
passage, around 15–16ft wide until the buildings were eventually removed.[31]
For hawkers, the slow-moving traffic provided a captive market, though the
City authorities were intolerant of potential obstructions. In 1617, Humphrey
Searle was imprisoned for selling apples on the bridge and he was far from
alone.[32] Fleet Bridge, which spanned the now-covered waterway that meets
the Thames at Blackfriars, was popular among sellers of oysters and fruit.[33]
In Ned Ward's *London Spy*, the bridge draws a grotesque rabble. When the
narrator and his companion cross the Fleet, they discover nuts, gingerbread,
oranges, and oysters 'Pil'd up in Moveable Shops that run upon Wheeles,
attended by ill-looking Fellows, some with but one Eye, and others without
Noses'.[34] I have found fewer instances of hawkers trading on bridges in the
nineteenth century, but Mayhew suggests they were still favoured. If there
was a decline, it may be explained by the ever-rising volume of traffic, which
might have made stopping to buy from a hawker impossibly disruptive.
Street sellers may have sought out emerging pinch-points elsewhere, including those offered by new forms of transport. By the 1870s, the Metropolitan
Railway Company was carrying 40 million passengers a year, part of a growing network of trains that ferried commuters in and out of wider London
above and below ground.[35] A hawker had a fruit stall against the wall of
Baker Street station. When the vestry of St Marylebone complained, the rail
firm wrote back to say that the vendor, one of many outside their stations,
paid a rent for the chance to tempt travellers.[36]

For most descriptions of street selling, we know only that they took
place on the street. We can read from their language that hawkers occupied
the highway in various ways. Some were more mobile, described as 'going
along' or roaming 'about the streets'.[37] Many were more static. Ann Carrol
sat with her fruit where her court met Rosemary Lane (with traffic coming
from several directions, corners were also regular haunts).[38] Asked whether

he carried his oranges all over or stayed in one spot, John Franks said, 'I stand in one place.'[39] When hawkers were said to run a 'stand' or 'standing', that could signify more than digging their heels in the dirt over time.[40] They used baskets, tables, and boards to substantiate their presence, or erected a more permanent stall. With a sturdier footing, these hawkers had much in common with the shopkeepers who worked in the houses just off the street. However different their shops might appear, they were all engaged in the business of selling.

Keeping score

As simple as a table, as elaborate as an awning-covered wheelbarrow, hawkers' stalls were scattered across London. In the mid-nineteenth century, Mayhew tried to count them. To take a sample, he trudged 46 miles and found 632 stalls, which worked out to 14 a mile. From that, he estimated a grand metropolitan total of 8,000 stalls piled with fish, vegetables, fruit, and more, not including those set up in the street markets.[41] Hawkers seemed to have combed the streets, stopped at a suitable place—plenty of passing custom, not too much traffic—and if they came back made a claim on a patch of ground. While living undercover as a street seller, the writer Olive Malvery thought she had hit on a promising location. But when she pulled up her barrow, Malvery heard the loud voice of a 'big, strong, red-faced girl' carrying potatoes and cabbages, and calling, 'Now then, missus, 'igher up; you're right on my pitch.'[42] From the brief descriptions of hawkers' work, we rarely know if there were financial arrangements involved. Did Marjery Carter pay to sell apples from the 'stall or shedd' outside Richard Coleman's house in seventeenth-century Westminster? By 1609, William Dawson had rented his 'shop or stall' against a tailor's for at least two years, but how much did he pay and how secure was his tenure?[43] These agreements clearly had meaning for street sellers and were acknowledged by rivals, landowners, and neighbours, even if they had little basis in law.

In comparison to brick-and-mortar shops, hawkers' roadside constructions appeared to be rickety. The disparity sharpened in the nineteenth century with the development of new spaces like the West End's shopping arcades, roofed with glass, patrolled by officers, and designed by architects, the epitome of modern retail.[44] But recognizable shops had in fact been multiplying across London since the medieval period and, from at least the seventeenth century, were becoming more sophisticated in design. Most were originally the front room of a house, entered directly off the street or from a passage. Inside, screens marked front and back rooms apart and shop-keepers employed boards, shelves, draws, fabric linings, and show-glasses to display their stock attractively. To separate themselves from the street, shops in well-heeled parts of town began to glaze their windows or put up a lat-tice to ward off pilferers. Even less fancy shops might have a sign, most likely a hanging one that swung in the breeze, an advertisement but also an indi-cation of status.[45] Victorian shopfronts became increasingly intricate with the use of columns, pilasters, and fascias, which framed transparent glass panes that became larger and more affordable with new methods of indus-trial production from the 1850s.[46] Later on, department stores combined glass with artificial light to create theatrical spectacles, worth visiting for their staging as much as the myriad services and wares under one roof.[47]

What counted as a shop, however, was not well defined. Many shop-keepers expanded their retail space into the street, by setting up tables out-side the front door, and exposing their goods through open windows, a drop-down board acting as an extendable counter. Fresh food sellers like fishmongers and butchers were among the last to introduce glazing. Only in the late Victorian period did they embrace sash and folding windows, which still allowed immediate access to passing customers.[48] Before then, the word 'shop' itself denoted various structures, such as a pavement table on trestles, a lock-up for storing supplies, a canvas-covered stall that could be folded away, and a wood or stone booth known as a 'bulk' that stood freely or leant against a building.[49] Many hawkers with more permanent pitches claimed to run 'shops', though it seems from the context of the descriptions that these were street-based establishments.[50] The distinction between four-walled shops and street stalls was fuzziest in the case of the cellars. Hawkers used these below-ground rooms, reached by steps or trapdoors, for storage and as shopfronts. Cellars were occupied most often by vendors of fruit and milk and were not just for retail. The 'milk cellar' was a place to go for a swift, refreshing beverage.[51]

Some hawkers' stalls had solid features. John Kirkland's Bow Street fruit standing must have been durable, perhaps with sides and a lockable front, because thieves 'broke open' the stall and took his oranges, lemons, and apples.[52] At first glance, most stalls looked basic. In the 1750s, Paul Sandby drew a cherry seller bent over a small, square table (Figure 10). Simple though it seems, she is using the top as a counter, somewhere to place a

Figure 10. A fruit seller weighs out cherries at a table with folding legs.

basket and weigh her fruit, while the folding legs allow her to move on at trading's end. Street retailers adapted whatever materials they had at hand to form a space for selling, which could be as makeshift as a couple of raised planks or a semicircle of baskets.[53] A wheelbarrow could be manipulated to build an enclosed stall. The shellfish vendor photographed by John Thomson in the late nineteenth century (Figure 11) has parked his barrow against the kerb. A fabric roof shelters his various pots and condiments. There is even a chair for someone to rest their legs. A pair of customers inspect the goods on the counter, the one in a bowler hat framed by the structure. Where street sellers gathered in irregular markets, similar vertical frames were used to hang food.[54]

Hawkers brought to the street the techniques of retail too. They may not have used ticketed prices or advertised with printed trade cards, but they organized and prepped their stock much like their more permanent counterparts. After buying what they needed for the day, hawkers spent a good deal of time arranging and prettifying their purchases. A watercress seller

Figure 11. The substantial stall of a shellfish seller in the late nineteenth century.

interviewed by Mayhew explained how, after buying several bunches at Farringdon Market, he washed them at a water pump in Hatton Garden 'to make them look nice and fresh all the morning, so that the wind shouldn't make them flag'. Others tied the stalks in halfpenny measures as they walked off to their pitches or sat on the steps of the nearby church of St Andrew Holborn.[55] One July morning in 1860, between seven and eight, hawker James Crawley was washing some fish in a public drinking fountain in Southwark. Crawley was spotted by the district's inspector of nuisances and, after refusing to stop, was called before the local magistrate. Because there was no law condemning his actions, the youth was let off with a warning.[56]

Street sellers also ran their businesses with precision. In printed images of hawkers, like Sandby's drawing of a cherry seller, fruit vendors' scales were a motif, typically a handheld, hanging balance. More than a visual joke about these traders' unreliability, such scales were listed among street sellers' belongings.[57] When it came to numbers, hawkers had their own systems of accounting. Nineteenth-century journalists described various techniques, from a cress seller knowing that a pennyworth was as much as she could carry in her arms, while a shilling would cover her lap, to specific notation for totting up purchases that only a hawker could decipher.[58] Most street transactions were carried out in cash, though from time to time hawkers mentioned exchangeable tokens and bills accumulated by regulars.[59] Milk sellers extended credit through a system of tallies or scores. When the hawker delivered to a house, they made a notch or chalked a mark on a doorframe, gatepost, or stick. In another example of the artist's eye for practicalities, Sandby's picture of a London dairy seller (Figure 3) showed this recording in progress, the retailer scratching a piece of wood while the housekeeper watches over. An alternative like this to counting with paper and arabic numerals was an obvious target for criticism: John Trusler warned newly arrived Londoners that a nefarious trader could add an extra notch or rub off the marks and charge what they fancied.[60] But as well as revealing bonds of trust between street sellers and their customers, the system could be surprisingly reliable. When the iron gate of Mary Brown's Soho house was stolen in 1773, her servant was able to identify the missing object by the 'milk score'. There were '15 chalks upon it', the servant said, and the milk seller had struck her finger down the middle to show the bill had been paid.[61]

Through the efforts of street sellers, retailing remained on the streets of London. It stayed there throughout the nineteenth century, even as London's traditional street-based markets were pushed into dedicated sites and permanent buildings, and shops became ubiquitous and well ordered. If street sellers fitted uneasily in the overarching narrative of how buying and selling modernized, that is largely because that story suggests a firm idea of what a shop should look like. By focusing instead on the practices of retailing, we can understand hawkers as members of a broader group, which took in shopkeepers with large stores along with market vendors, stallkeepers, basket carriers, and barrow pushers. Some of these traders had finer trappings, more up-to-date technology, and smarter reputations than others, but all used the resources at their disposal to draw in customers and sell on stock for a profit. Hawkers were part of the spectrum of London retailers.

Carnivals of shopping

By the late nineteenth century, the street markets where hawkers congregated were accepted as essential sites of urban retail. Even then, their character was maligned. Like the descriptions of Billingsgate and Covent Garden at early morning, a vivid report of a London street market was journalistic trope. Exploring the eastern edge of the City, George Augustus Sala stumbled upon 'an apparently interminable line of "standings" and "pitches," consisting of trucks, barrows, baskets, and boards on tressels, laden with almost every imaginable kind of small merchandise'. As well as oysters, vegetables, fruit, cakes, and fried fish, Sala found ballads, bibles, crockery, frying pans, firewood, and artificial flowers. The sound of this 'Whitechapel Bezesteen' inspired his most exuberant prose: 'But the noise! The yelling, screeching, howling, swearing, laughing, fighting saturnalia; the combination of commerce, fun, frolic, cheating, almsgiving, thieving, and devilry; the Geneva-laden, tobacco-charged atmosphere.'[62] Sala picks words that ring of festival and exoticism (a 'bezesteen' is an oriental bazaar), rather than serious business. In his slightly more sober account, Blanchard Jerrold called such markets 'street-fairs'.[63] Another writer christened the Saturday night market in Hammersmith's King Street the 'great weekly shopping carnival of the poor'.[64]

In their physical form, street markets seem the opposite of the new civic market halls built across Britain from the early nineteenth century. Made of cast iron, glass, and stone, these market halls had standard-sized fixed shops and stalls divided by wide passages, running water and drainage, lighting and ventilation, and surfaces that were easily wiped clean.[65] Unlike the new buildings at Covent Garden or Leadenhall, the street markets had no shelter, facilities for storage and sanitation, or salaried officers to oversee trading. Nor did they follow prescribed hours. But we can look past their ramshackle appearance. Historian Victoria Kelley has proposed that street markets were a type of 'fragile' or 'temporary' architecture. With business at its height, the assembled stalls and barrows created a coherent, bounded space, with a sense of interiority analogous to a market hall or shop. The brightness of the naphtha lamps contrasted the darkness of the gloomy streets beyond. The advertising cries, sales patter, and ripples of conversation gave the markets their own soundscape. Knots of stalls and people discouraged traffic, insulating certain streets from the rest of the city's flow. Street markets struck Londoners' senses, arguably in a more forceful, direct way than nearby shops, maybe more like the gaudy department stores. Both street markets and department stores, Kelley argues, were 'temporary collocations of diverse things, designed for spectacle and affect'.[66]

The markets varied widely. In its 1893 report, the London County Council (LCC) committee counted 5,292 stalls across the city's 112 street markets. Some of the stalls were owned by shopkeepers, but the majority were run by hawkers. Two-thirds of these stocked perishable goods, the most abundant being vegetables, fruit, fish, meat, and sweets, while the rest offered old clothes, haberdashery, cookware, books, music, and toys.[67] The stalls were spread unevenly. Seventy-five markets had fewer than fifty stalls, while the thirteen largest accounted for just over two-fifths of the London-wide total.[68] Their occupation of the street could be quite different. At tiny Lupus Street market in Pimlico (two barrows most days, six on Saturdays) there was no obstruction along the 40 ft broad road. Even at medium-sized Goodge Street (forty-five stalls down both sides), there was more than enough space for traffic, and room to access the surrounding shops. Wentworth Street was on another scale. Between Whitechapel and Spitalfields, London's biggest street market was packed with 335 stalls and ran throughout the week, with business peaking on Friday afternoons and Sunday mornings in this strongly Jewish area. With the market in full flight, when stalls were pitched off the two kerbs and along a central strip, passing traffic was 'entirely stopped'. The pavement too was lined with traders. At times, the LCC committee said, Wentworth street 'can hardly be considered a thoroughfare'.[69]

The likes of Wentworth Street, Berwick Street in Soho, and King Street in Hammersmith were vast and rambling. The 1893 report concluded that the largest street markets were 'of sufficient importance and do a sufficiently large and general trade to be regarded as retail markets in the ordinary acceptation of the term'.[70] Even the smaller markets like Lupus Street should be seen as retail institutions, which followed predictable patterns on which their customers could depend. Trade was usually heaviest on Saturday nights, but most markets served their communities, in some way, throughout the week. The street markets may not have been physically permanent, the stalls being carried off or wheeled away at the end of each day. But they were fixtures for the ordinary Londoners who knew their rhythms. As the LCC report demonstrates, London's governors were perfectly able to track these routines if they wished.[71] In 1884–5, during a long-running dispute over the disruption caused by the market in King Street, the Metropolitan Police made a detailed inquiry, which involved adding up the barrows present every hour on the market's busiest day, over several months. The resulting table, surviving among archived Home Office papers, shows a regular pattern, with the number of stalls rising from eleven in the morning and topping out between six and eight at night.[72] To the people who lived nearby and the customers who relied on them, the markets were anything but temporary. Just as shops opened and closed their doors, hawkers' stalls filled the streets and left again.

Street markets were bottom-up institutions with largely unspoken rules. This helps to explain why plans to attract hawkers to new, official markets failed. On 28 April 1869, Columbia Market opened in Bethnal Green, its inauguration celebrated with musical bands, the singing of hymns, a procession of volunteer troops, and a speech by the Archbishop of Canterbury. The press gushed about the neo-Gothic buildings, with their pointed arches and striking clock tower, comparing them to Westminster Abbey. Costing £250,000, the two-acre site included galleries of shops on two floors, a market hall with fixed stalls arranged in aisles, and an open courtyard. The market's philanthropist founder, Lady Angela Burdett-Coutts, hoped it would provide hawkers with a place to sell and residents with a place to shop, and so resolve the dearth of retail provision in the East End. Within six months Columbia had closed. After enticing neither traders nor customers, the buildings were converted into a fish market, taken over by the City Corporation, returned again to Burdett-Coutts, and shut for good in 1885. The structure was demolished in the 1950s.[73]

Commentators blamed Columbia's failure on street sellers' intransigence, which fitted the stereotype that they belonged to a dissolute underclass. Sarcastically, Blanchard Jerrold bemoaned how this gift from the 'Lady Bountiful of our time' (Burdett-Coutts) had been rejected by hawkers who proved their 'ignorance and wantonness of vice'.[74] Her plan certainly had moralizing intent, with motivational phrases printed on the market's walls, instructing vendors to 'Be Sober' and 'Be Courteous'. The real reasons for the flop were more rudimentary. Hawkers were unused to following market by-laws, sticking to set hours, and trading only where officers permitted.[75] The failure did not put politicians and planners off. The LCC's 1893 report included drawings for several alternative hawker markets designed by architect Arthur Cawston, the proponent of highly rational and futuristic improvements to London's streets that were never realized.[76] But hawkers' unauthorized meetings continued to flourish, as they did throughout the early decades of the twentieth century. Their strength was the antithesis of Columbia Market's strictures. Without a rigid structure, the street markets were able to grow and shrink and adapt, as hawkers responded to the wants of their customers and the attitudes of neighbours, government, and police.

The lasting importance of street markets and the way they resisted reform begs the question—why did they only appear in the nineteenth century? There may have been more demand for their services, as the patchiness of market provision became more frustrating as the city expanded, as old centres like Billingsgate relinquished their retail functions, and most shops did not sell the cheap portions of produce that poorer consumers required. There were also more hawkers. With the growth of the working population and the prevalence of casual labour, more of the city's poor turned to selling food to get by, their numbers providing greater opportunity to organize and coordinate. London was crying out for a working class retail institution and there were now enough hawkers to answer the call.

Another answer is that street markets may have a longer history. Though these gatherings became more regular and extensive after 1800, street sellers had previously come together where they knew Londoners might need them or where there was plenty of prospective custom. The huddles of street sellers outside the Royal Exchange, on Fleet Bridge, or by the doors of alehouses and taverns were street markets in all but name. Temple Bar was another. The boundary between the City and Westminster, where Fleet Street meets the Strand, divided one of London's busiest thoroughfares. Traffic had to slow down to squeeze through the ceremonial archway, which was only removed in 1878. Hawkers took advantage. In 1614, Adam Harrison was accused by local householders of 'selling of Fruite and roots in a Cellar neere Chauncerye Lane in Flete Streete to the annoyance of Passingers in the kings highwaye'. Harrison was charged repeatedly in later years, along with other sellers of apples and oysters obstructing passers-by with baskets and stalls.[77] A stone's throw from the hungry legal population of the Inns of Court, the area remained a favourite spot for oyster sellers into the eighteenth century.[78] The economic culture of this early period, with its emphasis on limited sites of buying and selling, had a more restrictive sense of what a market should look like. But by laying out their produce and assembling stalls out of boards, baskets, and barrows, hawkers made a stretch of London street a place of business.

6

Tools

Hawkers used equipment finely tuned to what they were selling. In the nineteenth century, baked potatoes were among the lengthening roster of ready-to-eat street foods. To warm their starchy snacks, hawkers employed 'potato cans', bulky tins raised on legs, within which a charcoal burner heated a boiler, its steam released through a chimney. Proud owners kept their cans smartly polished and some had theirs painted and trimmed with brass and silver fittings and coloured glass lamps. Many cans were branded by their manufacturer, with names like 'Royal Union Jack', 'Prince of Wales', and 'Royal George'.[1] Later street sellers made additional adjustments. A vendor photographed in 1892 (Figure 12) has set his can on wheels for mobility, added drawers to compartmentalize his stock, and spiked a row of spuds on top for decoration.[2] Potato cans were just the most sophisticated examples of the numerous braziers, pots, and kettles used over these centuries to keep food hot on the street.[3] Even simpler equipment fitted street work's specific demands. Hawkers walked back from cowbarns with milk swilling around in deep buckets or pails, which hung from wooden yokes slung across their shoulders. The yoke and pails might have carried connotations of manual labour and rusticity, but they were necessary tools in the capital's intensive dairy industry. They enabled roving retailers to haul a heavy, unstable weight several miles on foot.

Most often of all, street sellers used what might seem mundane vessels—baskets and wheelbarrows. From the mid-eighteenth century, they also used squat, scruffy donkeys to pull their loads. At a time when the number of shops was increasing and their owners were using new technology like glazed windows, lights, and printed advertisements, baskets, barrows, and donkeys were marks of backwardness. For critical observers, they were proof that hawkers lacked sophistication and should not be classed as retailers. Even so, street sellers still embraced these tools, used them in ingenious

Figure 12. A baked potato vendor stands beside a late iteration of street selling technology, a warming oven on wheels.

ways, and tweaked them to their needs, well into the twentieth century. Hawkers' equipment is the kind of cheap, rudimentary technology previously neglected by historians focused on invention and innovation. As scholars of technology now point out, many old tools are used more widely than their novel counterparts and in some cases are creatively updated. Paying attention to what the majority of people actually use can unsettle grand narratives of historical change, like how cities like London grow, modernize, and improve.[4]

Baskets, wheelbarrows, and donkeys were essential and enduring technologies for London retailers between the sixteenth and twentieth centuries. While shopkeepers smartened up their stores, hawkers used their old tools with deftness and care, adapting them to match the rigours of working on the streets. Food that sustained the expanding metropolis was ferried around in baskets and barrows and pulled along by the power of horses, donkeys, and humans. Considering the technologies hawkers used not only reveals more about how they did business in the street environment and how they were perceived by other Londoners. It also lets us see, at a fundamental level, the ways the material culture of the street transformed as well as stayed the same.

Shops on their heads

On first inspection, the baskets street sellers used were throwaway objects. Typically made of willow and cane woven into a variety of shapes, they were the simplest vessels for carrying all manner of goods.[5] When listed in inventories of Londoners' belongings, baskets tended to be grouped with other objects and not individually appraised, a hint that they were not valued highly.[6] Cheap though they may have been, baskets would have been valuable to a hawker whose income was low and inconsistent. Fish seller Ann Malone accused her servant of running off with one of her baskets, which she valued at sixpence and had inscribed with her name.[7] John Bravo prized his fruit baskets enough to pay a groat a week to store them in a cellar.[8]

Some baskets had special uses. Among those used by hawkers, the pottle was the most distinctive. This small, conical basket, holding a portion of soft fruit, was the emblem of the strawberry seller, recurring in many images of this particular vendor. In Francis Wheatley's 1795 print (Figure 13), the hawker dangles two pottles from her hand, with more just visible tucked into another basket on her head, the way that larger amounts were lugged around the city. Pottles may have been an early form of takeaway packaging. By one account, hawkers selling by the pottle added a penny to the price, which the customer could get back if they returned the basket, a further sign that these containers had value.[9] For artists like Wheatley, the odd-shaped

Figure 13. The small, conical baskets dangling from the strawberry seller's hand, known as pottles, were used for portions of soft fruit. More pottles sit inside the basket on her head.

pottle may have offered a link to a core theme of Cries genre, in which street sellers were frequently depicted as custodians of quaint, traditional practices, reminiscent of both London's history and an older, rural past.[10] But there is no doubt that pottles existed. In incidental evidence such as court reports, customers described buying strawberries on the streets by the pottle and hawkers priced them by the measure.[11] We also have physical evidence. The Museum of English Rural Life at Reading holds two pottles dating from the nineteenth century. Made of slit willow, they are just under 30 cm long and 8 cm wide at the top, with a looping handle. Each could have held somewhere between a half and a whole pint of berries.[12] Because soft fruit is expensive, pottles contained a reasonably priced portion, while protecting this delicate food from being bashed around.

The pottle was just one of an assortment of baskets used for different reasons. Far bigger were the deep and wide pots, sieves, and flats used to bring fruit and vegetables from suburban gardens.[13] Awkward to carry a long distance, in the city they worked best for arranging into a rough-and-ready stall, just as several hawkers have done in Pieter Angillis's panorama of Covent Garden (Figure 7). When we come across complaints from local officials about street sellers' baskets blocking the highway, it was probably these that they were using.[14] More mobile were the hand baskets that hawkers could hang from their arm or tie to their waist. Sometimes the contents were covered by a cloth.[15] Perhaps the most unusual, at least to modern eyes, were tall baskets strapped to street sellers' backs. While these make practical sense—spreading the load across the body but keeping the hands free—back baskets were more common in the Low Countries and Central Europe than Britain. For evidence of their use, we have to rely on a handful of contemporary images, which suggest that they may have been strapped on by a few enterprising vendors of hot baked goods and fish.[16]

One carrying technique was specifically associated with hawkers. An early example of the Cries, a printed grid of street characters from the mid-seventeenth century (Figure 6), contains thirty-seven figures. Nineteen of these are hawkers of food and more than half of those have baskets balanced on their heads. Employing this motif in depictions of street sellers, the anonymous artist is unconcerned with realism, showing hawkers with head baskets lifting improbable weights (an overflowing basket of turnips), carrying unlikely produce (milk), and holding jaunty poses (one fish seller seems to be pointing or dancing). In this print like most other representations, the head carriers are predominantly women. In addition to hawkers' shaky occupational identity and the fact that most were initially female, those wishing to demean street sellers as legitimate traders could point to this strange means of carrying a basket. After mocking the Billingsgate fishwives for their vulgarity, the satirist Donald Lupton called them 'Creatures [that] carry their shops on their heads'.

We might then ask whether carrying food on the head was simply a creative conceit.[17] But there are enough scraps of evidence to be confident that London street sellers really did raise their wares aloft. Testifying at the Old Bailey in 1781, Alice Powell described walking home from buying greens to sell later 'with a load of goods on my head'. On another occasion, Catherine Mackar said she was 'going down Long-acre with my basket of oysters upon my head', when she witnessed the aftermath of a burglary. Asked to explain his work, William Gill replied: 'I sell asparagus about the streets; sometimes I carry them upon my head, and sometimes upon an ass.'[18] Obviously this was not just for women. A photograph from the last decade of the nineteenth century shows a male muffin seller standing by a house. A board of muffins is balanced on his head, the warm stock protected by a cloth. His squashed hat cushions the weight and keeps the board stable. In one of his free hands, he clasps a bell, ready for warning customers of his arrival.[19]

Head-carrying was certainly a skill. It remains widely practised, particularly among women in parts of sub-Saharan Africa. In the 1980s, scientists developed what was called the 'free ride hypothesis', after experiments appeared to show that Luo and Kikuyu women were able to carry loads weighing up to a fifth of their body mass without expending any extra energy (usually energy use increases in direct proportion to a rise in weight carried).[20] Recent studies have questioned the extent of the energy saving and found that head-carrying is no more economical than wearing a backpack.[21] But it is a solution to carrying bulky containers, like the baskets used in London's markets, which would otherwise have been difficult for a walker to manage. And whether or not it was especially efficient, balancing a weight while moving required practice. To do so in a fast-moving metropolis, traversing uneven paving, dodging traffic, and watching out for customers, was even less straightforward.

It would also have been tiring. While making various calculations about the capital's trade in fresh produce, the seventeenth-century statistician Gregory King estimated that the women porters who carried fruit uphill from the Thameside wharves to the markets managed the equivalent of 35–40 kg at a time. The men lifted just under twice as much.[22] Two centuries later, George Dodd claimed that the women who walked strawberries from suburban market gardens into the West End on summer mornings did so with thirty- to forty-pound head baskets (13–18 kg).[23] Exactly how much street sellers could cope with depended on an individual's strength, the length of their route, and the heaviness of their chosen stock.

Carrying a load would have affected how hawkers were able to walk. Anyone who has gone even a short distance with a hefty rucksack will know it has an impact on your speed, posture, and how freely you are able to manoeuvre. Though donkeys, horses, and carts were plentiful, this was a period in London's history when great quantities of food, materials for building and manufacturing, and even water was still carried on foot, in the hands and on the backs of labouring people.[24] They would have been used to employing equipment and manipulating their bodies to support all this weight. Describing the women strawberry carriers, Dodd noted that they adopted a 'very erect posture' and moved at the brisk pace of five miles an hour. Those with other tools, such as a pole along which poultry was strung or the milk seller's yoke and pails, may have walked differently. They may have used a style similar to one typical in Japan up to the mid-twentieth century, which involved walking from the knees, while keeping the hips and arms relatively still. This hunched, shuffling style lowered the walker's centre of gravity, so was ideal for bearing loads across the shoulders.[25] However they moved, hawkers and other weighed-down workers would not have walked as easily as strollers drifting unburdened along the pavement.

Barrow wheelers

One solution for taking the load off was to push it along the ground. From the evidence we have, it seems that London hawkers began using wheelbarrows in the late seventeenth century. The earliest case I have found was in March 1688, when four men were brought before the lord mayor and charged with 'pestering the streetes with a wheelebarrow of Fruite'.[26] A year before, Marcellus Laroon had published his print series, *The Cryes of the City of London Drawne After the Life*, which included the first image we have of a hawker with a barrow, in this case packed with craggy-shelled oysters.[27] At first, most of these barrow pushers were young men. John Harris said he hawked fruit from a wheelbarrow 'to maintain his sick Mother'.[28] But from the start of the eighteenth century women street sellers were using barrows too, continuing to do so for foods as different as cherries and eels for the rest of London's hawking history.[29]

What took street sellers so long? The Western-style push barrow, with one or two wheels mounted at the front, is ancient technology, found on building sites in classical Greece and reaching England by the twelfth or thirteenth century at the latest.[30] Like baskets, when barrows were listed in inventories of Londoners' goods, they were generally bundled up with other objects.[31] Those employed by street sellers were simple constructions. Early versions were essentially wooden boxes on wheels, with a pair of arms for leverage and legs for resting on the floor. They were made of planks crudely nailed together, sometimes lined with a cloth to protect the food inside from dirt or to cushion it from bruising. As a sketch by Thomas Rowlandson (Figure 14) suggests, such basic barrows were still being used long into the nineteenth century.[32]

Gradually, hawkers made alterations and additions. Leather straps that stretched from the barrow's arms over the street seller's shoulders reduced the strain of lifting.[33] A vendor of hot puddings drawn by Paul Sandby around 1760 has turned his barrow into a portable oven. The print's caption that evokes the hawker's cry, 'The Grand Machine from Italy. Bake as I go', implies that this technology originated abroad.[34] The image anticipates the wheeled potato cans that appeared in the second half of the nineteenth century. By then, the original hawker's barrow had gone through a succession of improvements. The late Victorian model was longer and wider, with or without rails along the sides, its wheels shifted towards the middle, possibly with springs to soften the ride. The key change was the extension of the arms, which hawkers could use to push or, if they were fortunate, harness to a donkey for pulling. These cart-like 'coster's barrows', perfect for longer journeys and heavier weights, were ubiquitous in the first photographs of London street sellers (Figure 15).[35] When the capital cleaved more closely to its medieval boundaries, hawkers did not have to walk as far from the markets to seek out customers. As the built-up area expanded and street sellers took food into emerging districts, wheelbarrows may have let them cover more ground.

Pushing a barrow was not without its challenges. Much like carrying a basket on the head, directing the fully laden vessel required practice. This frustrated the writer Olive Malvery in her time undercover as a hawker. On her opening day of business, having gleefully tossed tomatoes and plums in her barrow, she could not push the load, the weight 'so ill-planned I could not push it'. A street-selling friend showed her the knack of careful packing, but even then Malvery struggled and had to ask a man for help.[36]

Figure 14. Several street selling technologies in one picture: a head basket, a pole strung with rabbits or poultry, and a basic, wooden wheelbarrow, in this case full of potatoes.

Figure 15. In the nineteenth century, hawkers' barrows took on a cart-like appearance. Some, like this one, had extended arms for harnessing to a donkey.

Once stopped, hawkers made their barrows into a counter, by laying boards or a cloth across the top.[37] The nineteenth-century street markets were really just long rows of parked barrows, pulled or pushed from across the metropolis. Once in position, hawkers accessorized these stalls with frames, canvas, drawers, boxes, and stacks of produce.[38]

Buying a barrow was an investment. It was the hawker's equivalent of setting up shop, the traditional process by which an artisan or tradesman, having completed an apprenticeship, founded an establishment of their own. Recounting his life story, Joseph Laycock described how he 'thinking himself big enough, as well as old enough, to Trade for himself, purchased a Wheelbarrow, and went about the Streets selling Oranges'. Laycock called the barrow his 'little Shop, not requiring a very large Stock', more proof of how the term 'shop' had a loose meaning throughout this period.[39] From the late eighteenth century, when hawkers' wheelbarrows were included in lists of stolen goods, their values ranged from 5s. to 15s. (whatever the monetary value they were clearly worth stealing).[40] By the 1850s, these barrows were more expensive, perhaps £2 for a new one and 30s. for a good example second hand, but these were probably the larger, cart-like versions that became common.[41] We can realistically say that purchasing a barrow cost a street seller at least a week's entire earnings, a serious outlay. But as the street trade developed a more complex hierarchy, it was an investment that many of these retailers were willing to make.

From the mid-nineteenth century, the barrow became the essential tool of the most respectable street seller, distinguishing a genuine costermonger from the occasional hawker who wandered along with a basket or tray. Full-time ownership was out of reach of many vendors. A Covent Garden informant told James Greenwood that hawkers often purchased one in early summer, when strawberries and cherries started coming to market, and sold it off again in late September, when the fruit and vegetable business began to dwindle.[42] There were alternatives to buying outright. Charities set up to help hawkers and their families, like the Costermongers' Mission run by Reverend Orsman, organized 'barrow clubs'. Similar to a building society, street sellers made regular payments, topped up by a bonus, so they could save and secure a barrow of their own.[43] The inevitable choice for the majority was to rent from one of the barrow markets, such as Lloyd's Row in Clerkenwell.[44] Renting cost around 3d. a day or a 1s. a week in winter, increasing to 4d. a day and 1s. 6d. a week in the more profitable summer season. Across their working lives, renting hawkers could have bought a barrow several times over. Many of the opportunistic lenders, who swallowed a significant share of hawkers' income, had risen from the street selling ranks themselves.[45]

The coster's companion

The most prosperous street sellers had a donkey. In practical terms, having a donkey allowed vendors to use the largest barrows, roughly 5 ft long and 3 ft wide, able to carry the bulkiest vegetables and fruit.[46] These were the street sellers' version of the horse-drawn carts owned by thousands of London shopkeepers and tradesmen, which allowed these retailers to extend their customer base throughout the newly built metropolis. The capital's streets and stables were full of equines kept for commercial and industrial purposes, with horse numbers rising markedly as the city's expansion took off. Even a small cart horse was too expensive for most street sellers.[47] But incidental descriptions suggest at least some used what they called a 'cart', pulled by a pony, for conveying milk, greens, and roots like turnips.[48]

Donkeys were a cheaper option. Like wheelbarrows, they were hardly unheard of before hawkers started using them. Their late uptake may be explained by the same reason, that London's sprawl made long-distance transport more necessary. The earliest depiction of a street seller accompanied by a donkey also appeared in Laroon's *Cryes*. The artist's hawker selling vinegar walks beside his animal, a skinny donkey with expressive eyes, upon which is strapped a saddle with barrels and cups.[49] We know that pedlars who traded from town to town and throughout the countryside used beasts of burden around this time.[50] But the first documentary evidence of street sellers using donkeys only appears from the 1760s. From that point on, numerous hawkers were described like Andrew Welch, a man who 'drives a jack-ass about, and sells greens and potatoes'.[51] Just a few years before, Sandby had sketched a lad walking beside a donkey (Figure 16), bearing a pannier so large it covers its whole flank. Many of the first street sellers who

Figure 16. A young man walks beside a skinny donkey loaded with baskets. With his mouth open, the boy may be crying in advertisement.

used donkeys were, like Sandby's boy, independent young men. John M'Namara and John Fisher were aged 14 and 15 respectively.[52] Donkey drivers remained mostly male, but soon included older street sellers calling themselves greengrocers and costermongers, who loaded their animals with baskets or made them draw barrows and carts.[53]

Only the most successful hawkers could justify the cost of buying and keeping a donkey. The kind of 'asses' hawkers owned were worth around £1–2 in the early 1800s, rising to maybe twice as much for a better quality 'moke' by the end of the century.[54] Henry Mayhew described the scene at the street sellers' donkey market at Smithfield on Friday afternoons, where the animals were trotted up and down the 'race course', an 80 ft strip lined with eager buyers, with as many as 200 donkeys changing hands on a busy day. At the same time, new owners could also pick up the requisite paraphernalia, such as harnesses and whips.[55] After the purchase price came the running costs. Donkeys needed feeding, with the luckiest receiving a blend of chaff, oats, beans, and hay, which would have added up to several pence a day.[56] They also needed stabling. Earlier in London's history, finding a patch of open ground to leave an animal to graze would have been easier. As late as 1819, William Davy left his donkey overnight in an orchard off Millbank Row, Westminster.[57] With inner-city housing becoming ever more densely packed, hawkers had to make other arrangements. An early twentieth-century photograph shows a back-street stable in Notting Hill, where donkeys were accommodated and groomed.[58] The pressure on space led to the scenes that so shocked those investigating the parlous state of working class homes, in which donkeys were housed in hawkers' front rooms and toilet blocks shared by the street.

How hawkers treated donkeys and other animals was used to demonstrate their barbarous nature. In the early nineteenth century, a few street sellers may have used dogs to drag barrows and carts, a practice eventually outlawed by Parliament.[59] Animal cruelty was among the most frequent charges faced by costermongers appearing at London's police courts. Forty-nine out of the 868 cases I have identified involved street sellers allegedly causing harm to a donkey, pony, or horse. Many of the cases were brought by officers of the Society for the Prevention of Cruelty to Animals (SPCA) or relied on their testimony. In October 1833, at Union Hall police court in Southwark, an SPCA official described seeing George Rolls 'beating his donkey with the butt end of his whip'. The donkey was delivered to the courtroom door and the magistrate inspected its injuries. Despite Rolls claiming that he had only hit the animal because it was acting 'cantankerous', he was fined 3s. and costs.[60] Some of the cases do suggest deliberate cruelty. In graphic language, witnesses recalled hawkers stabbing a donkey with knives, hitting a pony with a piece of a cartwheel and breaking its back and pelvis, and kicking a 'faithful' moke in the ribs.[61] The first comprehensive animal protection law was passed in 1822 and the SPCA was founded two years later (gaining the 'Royal' prefix in 1840), but these prosecutions were not merely signs of an upswell in sympathy for Londoners' fellow creatures. These accusations—and the selection of court cases to be written up in the newspapers—were influenced by deeper currents in metropolitan culture. They suggest an unease about the city's rapid growth and the way it changed relationships between humans and the natural world, along with fears about the unruliness and incivility of working London.[62]

There is plenty of evidence, however, that street sellers treated their donkeys with affection. In 1837, a costermonger from Wimbledon appealed to the lord mayor after a mischievous crowd had taken his donkey to the pound. The street seller had owned his 'Neddy' for seven years and promised he had 'never struck him a blow or gave him an unkind word in all that time'.[63] After buying an equine companion during her stint on the street, Olive Malvery reflected that, 'A coster's donkey is his friend, and it is only very rarely that they are ill-treated.'[64] Given the initial expense and the upkeep, it should not be surprising that these traders looked after their possessions. Like baskets, wheelbarrows, potato cans, and yokes and pails, donkeys held enormous value for their owners. They were substantial investments integral to their business on the street.

They also became icons of their work. In the second half of the nineteenth century, some hawkers began exhibiting their animals. The first Mule and Donkey Show opened in August 1864 at the Agricultural Hall in Islington (now the Business Design Centre). More than a hundred donkeys were entered in several classes, with those owned by hawkers shown alongside an Egyptian breed belonging to the Prince of Wales, gifted to His Highness by the Pacha. The middle of the hall was boarded off for racing, with costermonger jockeys racing five times around the track. A journalist from the *Morning Post* believed the show would correct the 'popular error' that street sellers mistreated their donkeys, citing the fond names they were given. 'Tom' and 'Tommy' were the most popular for males, while 'Jenny', 'Jane', and 'Poll' were typical for mares.[65] The event was repeated the following year and later editions were held at the Crystal Palace, the People's Palace in

Bethnal Green, and the gardens of Lambeth Palace, the latter event aimed exclusively at hawkers from south of the river.[66] Improving the welfare of donkeys was a stated aim of all these exhibitions. Lady Angela Burdett-Coutts, sponsor of other civilizing projects like the model dwellings movement and Columbia Market, handed out prizes for good treatment, alongside animal protection campaigners. But hawkers still attended in huge numbers, showing off their special tradition.

Because street sellers' working identity was slow to come together, the way they worked and the tools they used were especially meaningful. Baskets, barrows, and donkeys could appear to be throwbacks or curiosities, but they were what hawkers required to sell food on the move. Only in the early twentieth century, when the street markets in fixed locations became dominant, did these tools start to wane in prominence.[67] Even at the apogee of modernizing Victorian London, where trains and traffic roared and the arcades and department stores of the West End shimmered, this old technology helped thousands of retailers navigate the difficult conditions of the street.

7

7

Traffic

S treet sellers dressed for working amid muck and mess. In Marcellus
Laroon's print of a mackerel seller from the 1680s, the winking old
woman who embodies the fishwife stereotype (Figure 2), the hawker's
petticoat and gown are made of coarse, heavy fabric. A shawl is knotted
untidily around her shoulders and head, and her cuffs are roughly folded.
Notice the marks of wear: missing buttons, frayed edges, stitches from repair,
a wide hat crumpled from balancing a basket of fish. Her outfit has been
picked for practicality, not fashion, for warmth and for protection from sudden bursts of rain or sprays of dust and dirt from the street. To keep her
footing, she has a stick and sturdy boots. In his early career, Laroon specialized in drawing clothes and had an eye for such details, which helped him
suggest that hawkers were worthy of sympathy.[1] In all likelihood, like the
rest of poorer London, their clothes actually ranged from rags to flashes of
finery, perhaps found cheap or second hand.[2] Their costumes were similar
two centuries later. According to Henry Mayhew, the clothes of male
costermongers matched 'the durability of the warehouseman's, with the
quaintness of that of the stable-boy'. That meant corduroy waistcoats with
a colourful neckerchief called a 'king's man' tied loosely at the neck. The
women wore their neckerchiefs like shawls and their petticoats stopped at
their ankles, supposedly to show off their 'much-admired boots'.[3] A less
charming explanation is that the raised bottoms were really functional, to
stop their dresses trailing in the mud.

Most walkers would have had the same unpretentious concerns. Every
day, middling and working people took to the streets for practical reasons,
to reach their workplace, to run errands, and to shop. Yet the best-known
accounts of London pedestrianism have a blinkered point of view. From
Ned Ward's topographical romp, *The London Spy*, to John Gay's 1716 ode to
bipedalism, *Trivia*, to the writings of Pierce Egan, Thomas De Quincey, and

Charles Lamb in the early nineteenth century, the literature of metropolitan walking traces the movements of upper class men. These writers express a budding desire to withdraw from the jostling crowds and filth of the street. In their narratives, the thoroughfare became a theatre, where wandering spectators encountered, at a safe distance, a succession of characters and scenes. Mayhew and the investigators that followed him showed sensitivity to the unforgiving circumstances faced by Londoners labouring in the open air. But their analysis was still shaped by the concerns of social superiors, who saw the city's street culture as an object to be studied, not a reality they had to face.[4] They also give us little sense of the physical experience of moving through the city. They reflect what anthropologist Tim Ingold has called the 'fundamental groundlessness so characteristic of modern metropolitan dwelling'.[5] Benefiting from improvements like paving and lighting, these writers and their narrators drifted through the city with little effort. Most Londoners did not have that privilege.

Thinking about the conditions hawkers faced enlivens our knowledge of street life in the capital's past. Unlike those literary strollers, the women and men out hawking food were constantly aware of the material environment and the strain that walking and carrying placed on their bodies. In common with other ordinary walkers, street sellers manoeuvred the highways, roads, lanes, and alleys of the city with their senses alert to the shifting conditions and braced for risks they might confront, from rushing traffic to harassment by strangers. Hawkers experienced directly the ways that London's streets were improving, but would also have known that progress had a long way to go.

Broken pavements

Working outdoors, street sellers suffered the worst of the weather. Though many found different employment as summer turned to winter, others kept trading as the temperature plunged. A shrimp seller told Mayhew that the numbing effect of standing at her stall was worse than going on a round. 'My feet feels like lumps of ice,' she said.[6] Rain was unpredictable, a downpour soaking hawkers' clothes, tools, and produce, and reducing the number of customers willing to stop and make a purchase. A vendor of fish claimed that wet weather more than halved his takings, the patter of raindrops putting him 'in mind of drownding'.[7] Perishables like seafood would not keep more than a few days and, because street traders lived week to week, a run of soggy weekends forced many to sell their barrows and donkeys. This was a perennial problem, but the stakes were raised in the second half of the nineteenth century, with the greater importance of street markets that peaked on specific days. As one Edwardian journalist put it, 'A wet Saturday brings ruin to the coster'.[8] All most could do was wrap up in sensible clothes and a wide hat and, if they had a stand, hide beneath an awning. Jane Wood, who in 1824 ran a stall by the docks in Wapping, kept the rain off her fruit with an umbrella.[9]

Rainwater splashed into the streets, turning dust to mud and mingling with waste from houses nearby. This unpleasantness was a refrain in eighteenth-century literature, playing on the ancient comparison of the seedy town with the breezy countryside. In Jonathan Swift's 1710 poem 'A Description of a City Shower', London's bustle is halted by the elements. The rain is a leveller, driving 'various kinds, by various fortunes led' to bunch beneath whatever shelter they can find. In the poem's closing lines, the swollen gutters start to flow: 'Sweepings from butchers' stalls, dung, guts, and blood, | Drowned puppies, stinking sprats, all drenched in mud, | Dead cats, and turnip tops, come tumbling down the flood.'[10] Street sellers both contributed to the malaise and met its consequences. Matthew Bramble, an irritable countryman visiting the capital in Tobias Smollett's 1771 novel *The Expedition of Humphrey Clinker*, moans about most features of the city, including its food sellers. Watery London milk, Bramble writes in a letter, is 'carried through the streets in open pails, exposed to foul rinsings, discharged from doors and windows, spittle, snot, and tobacco-quids from foot-passengers, overflowings from mud-carts, spatterings from coach-wheels, dirt and trash chucked into it by roguish boys for the joke's sake'.[11] This literary hyperbole was rooted in problems that lingered into the nineteenth century. The streets were full of all sorts of unwelcome material: soil kicked up from unpaved roadways, sand and gravel poured for gritting, ashes and rubbish tossed by passers-by and residents, paving stones from attempted improvements loosened and cracked, and the unrelenting nuisance of animal manure. By one estimate, 1,000 tonnes of horse muck had to be cleared every day from London's streets in 1875. What could not be cleansed immediately was swept into piles on the roadside.[12]

It is little surprise that hawkers wore such a robust uniform. Anything they put on was liable to be splattered. In a less studied section of *London Labour* dedicated to the highways, Mayhew tried to work out, in painstaking detail, the cost to labouring people of cleaning street dirt from their clothes. He came to a figure of 2d. a week per head, which covered the coals for heating water, soda, soap, starch, blue, plus the labour, but not the expense of replacing what was tired.[13] Some street sellers put on special footwear to rise above the mud. Used in London since the twelfth century, pattens were elevated overshoes, made of wood or leather, with a chunky heel or ring of metal underneath.[14] They were strongly associated with women—in Gay's *Trivia*, the patten is called the 'female Implement'—which may have led to gendered differences in walking. Boot-wearing men remained nimbler than women forced to move on these miniature platforms.[15] Though pattens do appear in some early pictures of hawkers, we cannot know how widely they were worn.[16] They were one of several possible ways, like tugging a skirt-bottom above the ankles and draping a protective cloth across a basket, by which street sellers endured the grubbiness of their place of work.

The surface they stood on was slowly being improved. In the early seventeenth century, the city's streets were mostly made of compressed earth, with stones sometimes pressed into the ground to make a rudimentary pavement. In 1661, the Royalist writer John Evelyn complained of London's 'narrow and incommodious' highways, with their 'ill and uneasie' paving that drained so poorly that the city looked like a 'continual Wet-day after the Storm is over'. As a Royalist, Evelyn saw in the disrepair a metaphor for the recent political turmoil of the Civil Wars and Interregnum.[17] The Fire of 1666 is often seen as a turning point in the renewal of the capital's built environment. After over 400 acres burned down and tens of thousands of Londoners lost their homes, the City was comprehensively rebuilt in stone in the years that followed. But improvement began before the blaze.[18] An ambitious act of Parliament passed four years earlier took aim at the streets of London, Westminster, and their suburbs, empowering commissioners to order streets to be 'sufficiently paved' and 'kept sufficiently repaired'.[19] In the fallout from the Fire, Parliament and the Corporation sought to transform the City as it rose from the ashes. Acts and by-laws allowed local officials to set the precise paving materials and pitch for the streets within their jurisdiction and continued the straightening and widening of major routes that had already started. From then on, no street was meant to be less than 14 ft broad.[20] Later, the 1762 Westminster Paving Act formally extended these processes into London at large. In streets across the metropolis, teams of paviours ripped up pebbles and replaced them with flat blocks of stone. The central gutter, clogged with rubbish like the dead cats and turnip tops of

Swift's poem, was covered over, and the road cambered to let water run off into channels that ran down either side.[21] These cumulative changes were part of a major shift in how London's streets were managed. In all sorts of matters, from paving to cleaning to lighting, householders were initially responsible for the roadway outside their door. Over time, this responsibility was increasingly handled in collective fashion, at first by magistrates, parishes, and wards, then by appointed officials, whose work was funded by rates. The latter seems a modern way of managing urban space.[22]

But as hawkers knew full well, such improvement was sluggish and inconsistent. The City was generally ahead of other districts. In the lead up to the 1762 act, reform-minded writers pointed out how much ground still needed making up, particularly in Westminster and the Middlesex parishes beyond the Corporation's bounds. In one pamphlet, John Spranger decried the 'fatal Mischiefs' and 'dismal Accidents' still caused by 'rough, unequal, or broken Pavements'. Jonas Hanway claimed there were 'no such parishes' that had been 'effectually' paved, cleansed, or lit. To explain why the suburbs were lagging, Joseph Massie blamed the 'looser Government', the lack of a single metropolitan authority.[23] Even under the new laws, the paving materials varied widely. Within Westminster, some streets were laid with slabs of hard, blue whinstone, others with squares of Purbeck limestone, and many continued to be cobbled. Officials also had to cope with how London was creeping into new areas all the time, places where construction work to improve the streets began as soon as people moved on.[24] These fringe areas were those extremely reliant on hawkers.

For walkers, conditions in the nineteenth century were not necessarily easier. Two new paving technologies spread across London: John Loudon McAdam's technique of fusing small, granite pieces into a smooth surface with a roller (named macadam after its inventor), and Thomas Telford's method of laying rows of three- to four-inch granite blocks on top of a ballast base. In later decades, these forms of paving were joined by wooden blocks and asphalt, a mix of bitumen and aggregate used widely today.[25] Each of these materials had their drawbacks. Telford's blocks were simple to clean but noisy when wheels ran over them and slippery even when dry; asphalt and wood, by contrast, lost their grippiness when damp; wood had the extra problem of absorbing liquids like horse urine, swelling, and becoming noxious; macadam offered better footing but demanded continual maintenance, the stones coming up regularly and adding a novel component to the muddy cocktail of water, dust, and dung.[26] In the 1880s, while the City's roads were entirely paved (chiefly with granite blocks and asphalt) along with most of Westminster's main drags (mostly with macadam), less than half of the streets in the rest of London were lined with anything more than flints and gravel.[27] Variability was as much of an issue as the materials, making walkers, carts, and carriages adjust quickly from surface to surface. Commentators blamed this on the fragmentation of jurisdictions typical of the capital's government. In 1875, a Society of Arts committee mapped seven major routes east–west across London, 77 miles of streets in total. The investigation found they were under the charge of sixty-eight different local authorities. Oversight of some streets was split down the middle, so that 'one half of a street is paved at one time, and the other at another time, and sometimes by a different method'.[28] The lack of coordination affected other amenities like street cleaning. By the late nineteenth century, parishes and district boards employed teams of repairmen, sweepers, and orderlies, who brushed and watered the surfaces several times a week. But the level of cleanliness, like the quality of paving, fluctuated across the metropolis.[29]

Where paving was comprehensive and the streets were well looked after, travelling on foot became a smoother experience in the three centuries after 1600. But if we consider London as a whole and pay attention to what contemporaries said themselves about the limits of improvement, we realize that most walkers never moved without difficulty. Hawkers were just some of the ordinary pedestrians always conscious of the ever-changing conditions of the street.

Around the clock

Those conditions even shifted over the course of the day. Hawkers took to the street at different times, as they targeted specific customers, sold foods that suited certain hours, and dovetailed other jobs and domestic tasks. To match the more plentiful evidence of working times from the later nineteenth century, we can reconstruct the trading hours of earlier street sellers. Up to 1825, I have found 175 descriptions of hawking food which indicate the time of day. We can use these to pick out the sometimes surprising foods that street sellers were offering, as morning turned to afternoon and evening into night.[30]

Some hawkers tended to be out and about in the daytime. Their business being close to the pace of agriculture, milk sellers were usually on the streets in the morning and afternoon. Before sunrise much of the year, women and men walked to where the cows were milked, returning to the centre as the rest of London was waking up. In several cases, milk sellers were on the streets from as early as four. They kept these early hours throughout the nineteenth century.[31] Street sellers were part of the 'vanguard of the army of Labour', described evocatively by Blanchard Jerrold, 'black objects against the deep gloom, gliding out of the side-streets to the main thoroughfares', starting their pre-dawn trudge to the docks, factories, building sites, and corners where they hoped to make a living.[32] Later in the day they were joined by those who sold perishable produce, the cheaper sorts of fish, fruit, and vegetables that arrived at London's markets. Tellingly, Jerrold's sketch also features a baked potato vendor and a coffee stall, 'most welcome friends' for the labouring population in need of sustenance. Hawkers sold prepared staples and snacks throughout the day: among the descriptions from morning and afternoon are traders of fruit, oysters, shrimps, nuts, gingerbread, cakes, and hot drinks. The following century, Mayhew interviewed a seller of hot green peas who hawked 'morning, noon, and night'. The man fed other street vendors stocking up at Billingsgate first thing, lunchtime diners at the taprooms, and drinkers in the public houses in the evening.[33] Londoners were always hungry and hawkers were ready to satisfy them at all times.

The offering of street foods expanded as the working day ended. From the descriptions up to 1825, we know street sellers trading in the evening and at night also sold baked sheep's heads, pies, sausages, and puddings. Some vendors stayed out after twelve, notably around the alehouses, taverns, and theatres near Covent Garden.[34] Late-night street snacks were frequently described by journalists, who saw in the morsels arranged on stalls gustatory proof of London's strange liveliness after dark. In an early twentieth-century essay called 'Midnight London', Beckles Willson reported how barrows of baked potatoes, whelks, and oysters lined Whitechapel High Street. When the public houses shut, coffee proprietors opened sheds and stalls which remained busy 'until morning dawns'. Their customers, 'an incongruous and ill-assorted group', included cabbies, sailors, dockers, tramps, and police.[35] The street markets were at their buzziest on Saturday evenings. Their extended opening meant that poorer workers could pick up fresh foods outside the limited hours that shops and official markets operated. Thanks to hawkers, the end of the day was also a time to buy basics. In previous centuries, several hawkers were described as being out carrying milk, that most characteristic of daytime foods, even as night was falling.[36]

These street retailers were caught up in a sea-change in London's temporality. In the medieval capital, a bell signalled the nightly curfew and the City gates were shut. Around 1600, walkers still had to have a reason to be out, with watchmen patrolling the streets for miscreants and only essential tasks like carting waste supposed to continue.[37] In the first half of the seventeenth century, some hawkers were prosecuted for trading in the evening, but instances of being arrested for simply working late dry up from that point onwards.[38] Doing business after dark became normal. In a process that historian Craig Koslofsky has labelled 'nocturnalisation', city dwellers across Europe were staying out later and finding legitimate reasons to do so. At night, more and more Londoners were working and travelling, socializing in public houses, and enjoying new venues like the Pleasure Gardens at Vauxhall. While out, they could pick up snacks and treats from street stalls and roving hawkers.[39] By the nineteenth century, this shift became so ingrained that it prompted a backlash, with initiatives such as the Early Closing Association formed in the 1840s, which blamed London's worryingly late hours on innovations like streetlights fuelled by gas.[40]

The quality and extent of street lighting made enormous steps forward over these centuries, following a similar route to that of paving, from individual responsibility to collective organization. A 1599 by-law ordered all City householders to hang outside their door a lantern—at that time, a box with translucent sides containing a candle—from five or six in the afternoon until nine in the evening, on nights when the moon was dark, for five months of the year. Subsequent acts and orders from the Corporation and Parliament lengthened the necessary hours of illumination, extended lighting to Westminster, and allowed contractors to erect large numbers of lanterns and, later, oil lamps. This culminated in a 1736 act of Parliament that permitted the City to charge a special rate to cover public provision and stretched the lighting season to the whole year. Soon, there were 4,800 oil lamps installed within its wards, ideally no more than 25 yards apart on busy streets and 35 yards distant everywhere else.[41] Additional laws handed the same powers to Westminster and growing parishes like Marylebone.[42] Eventually, lighting companies replaced lanterns and lamps with gas burners that produced ten to twelve times as much radiance, technology that was trialled in Pall Mall in the first decade of the nineteenth century. In 1823, there were just under 40,000 lamps lighting 215 miles of streets across the metropolis. By century's end, the number of gas lamps more than doubled again, now supplemented by electric lights, servicing not just streets but factories, hotels, train stations, and shops.[43] Compared to the late Elizabethan capital, London was aglow. Those taking to the night-time streets, such as hawkers, would have more clearly found their way.

They would have known, however, that London was never fully lit up. Lighting was much slower to reach some parts of the metropolis than others. For all the radical impact of the 1736 act on the City, Westminster was once more behind. John Spranger complained that the district's inhabitants were 'exposed, every Night we pass through our Streets, to frequent Insults, Assaults, and Robberies'.[44] Throughout the eighteenth century, swathes of the northern and eastern suburbs relied on moonlight to guide walkers and carriage drivers after nightfall.[45] In the course of their work, bringing food to underserved neighbourhoods, hawkers would commonly have found themselves in London's gloomiest localities. About seven o'clock on New Year's Day 1737, Thomas Gwillim was on his way out to Stepney guided only by 'Star-light', when he was robbed and stripped of his clothes. Staggering away naked he caused a passing man, an oyster seller, to jump with surprise.[46]

Hawkers had to carry lamps themselves. Paul Sandby's drawing of a fruit stall at night (Figure 17) is a good example of both his gritty, observational style and his sense of play. Several customers, one with a head basket perhaps a hawker herself, gather around a street seller's barrow. A lamp is attached to the movable stall, shedding light on all the characters' faces. Sandby demonstrates a practical aspect of street work, while pointing out the artifice and illusion of a highly conventional genre like the Cries. Without the lamp, of course, the scene would be invisible.[47] From incidental descriptions, we know street sellers used similar lights. One evening in late April 1787, a china and glass dealer was returning home from Drury Lane to Newgate Street. On his way, just as the watchman was crying ten o'clock, he saw a group of hawkers 'selling fish at the end of Blackmoor-street, with lights in their baskets'.[48]

In the nineteenth century, flickering lamps were hallmarks of the street markets. Passing through a row of traders in Whitechapel, George Augustus Sala described how each stallholder employed lights in their own 'peculiar manner', some had gas burners, some primitive devices like a 'rushlight stuck in a lump of clay, or a turnip cut in half'.[49] Naphtha lamps, portable burners with vivid, whispering flames, became the most widely used. The liquid fuel was a by-product of burning coal to supply the gas lamps of the City and West End, a material indication of how these markets were the inverse of respectable London.[50] But the use of naphtha also tells us about the limits of public lighting and how darkness still engulfed much of the capital. To serve citizens after dark, hawkers resorted to using a volatile fuel

Figure 17. A hawker's fruit stall with a lamp attached to illuminate night-time business.

close to flammable wood and fabric amid the scramble of market trading. In a sad accident investigated by the City coroner in 1873, an oyster seller overfilled his lamp, which flared violently forcing him to toss it into the gutter. The flames hit three boys standing close by, all of whom were taken to St Bart's hospital. One, a 10-year-old, died from his injuries.[51] Where street sellers worked, danger could strike at any moment.

Crossing the road

Onrushing pedestrians, carriages, and carts were a constant threat. Many of the descriptions of street sellers in action recount the moment just before they met with misfortune. Men and women heaving full baskets or pushing wobbly barrows were bumped by fleeing felons and knocked down by drunkards.[52] Accidents involved fast-flying vehicles. In 1855, a 'furiously driving' horse and cart crashed into a fruit vendor and his stall on Hackney Road.[53] Sometimes these collisions were lethal. One day in 1722, milk seller Joan Cornish was crossing the road near Shoreditch. Probably slowed by her yoke and pails, Cornish was struck by a coach, trampled by the horses, and run over by the front wheel. She died a few days later.[54] Throughout London's history, venturing on to the street was perilous. While children and the elderly were the most common victims of fatal accidents in the seventeenth and eighteenth centuries, poor street workers, such as beggars and hawkers, also faced outsized risks.[55] Between 1869 and 1874, an average of 206 people a year were killed due to street conditions or traffic, with more than ten times that injured or maimed. By the end of the nineteenth century, the rates were higher still.[56]

Writing about the city stressed the ever-present hazards. In Gay's *Trivia*, hawkers themselves are described as a risk for pedestrians. The poem's narrator warns walkers not to trip on a step or cellar door and 'overturn the scolding Huckster's Stall', otherwise the street seller 'shall not o'er thee moan, | But Pence exact for Nuts and Pears o'erthrown'.[57] Bundled-over hawkers were made into figures of fun. But writers acknowledged too that street sellers were forced to deal with London's traffic problems at the same time as adding to those problems themselves. Seeking to explain the 'disagreeable, dangerous, and disgraceful condition' of the late Victorian roads, Sala argued that the presence of costermongers ('their barrows have grown much longer than of yore, and their trade impedes the traffic to a much greater extent') was a factor.[58] Just getting from one side of the street to the other was believed to be a challenge, with some spots causing more nervousness than others. The narrator of Ward's *London Spy* warns his companion about crossing Fleet Street, a road we know was popular with hawkers, which gave him 'much dread of having my Bones broke'.[59] Charles Dickens opened his 1866 essay 'The Dangers of the Streets', citing the 'no end of nerve' required to pass over the same highway. Moving to the heart of the City, Dickens describes the dispiriting wait on the kerbside to cross another busy junction. 'But as bus succeeds cab,' he writes, 'and butcher's cart bus, and Great Northern van butcher's cart, and another bus the Great Northern van, and a private carriage the other bus, and a Hansom the private carriage, and a third bus the Hansom, and a fourth bus the third bus, you shrink back in despair.'[60]

Even as traffic was intensifying, hawkers could never step away. The problems of circulation became acute from the mid-nineteenth century, the irregular grumbling of earlier periods rising to a persistent wail. By sheer numbers, the volume of travel was shooting upwards. In 1867, Londoners were each making on average more than 22.7 journeys a year by horse-drawn and other forms of transport; by 1896, they were making more than five times as many.[61] This does not even account for the innumerable trips on foot and the carts, wagons, and animals that hauled food, materials, and manufactured goods to and fro. Parliament passed legislation to reduce the crush, but the effect of such laws was minimal. Eventually a Royal Commission was appointed. First reporting in 1905, the inquiry churned out several tomes of evidence about the mayhem of London's traffic, including hundreds of pages of testimony, reams of statistics, and dozens of diagrams and maps.[62]

New on-street transport added to the scrum. By the 1850s, the capital's streets were home to more than a thousand horse-drawn omnibuses, the preferred means of commuting for those who could afford the fare. Shortly after its formation in 1856, the London General Omnibus Company (LGOC) was carrying 40 million passengers a year. Two decades later, trams arrived as competition, pulled on tracks laid down in the centre of the street, powered first by horses and later by electricity.[63] The effects of these technologies on other street-goers are best observed at a local level. In February 1906, Hammersmith Borough Council composed a brief history of the long-running conflict between the hawkers on King Street and the local authority. In part thanks to the erection of two omnibus stables and a line of electric trams ('the road being too narrow to admit of a double line'), traffic had reportedly doubled or tripled over thirty years. On King Street's south side, according to the council's measurements, there was not enough room for an ordinary 6 ft 6 in cart to pass between the tram rails and the barrows of produce pressed against the kerb.[64]

Hawkers had dealt with competitors for street space before. In the seventeenth century, more numerous hackney carriages caught the attention of the City and Parliament, which through successive laws capped their numbers, made the drivers take out licences, and regulated fares and pick-up locations. Like the omnibus and tram would do later, hackney carriages promised swifter travel and encouraged new social and cultural practices, but also had the effect of worsening congestion.[65] Many of the accidents sustained by hawkers in late Victorian London, like barrows and stalls being upended by Pickfords vans and Hansom cabs, could have happened in earlier centuries.[66] In 1894, a street seller named Field successfully sued the LGOC for damages, after an accident the year before when he was run over by an omnibus and his leg had to be amputated. The High Court heard how Field, after buying early season strawberries at Covent Garden, headed west towards Piccadilly. Needing to cross the road, he waited for a break in traffic, before stepping out with his barrow and being hit.[67] He was doing what hawkers had done countless times a day for at least 300 years.

This takes us to an important continuity. Between the late sixteenth and early twentieth centuries, the vast majority of Londoners got around on foot or by horse-powered transport. This is not to downplay the revolutions of the Victorian era. In the 1860s, the Metropolitan Railway and the South London line began to ferry passengers in and out of the wider sprawl. The first underground route, the District line connecting to the subterranean parts of the Metropolitan, cut beneath the built-up centre. Whisking travellers from place to place, the railways unsettled conceptions of time and space.[68] But within this span of London history the trains appeared relatively late. And far from eclipsing older forms of transport, they raised demand for their services. Horses were needed for haulage during construction, and carriages, carts, wagons, and vans were still the primary way for goods and people to get around, especially on the shorter trips for which railways were not useful. The total number of horses across London may have quadrupled in the second half of the nineteenth century.[69] Throughout the period in which hawkers were integral to the food supply, horses, donkeys, carts, coaches, barrows, and baskets, to say nothing of boots and shoes, were the key technologies of London's streets. A newcomer that would alter street life more profoundly only arrived in the twilight of Victorian London. Motor vehicles were first seen on the capital's roads in the 1890s and their uptake was rapid. In 1904, the metropolis had just thirty-one omnibuses propelled by steam, petrol, or electricity; two years later, there were more than 700. On the eve of the First World War, the London of horses and hawkers was primed for a step change in speed.[70]

It was not just vehicles that street sellers had to look out for. London's streets were full of people, some of whom were eager to take advantage of hawkers working alone. Many mobile vendors had their stock stolen by opportunists, a risk that no doubt heightened after dark. One autumn evening in 1671, between eight and nine o'clock, Elizabeth Dixon was 'crying of Pyes' on Gray's Inn Lane. When Dixon stopped to serve a customer, a man slipped a pie from her basket, forcing the 20-year-old hawker to chase him down the street demanding payment.[71] Street sellers lacked the security offered by a permanent shop and even those with substantial equipment were vulnerable. Some had whole cod, pounds of pickled salmon, and gallons of plums swiped off their stallboards, while others had figs and hot potatoes lifted from the beds of their barrows.[72] The tools they used, so readily mocked in art and literature, were deemed worth stealing too. Milk sellers were frequent targets, perhaps because their pails and cans were made of more valuable metal.[73]

Many suffered harassment as they went about their business, with angry words and insults often leading to violence. In the nineteenth century, a significant proportion of the police court cases in which costermongers were prosecuted involved scuffles and brawls between street sellers, shopkeepers, customers, and officers of the law.[74] The most shocking attacks took place against women. In July 1899, Clerkenwell police court heard how Sophia Willsher, who kept a fruit stall in Islington's Chapel Street, was assaulted by three men. On a Tuesday afternoon, the men started abusing the trader, before one stooped down and with his shoulders overturned her stall, sending grapes, cherries, and greengages shooting down the road. In the tussle that ensued, they kicked Willsher in the stomach and 'struck her a heavy blow in the chest'.[75]

In the Victorian city, women walkers were harassed and threatened with assault, dangers that did not obviously decline despite improvements to lighting, transport, and policing. Books and newspapers characterized women journeying alone either as the potential victims of predatory male attention or temptresses who offered up their bodies to passing men. Their behaviour was to be observed and regulated. New forms of consumption, like department stores, at first induced anxiety, because they encouraged middle class women to shop, pursue pleasures, and diverge from the respectable ideals of femininity.[76] Regardless of contemporary rhetoric, middle and working class women continued to take to the streets out of necessity. However else could they get around? This contradiction was not a recent development. Women's constant presence in the streets, for work and play, had provoked unease and aggression since at least the sixteenth century.[77] The vulgar stereotype of the fishwife, an independent, working woman, was one example of how these attitudes were expressed.

These anxieties affected hawkers as they tried to do their work. In June 1671, one morning around ten o'clock, a street seller called Mrs Prescott was selling cherries at a stall pitched outside a tallow chandler's shop, between Charing Cross and Pall Mall. William Budge, who lived next door, was returning home and hissed to the customer Prescott was serving, 'Looke to your weight, for shee...will Cosen you.' Defending herself from accusations of trickery, Prescott may have called Budge 'old knave' or 'Anni-seed Robin', a hermaphrodite character in popular culture.[78] He launched a tirade in response, pointing at the street seller and shouting, 'You are a whore, you are a private whore, and you Know your self to be a whore.' Two witnesses explained that the slander had wrecked Prescott's reputation and her husband had deserted her.[79] We know what happened in such detail because Prescott sued Budge at one of London's church courts, which at this time had jurisdiction over various moral issues. Prescott was criticized using the complex terminology of sexual deviance—'whore' did not automatically mean she was a prostitute, just that she was subverting the expectations of her gender—and used that same vocabulary to argue back.[80] Accused of cheating her customer, the hawker's integrity as a retailer was bound up with her status as a dutiful wife. Well into the eighteenth century, most disputes of this type took place outdoors, in view of neighbours and passers-by, making the street an arena for the judgement of status and morality.[81] Working in the glare of public scrutiny, the honour of women street sellers could be called into question.

That harassment went beyond words. One night in January 1735, Grace Long was sitting with oysters by Temple Bar, when a man called Evan Edwards came out of the nearby Devil Tavern and called her over. He asked if they could spend the night together and, when Long refused, Edwards threw her shellfish across the street. After eventually going back to Long's cellar in St Giles, the next morning Edwards alleged that the oyster seller had filched his silver watch and gold ring. The report from the subsequent trial does not give the full context, but the unspoken suggestion was that this hawker, hanging around after dark in a district known for low-life and crime, was really selling sex.[82] Whether or not Long was doing exactly that, a woman loitering on the street was still deemed worthy of suspicion.

Bringing food indoors was not always safer. Another oyster seller was invited into a Newgate Street alehouse to serve the customers. Shown into a room with three men, they shut the door, threatened to kill her if she cried out, and raped her.[83]

Horrific cases such as these are the worst situations in which street sellers found themselves. Though it does not seem to have deterred them, the women and girls who hawked food clearly faced the greatest risks. They also endured the struggles of all street vendors, whose foothold in the highway was never entirely stable. Being allowed to sell food in a particular place had no foundation in law, but rested on arrangements between residents, street sellers, and governing authorities. Even hawkers contested each other's claims to patches of dirt. In 1609, two vegetable dealers in St Clement Danes, William Dawson and Joan Granger, started arguing about one of them serving their counterpart's customers. When Dawson told Granger to 'kepe her owne p[ar]ishe', she shot back that the street 'was as free for her as for him'.[84] The following century, Catherine Russell charged Frances Dempsey with assault before one of the City aldermen. The two women both kept fruit stands in Cheapside and had fallen to fighting.[85] On Christmas Eve 1887, Philip Cohen was roughed up when he tried to park his barrow in Brick Lane. Some other hawkers had stayed all night to guarantee a pitch, but Cohen turned up at five in the morning and pushed his way into the line. An argument followed, a police constable stepped in, and Cohen was grabbed by the throat. In court, he was branded a 'trespasser on the spot'.[86]

Spread across three centuries, these confrontations remind us that, most of the time, hawkers' occupation of the street was customary and contingent. Not only did they have to face inclement weather, uneven ground, and streaming traffic, their very right to stop on the roadside and sell food could be disputed. Hawkers might dress their claims in the language of ownership or tradition, but if their presence was challenged by a rival, a displeased neighbour, or an officer of the law, they were left with little to stand on.

8

Nuisances

From time to time, street sellers were dragged into a courtroom before one of London's magistrates. Depending on the era, this could have been inside daunting Bridewell prison, the Tudor palace turned into a house of correction; or the dedicated chambers at the City's Guildhall and Mansion House, where the aldermen and mayor ruled on minor crimes in the heart of Georgian London; or one of the several police courts dotted across the metropolis which acted, from the late eighteenth century, as the capital's first tier of justice.[1] At this level of the legal system, where magistrates made decisions without the rigmarole of jury trials, the records are generally partial or brief. When hawkers were in trouble, we often lack the street seller's side of the story. But in many cases for which reports exist, like those of Margaret Sadler charged with selling apples at night, Jane Murta acting suspiciously as she dealt oysters on a bridge, and John Crowther blocking the road at King's Cross with his barrow of nuts, we have a sense that officers did not rush to judgement.[2] They seem to have weighed the evidence, balancing the laws of the City and the country with a broader sense of public order and fairness. Sadler, Murta, and Crowther, like many street sellers before and after, were let go with a warning on the promise not to reoffend.

There are reasons why they might have faced tougher treatment. Street sellers broke the tenets of traditional, market-based trading central to the capital's early economy. They stopped in the highways where traffic was supposed to flow freely. And they were associated with the down-and-outs and dissolutes who made aldermen and justices nervous. As part of London's modernization, we might expect its governors to have taken a more uncompromising attitude towards such deviants. Historians of the late sixteenth and early seventeenth centuries have described a crackdown on irregular retailers.[3] Scholars of later periods have explored how government reactions to hawkers and their markets were ambiguous, at best allowing them freedom, at worst leaving them in legal limbo.[4] Questions about regulation are important because they are, basically, about politics and power. They tell us about street sellers' relationship to authority and their position within London society. And they still matter very much today, in a world where the status of street vendors is still precarious, where in places as different as New York, Delhi, and Bangkok they are harassed, evicted, and arrested.

Looking at these issues in the long run gives a fresh perspective on the policing of street selling in London. Over three centuries, hawkers were roughed up by constables, cleared from areas where they gathered, forced to pay fines, and locked up for days or weeks. But London's governors never tried to stop food hawking altogether. Instead, they tried to regulate how street sellers traded. This regulation was light-touch, with the fiercest interventions only when neighbours complained or when hawkers were causing specific problems in particular parts of the city. The rules street sellers followed were largely unwritten, reliant on aldermen, magistrates, and police applying discretion. This was a delicate balance, which endured as London expanded, and only shifted decisively as the twentieth century approached.

The costermongers' charter

The 300 years of street selling's heyday were bookended by two legal landmarks: an act of the City's Common Council in 1612 and a pair of parliamentary acts in 1867. The Common Council act has been described as the culmination of efforts to restrict hawkers in late Elizabethan and early Stuart London, while the furore that surrounded the later laws has been seen as indicative of hawkers' uneasy position on the Victorian streets. By examining these episodes alongside each other and in the context of street selling's longer history, we can see them in another light. Put together, they show how the capital's governors were content to leave food hawkers alone, as long as they were deemed to be behaving.

The decades before 1612 were a tense period in London. Recurring outbreaks of plague and the perception that vagrancy, crime, and prostitution were on the rise created a pervasive sense of a city on the brink, even if it never broke down. A run of bad weather and poor harvests caused food prices to spike and heightened tensions in the marketplaces.[5] As they tried to keep the rising population fed and happy, the City aldermen attempted to reinforce the old market system, which aimed to keep buying and selling in fixed locations at set hours. By-laws criticized 'hucksters hawkers haglers and wanderers' walking 'up and downe the Streets', empowering aldermen to demolish stalls, tables, and stools erected for street trading, and ordered hefty fines for those caught.[6] Hawkers were a handy scapegoat. London avoided much of the food rioting that spread across England, but one of its most famous eruptions was directed at street sellers. One day in June 1595, several dozen apprentices arrived at Billingsgate to buy fish for their masters and discovered that women hawkers had already bought most of the supply. Stirring up a crowd, the apprentices chased the women across the river into Southwark and forced them to give up their purchases.[7]

The aldermen tried out various schemes to control women hawkers' activities, including capping their citywide numbers.[8] The climax of these efforts came in March 1612 when, after pressure from London's fishmongers, the Common Council passed the most substantial by-law yet. After a feisty preamble, which complained about the 'manie and sundrie abuses & disorders' committed by the 'Greate & excessive number of men women widowes & maides w[hi]ch have beene tolerated & p[er]mitted to carrie & convey oysters fishes fruite Roots, & other victuals about the streets', the act's nineteen subsections laid out thorough regulations. Each ward's alderman was to identify respectable street sellers, who had to be aged at least 30 and be the wife or widow of a City freeman—an enfranchised citizen who belonged to one of the guilds or livery companies. The list of those chosen would be kept by Bridewell's treasurer, who was to issue the women with tin badges, for which they each paid sixpence. While trading, hawkers had to wear their badge 'in Open sight' and stick to extra rules, such as not selling in the streets around Billingsgate and only offering good quality food that was properly weighed and measured. Transgressors risked forfeiting their stock, losing their badge, and imprisonment for twenty-four hours. Hawking food without a licence was prohibited.[9]

Gaps in the evidence make it hard to know how fiercely the new law was enforced. Though the minutes of Bridewell's court for the immediate aftermath of its passage do not survive, when the records pick up there is no surge in hawker-related business.[10] We know the aldermen tried to get the system up and running. Shortly after, they told the chief engraver of the Royal Mint to fashion the badges and commanded constables and beadles to arrest underage street sellers breaking the 'lately made' act.[11] Half a century on, the law was still an important point of reference. During the arguments in the 1660s over the right to use Billingsgate, the aldermen ordered the act reprinted and new badges to be produced, each with the retailer's name on one side and the City coat of arms on the other.[12] The power to issue licences passed to London's justices of the peace, who in the decades after received several petitions from women asking for their work to be recognized.[13] But the most important legacy was the principle that the act established: food hawkers, if they followed the aldermen's instructions, were allowed to keep on selling.

Licensing would not have worked to all street sellers' advantage. The 1612 act distinguished those who qualified for badges from those who did not. Social scientists studying street vending in the present day have demonstrated that licensed or unionized traders can behave like guilds, opposing those who remain unregistered. When given the chance, most hawkers end up paying for a licence, but there is a typically a sizeable group who, by choice or compulsion, stay in the shadows, in danger of prosecution.[14] In the seventeenth century, the Corporation also introduced licences for porters, cart drivers, and hackney coaches.[15] Handing out licences to hawkers may have been less feasible. In contrast to those other trades, street selling took different forms and no self-governing institution was founded to oversee hawkers' business, perhaps because most of them were women. By the end of the century, the idea of licensing was abandoned. In 1696–7, Parliament passed an act which required itinerant retailers across the kingdom to pay a £4 fee, plus another £4 for any horse or other animal they employed. The act expressly stated that its demands did not apply to those selling fish, fruit, or any other food.[16] From that point onwards, London's street sellers, whoever they were, had tacit permission to trade.

Because this remained the position up to the mid-nineteenth century, what happened in 1867 was a shock. In the early part of that year, when Parliament was preparing to take action against the scourge of traffic and congestion that seemed to worsen ever year, food hawkers were not at the centre of the conversation. Giving evidence to a House of Lords committee on a potential bill, neither the Metropolitan Police commissioner nor his City counterpart mentioned street selling as a major problem.[17] By late summer, the Metropolitan Streets Act passed into law, without any explicit mention of street sellers. However, its sixth section said that no goods should be placed on the street or cause inconvenience to passers-by, for any longer than was needed to load or unload. The act came into operation on 1 November, after which rule-breakers faced a maximum fine of 40s.[18]

Street sellers may not have been the intended target but, if the broad wording was strictly enforced, their livelihoods were under threat.

In its hawking-related provisions, the new law was not dissimilar to earlier statutes that dealt with obstruction. And there was no sudden uptick in arrests. A week before the act came into force, police officers served notice on street sellers near Paddington, but seven days later the retailers were still pushing their barrows together, both there and all over London.[19] But there was widespread concern that the act imperilled the future of street selling in the capital. Throughout November, supported by local tradespeople and priests, hawkers called for crisis meetings, cramming into schoolrooms in Stepney and Whitechapel and drinking houses like the Nag's Head in Leather Lane.[20] A deputation of East End street sellers visited the Home Secretary, Gathorne Hardy, warning him that thousands of hawkers and their families were at risk of destitution. Hardy told the petitioners that he had no power to suspend the act and that the damaging effects of its sixth clause should have been brought up during parliamentary scrutiny. He merely promised to ask the police to show lenience.[21] Meanwhile, the legislation was attacked in the editorials of newspapers across the political spectrum. The *Standard* saved its most withering disapproval for the 'bungling section' that would do away with street sellers, those 'servants of the public' who were 'at present indispensable' for feeding the labouring classes. Under the shocking headline, 'The Wholesale Starvation of the Poor', the radical *Reynold's Newspaper* predicted a cold, lean winter ahead.[22]

The government was forced to react, wary of the mass protests in Hyde Park earlier that year and at pains not to immediately annoy all the city-dwelling men enfranchised by the 1867 Reform Act. Home Secretary Hardy introduced a fresh bill on 21 November and, at the start of December, barely a month after the first Metropolitan Streets Act had come into effect, Parliament passed the amendment. It was short, stating only that the sixth section of the first act 'shall not apply to Costermongers, Street Hawkers, or Itinerant Traders, so long as they carry on their Business in accordance with the Regulations from Time to Time made by the Commissioner of Police'.[23] Two years later, those regulations were published.

The amended act did not go unchallenged. Vestries and district boards of works urged the police and Home Office to be bolder in policing street sellers or, at least, let them clear away hawkers themselves. In the 1890s, two cases of irregular retailers accused of blocking the streets, first prosecuted by local authorities in Holborn and the parish of St Mary Newington, were ruled on in the higher courts. The courts decided that the amended Metropolitan Streets Act superseded earlier laws that touched on hawkers, which meant that the district bodies had no right to move them on, unless they breached the police regulations. Referring to these decisions, a Metropolitan Police memo called the second 1867 act the 'costermongers' charter'.[24] For the first time, food hawkers' right to do business was enshrined in law.

Both the Victorian statute and the City's early attempt to license street sellers allowed food hawking, most of the time, to continue. Reading the two episodes in this more positive way helps explain what might otherwise seem a conundrum. In all the capital's courtrooms across these centuries, street sellers were rarely prosecuted for the simple act of selling food. Take the busy first decade of the seventeenth century. During that time, just thirty-one men and women identified as food hawkers appeared before Bridewell's court of governors. Over half the cases mentioned only that the defendants were selling food, usually fish, while others were primarily charged for sexual impropriety, excessive drinking, and vagrancy.[25] Even if the court books show just a minimum of those arrested, the numbers are still remarkably low. Later on, the rate fell to a handful of hawkers appearing every ten years.[26]

The picture was similar at the Guildhall, where from the late seventeenth century the lord mayor sat to hear cases for several hours most days of the week.[27] Fewer than ten hawkers appeared each year, when the mayor was ruling on several hundred cases annually, and most of those were for other offences.[28] This stayed the situation as the mayor's court developed by the mid-eighteenth century into two justice rooms, at the Mansion House, where the mayor presided at his residence, and the Guildhall, where the aldermen sat as magistrates in rotation.[29] The people hawking fruit and pushing barrows who were occasionally summoned were charged with driving on the foot pavement, blocking passageways, and breaking the Sabbath—not the fact that they were offering food.[30] Throughout this period, wards and parishes could also deal with minor troublemakers, ordering them to pay fines at the annual meetings of householders or instructing officers to have them removed. From the remaining evidence, it is clear that these local bodies took action only when hawkers were causing an acute issue, like outside the Royal Exchange in Cornhill or the stretch of Fleet Street near the church of St Dunstan in the West. They were not concerned with food hawking in general.

The regulation of street activity was blighted by the same problems of fragmented and overlapping jurisdictions that affected matters like paving and lighting. Over time, London became more thoroughly policed. Before 1700, most policing had been done part-time, with men from the neighbourhood serving in rotation as constables, beadles, or in the night watch. The City led the way with more extensive and organized policing, but beyond the Corporation's boundaries certain Westminster parishes showed initiative, with the vestries of St James Piccadilly and St George Hanover Square in 1735 the first to secure an act of Parliament that let them raise a rate to pay for a permanent night-time patrol.[31] With the memory of the anti-Catholic Gordon Riots still raw and fears about criminality festering, Parliament eventually passed the Middlesex Justices Act in 1792. This created seven new public offices, each staffed with three stipendiary magistrates and six constables. These constables did not troop around the streets but investigated crimes and brought the accused to the magistrates.[32] The formation of the Metropolitan Police in 1829 was the great leap forward in terms of centralization. Organized under two commissioners, the new force was split into divisions and sections, and the full-time officers were ranked as superintendents, inspectors, sergeants, and constables. Patrolling regularly throughout the day and night, the police now had a wider remit for keeping peace and order in the streets.[33] The London magistracy was also transforming from an old roster of amateur justices towards a staff of professional lawyers. The public offices of 1792 became 'police offices' and then 'police courts'. By the 1850s, there were thirteen police courts across the metropolis, anticipating the magistrates' courts of today.[34]

Even with this extension of justice and policing, street sellers were still left largely alone. To think about the police courts systematically, I have used the digital archives of several newspapers that reported on their proceedings to find 868 cases between 1816 and 1900 in which men and women described as costermongers appeared as defendants. With at most a few cases from each court written up every day and the courts holding collectively as many as 100,000 hearings every year, it is hard to be sure how representative this sample might be.[35] But it does reveal that food hawkers appeared for the full range of offences with which we might expect poorer Londoners to be charged, from dangerous driving and drunkenness to theft, assault, and murder. They were accused of causing disorder in the streets, by hawking food on Sundays, tempting customers to gamble, or stopping up traffic with barrows and stalls. But none at all were called to answer for simply selling food.[36]

The assumption that constables and sergeants were set against hawkers owes much to Henry Mayhew, who described the 'continual warfare' between street sellers and the police.[37] Reflecting this stereotypical tension, numerous cases of hawkers assaulting officers were recounted by newspapers, along with instances in which constables turned violent, beating street sellers with their sticks, upsetting barrows, and tumbling food like turnips into the mud.[38] There is, however, more evidence to the contrary. On the whole, police were reluctant to go too far in their supervision of street sellers. The 1839 Police Act gave officers wide-ranging powers to clamp down on aspects of working class culture, such as drinking and gambling. But in matters like street trading the police were careful and considered, possibly because of the few officers out on patrol at any one time (under a thousand men in mid-century).[39]

Those tasked with watching over the streets had plenty of leeway in dealing with food hawkers. Before they reached the courtroom, street sellers encountered officers belonging to the City, ward, parish, or Metropolitan Police, who could order them to move, confiscate goods and tools, perhaps even push them around, then decide whether to make an arrest. Such street-level regulation has made almost no dent on the historical record.[40] In the seventeenth and eighteenth centuries, more and more offences were being handled summarily by magistrates who sat alone, in formal settings like Bridewell and the Guildhall as well as in places like taverns, handing out punishments or dismissing charges without recourse to a trial.[41] Offences related to hawking, such as obstruction and Sunday trading, were mostly dealt with in this way.

In practice, this meant that magistrates could show discretion, considering the context of a case and being flexible with the punishments they applied. Irregular food sellers summoned to answer a multiplicity of charges were frequently allowed to walk free. In October 1732, Thomas Russell was brought before the mayor, accused by a constable of 'Selling Rabbitts and other Poultry in the streets as a Hawker'. Russell was discharged on the promise not to reoffend.[42] Even as the system of summary justice became more standardized in the nineteenth century, magistrates could exercise judgement, mediate between disgruntled parties, and express their opinion. And they often came down on street sellers' side. In December 1867, when dealing with a complaint against a traffic-blocking hawker, the magistrate of Westminster police court chose to comment on the recent parliamentary upheaval. 'It was never the intention of the Legislature to prevent costermongers plying their trade in the street,' he said. 'Standing with a barrow in the street, and not causing an obstruction was not an offence in law.'[43]

Infamous wretches

This did not exempt food hawkers from suspicion. Magistrates, local officials, and police intervened if they felt that street sellers were up to no good. Useful as they proved themselves as retailers, hawkers were thought to associate with the most disreputable elements of metropolitan society. In the seventeenth century, the character of the fishwife, developed by writers like Donald Lupton and Ned Ward, was depicted drinking, swearing, and upbraiding men in a violation of the period's expectations for women. In a 1797 edition of his treatise on London policing, Patrick Colquhoun claimed that hundreds of men and women pretended to be 'Costard Mongers', 'Ass Drivers', and vendors of rabbits, fish, and fruit, but were really thieves and pedlars of counterfeit money.[44] Introducing the published volumes of *London Labour*, Mayhew explained that he sought to uncover the class of 'urban and suburban wanderers' of which hawkers were part, alongside pickpockets, beggars, prostitutes, cabmen, and street performers.[45]

Early on, women street sellers were accused of selling sex. In the minutes of Bridewell's court from January 1603, Agnes Bynks was labelled a 'fish-woman', but the charge against her was that a man had enjoyed 'th'use and carnall knowledge of her bodie'.[46] Another fishwife, Elizabeth Phillips, was named a 'nightwalker', which in the early seventeenth century was a code-word for nocturnal depravity.[47] On top of issuing licences to food hawkers, the hospital's governors were the main arm of the City's efforts to regulate the sex trade. As much as it riled the aldermen and other elites, prostitution was an unremarkable feature of life in the capital. For poor women, selling sex was part-time work that could be paired with other makeshift jobs, such as hawking food. Many street-vending hotspots, like the highway between Fleet Bridge and Temple Bar, were also known for soliciting. Eroticized depictions of young women hawkers, especially those selling aphrodisiacs like oysters, further buttressed the connection.[48] By the later nineteenth century, the ties between street selling and sex seem to have loosened, though similar sorts of women still turned to these difficult means of making a living.[49]

Other perceptions were harder to shake. London's rulers had always worried about the quality of what was sold in its markets and shops and on the streets. Pledging only to sell food that was 'wholesome for mansbodie' was one of the rules that the 1612 licensing act made sanctioned hawkers follow. One of the oldest accusations was that milk sellers watered down the contents of their pails. John Middleton described the process in fine detail in his 1798 survey of Middlesex agriculture. He claimed that most barns had a special pump, known as the 'famous black cow' for the colour it was painted, from which hawkers 'not secretly but openly' added as much water as they wished. Those without access to a pump dipped their pails into horse troughs and the dung-filled streams next to which the cows grazed.[50] As the dairy industry became more sophisticated over the nineteenth century, watering-down remained widespread, along with other adulterations like adding flour for thickness, chalk for whiteness, or pigment to turn pale milk a creamy gold.[51] A complex trade, with lots of intermediaries like street traders, offered copious opportunities for fraud.

Vending unfit food was one of the common reasons for which street sellers were brought before the police courts. Some of the questionable wares sound objectively vile, like fish described as 'rotten and quite green' (the hawker's shaky defence was that the fried fish shops sold no better).[52] But offering lower grades of fish, fruit, and greens was street traders' specialism. In 1897, Islington's sanitary inspector charged Essex Road hawker John Hurley with selling bad quality pears and greengages, having seen some children approach him and ask for a few 'farthingworths of specks'. From beneath his stall, Hurley had slid out a box of damaged but not necessarily unsound fruit. For giving his customers what they wanted, the hawker was fined £5.[53]

Street sellers were believed to cover up flaws with deception. At once delighted and appalled, Mayhew rattled off the ruses that costermongers tried: boiling oranges to make them puff up, mingling cherries of variable quality, and stuffing the bottom half of containers with detritus such as cabbage leaves.[54] From police court proceedings, we know some of these techniques were actually employed, most often of all the manipulation of weights and measures. One man selling grapes in Camden Town set his scales on an incline, so that every pound of fruit weighed an ounce and a half less than he claimed.[55] Giving evidence at the Guildhall in 1842, a City policeman recalled how he had investigated a cherry seller's weights and discovered that they had holes scooped out, replaced by cork, and painted over.[56] But this problem went beyond the streets. When hawkers were named and shamed at special weights and measures hearings, they were joined by supposedly more upstanding shopkeepers and market traders.

A more particular accusation levelled at hawkers was gaming. From the late seventeenth century, the Middlesex justices of the peace issued repeated orders instructing constables to arrest street sellers pushing wheelbarrows with oysters, oranges, apples, and nuts. The hawkers carried dice and tempted customers to play for their purchases.[57] With flat bottoms and raised sides, wheelbarrows made perfect portable gambling tables. In February 1693, John Hames, described as a 'Barrow wheeler', was brought before the lord mayor for 'carrying dice & Marbles'.[58] This was a period of intensive activism by groups of citizens trying to suppress what they saw as immoral behaviour, such as prostitution, swearing, and gambling. Driven by fervent religious belief and fears of social disorder within the metropolis, the self-described campaigns for the 'reformation of manners' made accusations against tens of thousands of mostly poor Londoners.[59] Street sellers were not put off using their equipment and stock in creative ways. Nineteenth-century hawkers used coconut shells to shake dice.[60] A simple, long-running game was tossing for pies. Customers paid a penny for the street seller to flip a coin. If the player guessed heads or tails correctly, they received a pie; if they lost, the hawker pocketed the cash.[61]

Moralizing reformers also fretted about Sunday trading. Not hemmed in by standard market days and hours, hawkers were an easy target for prosecution. Early on, street sellers were charged at Bridewell with crying milk, fruit, and wheat on Sundays.[62] Though restrictions on work and rowdy behaviour on the Sabbath were already established in the Elizabethan and early Stuart city, allegations of Sunday business seem to have accumulated, like those about gambling, from the late seventeenth century.[63] When parish vestries told their officers to clear orange sellers and other street traders from their churchyards, the unrest tended to be around the time of weekly worship.[64]

Sunday food selling became even more contentious in the nineteenth century. Speaking in 1850, at one of the parliamentary committees convened to discuss whether new laws were needed, a barber described the scene at Whitecross Street at eleven o'clock on a Sunday morning. He claimed that more than 130 shops and stalls were open, turning the street into 'one mass of persons, crying "buy, buy!" from gridirons to halfpenny pies'. Churchgoers on the way to nearby St Luke's were forced to take a circuitous route.[65] The Metropolitan Police were reluctant to intervene, their senior officers playing down the extent of Sunday disruption and warning that seizing traders' goods could trigger furious resistance. With many London workers paid on Saturday evenings, their families had to shop the following day.[66] The commissioners were right to be cautious. In early summer 1855, a bill that would ban all Sunday trading apart from a few ungenerous exemptions was introduced to Parliament. Over successive weekends, protesters packed Hyde Park, voicing their anger and scrapping with police. The bill was finally withdrawn.[67] Until the end of the Victorian period, food hawkers continued to be prosecuted intermittently under the Sunday trading act passed under Charles II, back in the seventeenth century, a law out of tune with the practicalities of urban existence. An unnamed muffin seller charged with Sunday trading at Hammersmith police court defended his actions by saying, 'They were not living in the times of Adam and Eve, but of civilization.' The magistrate disagreed and sent him off with a fine.[68]

Complaints about Sunday trading are typical of how most street selling problems were handled. London's governors and police never had a blanket policy for repressing the activities of hawkers, but reacted to accusations that bubbled up from individuals and communities. In response, the capital's authorities carved a middle path, addressing the worries of those complaining, as well as the need to keep order in the streets and allow poor Londoners to stay afloat.

The New Cut, which now runs between the Old Vic theatre and Southwark station, was one of the street markets where Sunday trading was deemed too boisterous. One morning in December 1871, the Lambeth vestry sent a team of uniformed nuisance inspectors, protected by two dozen police, to make the street traders remove their stalls. The hawkers who refused had their names taken down and were later summoned to face charges.[69] After the magistrate at Southwark police court adjourned the proceedings against the forty-eight street sellers, the first January meeting of the vestry received three deputations on the matter. Two were from shop assistants and tradesmen in favour of an enforced day of rest; the third, signed by 250 hawkers and more than 2,000 residents, took the street traders' side. The vestry voted for a compromise, committing to drop the charges if the stallholders left the New Cut by half ten every Sunday.[70] Perhaps a sign the truce would not hold, the following month the magistrate dealt with two of the costermongers in a test case and fined them both.[71] Showing their organization and legal nous, the Lambeth street traders applied to the Court of Queen's Bench, asking for a ruling that would force the local authority to provide proof that they were behind the New Cut problems. The Lord Chief Justice refused, saying the hawkers were causing an obstruction, regardless of the day of the week.[72] Back in Southwark, the remaining defendants were handed fines. The magistrate said the vestry had acted with 'great kindness' and the half-past-ten deal was 'reasonable'.[73] A newspaper reported the scene in the market street one Sunday in late July: at the cut-off time, there was a 'considerable amount of discontent and grumbling', but most hawkers moved elsewhere in the neighbourhood. In the afternoon, a crowd massed outside the open shop of one of the tradesmen who had called for the Sabbath day closure, 'hooting and groaning' at the hypocrisy until the owner put up his shutters.[74]

The Lambeth affair fits a pattern. First, prominent residents pushed local officials to act against misbehaving hawkers, accused of selling sex, gambling, cheating, or disrupting the calm of a Sunday. Police officers and magistrates were hesitant to step in. When a decision was ultimately made, hawkers were usually allowed to keep working as long as they followed a few restrictions. The situation remained settled until another complaint came along. Heavy-handed reactions sparked an outcry from both street sellers and the working and middling Londoners who relied on them.

Preventing free passage

The simplest charge to make against hawkers was that they were blocking the highway. Within the City, orders issued in the early seventeenth century against mobile traders were as much about obstructing citizens' doors as they were concerned with improper selling. When London's official markets were taking place on the street, the management of trading and city space were closely intertwined.[75] Beyond the Square Mile, where until the mid-nineteenth century there was no overarching metropolitan authority, problems like obstruction were mostly handled at a local level. Only a selection of the records of parishes, wards, and other jurisdictions have survived, but those that have suggest that residents actively managed the streets around where they lived.[76]

Across the metropolis, these powers were eventually formalized by acts of Parliament. The 1817 statute popularly known as Michael Angelo Taylor's Act listed a variety of nuisances and obstructions, such as placing baskets, barrows, and boards on the foot pavement or roadway. If the offenders did not move when requested, they could be summoned to a justice of the peace, receive a fine of up to £5, and have their tools and animals impounded, with any perishable food given to the district's poor.[77] In addition to outlining a host of other street offences that warranted a fine of up to 40s., the fifty-fourth section of the 1839 Police Act took aim at those who pushed barrows, carts, and trucks. They were not to pause for longer than was needed for loading or 'wilfully interrupt any public Crossing, or wilfully cause any Obstruction in any Thoroughfare'.[78] These laws cast a broad net in which hawkers could be readily caught.

Despite this, enforcement remained for the most part sporadic. In the seventeenth and eighteenth centuries, local officials and police tried to stop blockages and nuisances that flared up throughout London's sprawl. At annual meetings of householders and before magistrates like the mayor, food hawkers were blamed for laying out stalls and baskets 'to the Annoyance of passengers in the kings highwaie' or 'preventing the free Passage of his Majestys subjects'.[79] With a little variation, these are stock phrases that appear time and again in the records. Not least because most incidents would have ended with an instruction to move on, estimating the extent of the disruption is difficult, even in the nineteenth century. According to the London Statistical Society, 334 'basket people' carrying goods for sale were brought before magistrates in 1837.[80] There must have been thousands more minor infractions every year which did not even get that far.

Efforts to prevent obstruction centred on a series of specific problems. One of these was wheelbarrows. As soon as hawkers began to embrace the equipment, every tier of metropolitan government, from vestries up to county justices, was involved in trying to halt their use.[81] As well as being used for gambling, wheelbarrows were also causing issues on the roads. In the City, street sellers were charged with driving on the 'foot pavement', a sign of how the street surface was improving and the authorities were attempting to separate where vehicles rolled and pedestrians walked.[82] In the nineteenth century, police confiscated barrows and took them to the 'green yard' or pound. An earlier punishment was to let hawkers keep their barrows, but only after 'taking off the Wheels'.[83] Street sellers sometimes turned the tables on barrow-seizing policemen. When the constable went to call for assistance, the owner would whip off a wheel, making the vessel awkward for the officer to carry away.[84]

The most dogged problem for London's different authorities were places where hawkers consistently slowed down traffic. This is part of the reason why we know that street sellers for hundreds of years gathered in great numbers along Fleet Street, on the city's bridges, at the gates of the

Royal Exchange, and in and around churches. Vestries, householders, and officers repeatedly complained about the presence of hawkers within particular parts of their neighbourhoods, creating evidence that we have been able to read against the grain to learn about street selling in practice. Even in the nineteenth century, authorities maintained their focus on these blackspots. In 1863, the mayor and aldermen passed a by-law that banned anyone selling from barrows or carts from a list of the City's thoroughfares, including both London and Blackfriars bridges, Cornhill, and Fleet Street, between nine in the morning and six at night.[85] From reports in the papers, we can tell that hawkers were still upbraided for trading in those streets, but also responded by taking their business to the fringes of the Corporation's authority, to the likes of Liverpool Street and Farringdon Road.[86] In the metropolis at large, the street markets drew most attention. In a memo submitted to the Royal Commission on London Traffic that reported in 1905, Metropolitan Police commissioner Alexander Bruce noted that the 7,500 costermongers used 142 different streets, but only in a handful were they causing obstruction.[87]

When whinging about hawkers turned to prosecutions, it tended to be when they were causing a nuisance. In legal terms, a 'nuisance' was any activity that caused harm or offence to a community or the individuals within it. Before the nineteenth century, nuisances were not defined in statute but worked out through a combination of court rulings, by-laws, and decisions by on-the-ground officers.[88] Wards and parishes dealt with most annoyances and magistrates ruled in disputes between individuals. If someone living or working nearby decided to cause a fuss, just placing a basket of apples on the roadside, parking a barrow full of potatoes, or constructing a shellfish stall out of planks and boxes could be considered a nuisance. Obstruction was far from the only problem. In June 1875, eight hawkers were summoned to Thames police court for selling fish in Poplar. The charge against them was blocking the street, but the case revealed how several neighbours had complained about the 'very offensive' stink of the fish, worsened by the heat of early summer and the way the barrows were pressed together.[89] As we shall see, hawkers' advertising cries were another source of trouble.

Nineteenth-century laws like the 1839 Police Act were more exacting about what nuisances were problematic and what steps officers could take. But the police were unwilling to use these powers unless they were responding to a specific complaint. Mayhew described how, if street sellers were 'in the habit' of standing somewhere, the unspoken agreement was that they would not be disturbed unless a nearby shopkeeper or resident raised the alarm.[90] Orders sent to officers of the Metropolitan Police in 1882 stated that they should deal directly with 'casual' obstructions, but 'habitual', 'permanent', or 'oft-repeated' blockages should be referred to the local authority.[91] Some of these authorities became frustrated and took their own initiative. In 1885, the vestry of St Mary Newington complained to the Home Office about the police leaving to neighbourhood officials the 'very unpleasant duty' of clearing hawkers' barrows and stalls from Walworth Road, a busy thorough-fare that now also had a tramway. With no response forthcoming, the vestry ordered its street keeper to march down the road in question one morning and take down any stall he found open.[92] In the years leading up to the First World War, such bodies were still agitating for more determined action. A Metropolitan Police response to one set of proposals counselled against rashness: 'It must not be forgotten that the proposals made by the Local Authorities represent in the main the views of the tradespeople rather than the views of those who depend for many of the necessaries of life upon the street traders.'[93]

Obvious acts of repression, like in the 1850s when teams of officers were dispatched to shut down Somers Town street market and arrested dozens of retailers, were violent exceptions.[94] On most occasions when vestries and district boards pushed for harsher enforcement, police officers denied there was a much of a nuisance at all. Archived among Home Office and Metropolitan Police papers, reports from local police stations, scrawled on blue paper, explained that most street sellers behaved and stuck to the regu-lations.[95] Hawkers noticed this permissiveness too. Speaking to the Royal Commission on Markets in 1888, door-to-door fruit and vegetable seller George Shave said that he was 'never interfered with', when stopping for up to half an hour to serve a house.[96] John Denton, who had a stall in Islington's Chapel Street, agreed that, 'As long as we keep the place clean, and there are no rows, nobody interferes with us.' He added that the police kept as close a watch on the shopkeepers nearby.[97] Some admitted to being hassled, but all of these street sellers knew exactly what the police regulations were, down to the precise dimensions of the stalls and barrows allowed.[98]

Towards the end of our period, the room for manoeuvre given to officers of the law began to shrink. What was deemed correct or incorrect behav-iour was set down in more detail, as regulation became more prescriptive. This began with the list of rules for street sellers drawn up after the 1867 act of Parliament. The first three points stated that no barrow, cart, or stall should be larger than 9 ft long and 3 ft wide, that no more than one line of traders was permitted along the side of a street, and that every vendor should stay at least 4 ft from their neighbour. The three remaining rules said that hawkers should move when a resident needed to load or unload a vehicle at their door, should never stand at a street crossing, and were liable to have their equipment removed from anywhere that they obstructed the traffic or annoyed those living nearby.[99]

In some ways, the regulations are striking for their restraint. They do not touch on any of the issues of immorality with which street sellers were historically linked. A rule against hawking on Sundays was included in a draft but excluded from the final version.[100] But the regulations were a departure from how obstructions had been handled up to then. Formerly, local authorities, magistrates, and police had some flexibility when deciding how hawkers should occupy the street. Now, the way that these men and women could trade was predetermined and laid down in strict measurements. This more rigorous framework recalled an older piece of London legislation. In 1612, the City by-law that licensed women street sellers set out how these retailers should go about business (not stocking up before six in the morning, charging only the agreed market prices, not employing others to help sell) and how constables, beadles, and market officers should enforce the act's provisions. That rigid approach was soon abandoned in favour of pragmatism. This endured until the niggling effects of congestion and unruly street behaviour were felt to be too much to bear.

In the early twentieth century, the regulation of food hawking became even more onerous, marking the end of the era of discretion. Local authorities experimented with different models. Greenwich banned hawking everywhere in the parish apart from a central marketplace, where street traders were allowed to pay half the tolls of regular shopkeepers.[101] Shoreditch Borough Council erected permanent stalls with electric lights in Nile Street, but hawkers were unwilling to pay the small rent.[102] The City revived the notion of licensing attempted three centuries earlier. From 1911, all food hawkers trading within the Corporation's boundaries had to be registered. The following decade, a House of Commons committee explored the potential for a similar scheme for wider London.[103] Their proposals were never introduced but licensing became the dominant approach. After a 1927 act of Parliament, each borough council was left to decide how hawkers should be registered and how they should go about business.[104]

This was a clean break from what came before. Not only had the rules about how hawkers could fill streets become more precise, but the basis on which street sellers could keep trading had shifted. With stricter rules about obstructions and the London-wide introduction of licensing, a poor man or woman could no longer scrape together some cash for a basket and some fish or fruit and make a start in the street trade. They had to seek permission to sell food. To use the language of social scientists, food hawkers had been 'formalized'. In the process, those who could afford to take on a licence gained more in common with shopkeepers and market traders, who had a fixed address for their business and coughed up for rates and rent.[105] This did not hurt the prospects of individual street sellers. But the trade itself was changed for good. Previously open to newcomers, food hawking had been a loosely regulated business which had organized itself to feed the growing capital, with little oversight from London's governors. As the capital became unambiguously modern, the working lives of hawkers became structured from above.

9

Voices

A barrow-pushing fruit seller trudging through the suburbs, a fish seller carrying that day's haul house to house, and a hot potato vendor at a roadside stall—all used their voice to advertise their stock. Cried out above the tumult of streets, calls of 'New Wallfleet oysters!', 'Four for six pence mackrell!', and 'Come buy my watercresses!' signalled more than a chance to pick up provisions. 'Every morning, as surely as the sun rises, am I woke up at six o'clock by the melancholy shrick of the milkman,' a West Brompton resident whined in 1876, in a letter to the *Pall Mall Gazette*. 'The agony which he is capable of throwing into the final syllable of his formula is indescribable. The word milk is uttered in a shrill key and rather rapidly, but the "ho" is prolonged into something which is neither a hoot nor a moan nor a screech, but partakes of all three, and unquestionably can only have been acquired by long and assiduous practice.'[1] The letter writer joined a long list of Londoners who complained about hawkers' advertising cries, but in doing so revealed that they listened with care. Like it or not, the milk seller had become part of the correspondent's daily routine. And they had noticed too the sound's distinctive shape, the effort required to be heard, and the way that calling out to catch attention was a skill that took experience.

All the complex reasons why hawkers mattered to London's history are encapsulated in their voices. Reactions to their cries were bound up with how metropolitans thought about their changing city. Calling out was part of a trading toolkit particular to food hawkers' work. Throughout these centuries, cries were central to the soundscape, providing a sense of time and place, and lodging street sellers firmly in city culture and myth. Though other dealers enticed customers with their voices, such as ballad singers and newsboys, the cry was the hawker's trademark.[2] After all, the genre of visual art, music, and poetry with street sellers as its subject was known as the

Cries. Still popular well into the twentieth century, when street selling was beginning to decline and hawkers' calls were finally muffled, the Cries seemed to echo the capital's past.

Tortures of the ear

Like that disgruntled West Brompton reader, Londoners had bemoaned the racket for as long as street vendors had cried. In his 1609 play *Epicœne*, Ben Jonson created the character of Morose, a gentleman who so hated noise that he struck a deal with London's 'Fish-wives, and Orange-women' to shut them up.[3] A hundred years on, a satirical note in the *Spectator* observed how 'Vocal Cries are of a much larger Extent, and indeed so full of Incongruities and Barbarisms, that we appear a distracted City, to Foreigners, who do not comprehend the Meaning of such Enormous Outcries'.[4] Around the same time, while living just south of St Paul's, Jonathan Swift blamed his difficulties getting up on the 'restless dog crying Cabbages and Savoys' who disrupted his sleep. 'I wish his largest Cabbage was sticking in his Throat', the poet wrote.[5] Swift's foe had a counterpart in Tobias Smollett's 1771 novel *Humphrey Clinker*. Matthew Bramble, the countryman staying in London, was shaken from bed by the 'noisy rustics bellowing green pease below my window'.[6]

In all these complaints, hawkers' cries are 'noise', unwanted sound that confuses or annoys the listener. Reworking anthropologist Mary Douglas's classic description of dirt, Peter Bailey has suggested that noise could be defined as 'sound out of place'. Noise lacks the precise pitch of formal music and falls outside those sounds acceptable or useful to a community. Those that make it are deemed vulgar or degenerate.[7] Historians interested in sound stress that noise, like other aspects of sensory perception, is a specific cultural construct.[8] When Londoners labelled cries 'noise', they gave away what they thought about roving retailers, as well as preoccupations about their society and its sound.

Early criticism was linked to stereotypes of street sellers. One mid-seventeenth-century ballad, 'The Common Cries of London Town', described how a fishwife 'had need to have her tongue be greas'd | For she rattles in the throat'.[9] Another song claimed that the sound of women selling seafood, who 'each brabled with other', was enough to scare off the devil.[10] Brabbling, rattling, loud, and high-pitched, the fishwife's cry was a feature of her unruly caricature, just as activities of retailers like her were being closely watched in the Stuart capital.[11] At that time, audiences understood the sounds of the earthly world to have cosmic resonances: learned, well-tuned music indicated good order in society, while street songs and poor-playing were signs of unrest. The upheaval in the markets that so worried the City aldermen possessed a sonic counterpart.[12]

In the eighteenth century, the metropolitan middle classes used opposition to coarse music to shore up their emergent identity. Urban elites enjoyed a polite musical culture involving professional performers, which stood against the raucous sounds of the street.[13] Ralph Crochett, the imagined complainant writing in the *Spectator* in 1711, proposed himself as 'Comptroller general of the London Cries' to bring the discordant choir into harmony.[14] Several decades later, a comic letter by a musician named Joel Collier to the *St James Chronicle* criticized the limited progress since Crochett's warnings. Collier discusses a series of street calls, explaining their faults by reference to the standards of learned music. Spinach and muffins were bafflingly sung in the same key, smelts and mackerel were cried in absurd cadence, and the shout of fresh salmon was a 'mangled' interpretation of 'the celebrated Water-Piece' (presumably the work of Handel) with the addition of 'an unpleasant Semi-quaver'. 'This is a musical Age,' Collier writes, 'and it much becomes us to reform the present barbarous System of Cries.' The musician does not wish to silence street sellers, but wants to bring them in line with educated music, going as far as composing 'appropriate Airs' for each commodity.[15] It is unclear, however, exactly who is the butt of the article's satire. Like Hogarth's print *The Enraged Musician*, in which a bewigged violinist's practice is broken up by the noise outside his window, Collier's letter needles the sensitivity and pretensions of polite London.[16]

Later critics hoped to hush the cries once and for all. In familiar terms, *The Times* in 1856 attacked 'incessant cries, at the highest pitch of the vulgarest throats', which it thought 'absolutely unnecessary, and, what is more, an offence against the first principles of social life in England'. The paper asserted that the literary, political, and professional classes were unable to maintain the concentration that their work demanded.[17] Soon after, under the headline 'The Tortures of the Ear', the *Examiner* called for legislation to prevent a nuisance that, by irritating the mind and interrupting sleep, was 'a far more potent cause of ill-health than the bad drainage and universal smoke of which we hear so much'.[18] On the letters pages, the editorials drew supportive responses, which kept dribbling in over the following half-century. In particular, correspondents lamented how boisterous cries wrecked the tranquillity of London's leafy suburbs and the repose of Sunday mornings.[19] Their irritation is another reminder that, when hawkers were described as a nuisance, it was usually for a specific, rather than a general problem.

If this griping shares much with the fictional complaints of Morose and Crochett, it also hints at a different way of thinking about sound altogether. Previously, music and speech were considered ideal forms of sound, of which noises like cries were an inversion. In the first half of the nineteenth century, developments in the connected fields of acoustics, physiology, and otology meant sound was increasingly understood as a waveform and hearing as a mechanical function, the vibration of the eardrum.[20] Victorians listened more attentively and isolated individual sounds, which had the effect of sharpening attitudes towards urban nuisances.[21] These novel ways of listening interacted with social tensions old and new. The editorials in *The Times* and *Examiner* were early skirmishes in the anti-street music campaign that resulted in an 1864 act of Parliament. Among the advocates for action against Italian organ grinders and other instrumentalists were writers, artists, and thinkers, most famously Charles Dickens, Thomas Carlyle, and the mathematician Charles Babbage. Their arguments can be read as a defence of the expanding realm of home-based work, carried out by intellectuals and professionals, who needed quiet in order to think. With a firmer grasp of sound's physicality, they believed the noise outside their houses directly affected their bodies. To protect himself, Carlyle spent £170 building a soundproof study. On his deathbed, the *Punch* artist John Leech claimed his demise was hastened by the clamour of street musicians.[22] To these sensitive listeners, hawkers were no longer an occasional frustration; they were part of London's life-threatening roar.

It is wrong to simply say, as some sound scholars contend, that street cries became more of a nuisance over time.[23] What changed was what Londoners meant when they called a sound annoying. However, we know that there were many more hawkers on the streets, and those hawkers' advertising calls may have had to become louder, as they tried to break through a fiercer din. Around 1600, London already throbbed with sounds, from clip-clopping hooves and barking dogs to voices reflecting off close-packed buildings and the regular clang of bells. The ambient sound may not have gone higher than 70 decibels, softer than a modern-day vacuum cleaner.[24] As more of the city was paved and rebuilt in stone (instead of absorbent wood, plaster, and mud), traffic sounds reverberated with greater vigour. That traffic also grew unrelentingly.[25] The city's amplification continued with the new transport of the nineteenth century, the omnibuses, trams, and loudest of all the railways, which rumbled through the metropolis.[26] As with the persistent problems of traffic, street sellers contributed to the rising volume while also suffering its effects. But shouting with more force was not their only option. To cut through the hubbub, street sellers learned to make their calls ring out and catch the listener's ear.

The crying art

As well as heaving cumbersome loads around London, hawkers had to call loud enough to be heard, possibly for several hours a day. Consider the strain of this exertion. Henry Mayhew described one young woman as 'husky from shouting apples', while other street selling interviewees had cracked voices and were short of breath. Hoarseness, Mayhew wrote, was 'one of the peculiar characteristics of hawkers'. Some resorted to labour-saving alternatives, like using a drum or hiring boys to shout. The muffin seller, most memorably, walked along with a bell.[27] In 2004, a scrap metal collector in Mexico City, who found the constant calling had damaged his voice, recorded his 10-year-old daughter crying, 'Se compran colchones, tambores, refrigeradores...o algo de fierro viejo que vendan!' Blasted on a loudspeaker and copied countless times, the recording has become the signature call of such traders across Mexico and beyond.[28]

Crying was not aimless effort. The special manner of calling was a skill, one of the techniques used by hawkers to retail food. Though we cannot hear these sounds for ourselves, we can make careful use of songs and music written in previous centuries that claimed to capture street sellers' calls. While not offering direct access to these voices, the lyrics and melodies hint at how hawkers sounded as they moved through the city.

In the eighteenth-century ballad 'The Cries of London', every line of each verse, apart from a brief introduction, is devoted to a hawker's call. Depending on how they are counted, the song may contain more than a hundred different cries, all of them short and passing quickly from one to next. On listening, the effect is intense and bewildering, like walking down a street full of traders and hearing call after call from every side. But amid the aural onslaught, there are patterns to how the voices cry out. They either

begin with 'Come buy', 'Here's', 'Will you buy', or 'Do you want' before
listing a commodity, or give a price or quantity, such as 'Two-pence a bunch
young carrots, ho'. Some cries boast of qualities: the pears are 'dainty', the
cherries are 'round, and very sound', and the salop is 'hot and good'. Others,
like 'Newcastle salmon', 'Yorkshire muffins', and 'Windsor beans', commu-
nicate a variety or geographical provenance.[29]

Ballads could be witty, rife with playful inversion and double-meaning,
and 'The Cries of London' is no exception ('Wives, shall I mend your
husbands' horns?' one caller saucily enquires).[30] But the song does let us hear
how hawkers packed information into a few words and a burst of sound.
Like judging supplies in the market or displaying stock appealingly, crying
was a retail practice, a form of advertisement essential for those without a
fixed business address.[31] Seen this way, cries are further evidence of hawkers'
credentials as retailers. This advertising language may have changed over
time. In his nineteenth-century history of crying, Andrew Tuer argued that
putting the price before the quantity ('A penny for ten, fine warnuts') was
'quite a recent innovation' or maybe the restoration of an ancient practice.[32]
Early fish cries that indicated freshness, such as 'New mackerel', may have
been supplanted by 'Mackerel alive, alive ho', recalling the famous Irish folk
song 'Molly Malone'.[33]

In other Cries mediums, we can go beyond the words to consider the
ways that street vendors used rhythm and pitch. Ballads are less helpful here,
because their rhymes were sung to well-known tunes, customarily listed
below the song's title. Instead, we can examine other pieces that supposedly
reproduced cries from the street, including the series of seventeenth-century
compositions for voices and viols and a number of rounds written for
groups of singers.

Trying to hear these sounds, we join an ethnographic tradition that
peaked just after the First World War, when members of the Folk Song
Society tried to record the remaining cries and compare them with tunes
from the past. Practitioners like Lucy Broadwood, one of the society's
founding members, saw cries as genuine music.[34] The 1919 edition of the
Society's journal lists transcribed calls of chickweed, cat's meat, feather
brooms, goldfish, flowers and pot plants, strawberries, knives, bottles, rags,
lumber and old iron, rags and bones, small coal, fire logs, lettuces and
shrimps, peas, toy lambs, and a chair mender. Mostly collected in Chelsea
and Westminster, the transcriptions are written on staves and dated, some of
them giving a street location and account of the singer.[35] Intriguing as these

investigations appear, we should be cautious about their conclusions. Like commentators on the Parisian cries, who related nineteenth-century street sounds to forms like medieval plainchant, Broadwood and her collaborators were looking out for musical touchstones and made ambitious historical connections. 'Early cries seem to have been more enterprising in melody and less melancholy in character than those one hears nowadays,' song collector Anne Geddes Gilchrist noted.[36] Some listeners may well have heard music in the shouts of street sellers, but the cry's primary purpose was to grab the attention of customers.

Hawkers may have done this with distinctive phrasing, as suggested by the pieces for voices and strings written by Richard Dering, Orlando Gibbons, and Thomas Weelkes, sometime around 1600.[37] Similar to the 'Cries of London' ballad, the compositions each incorporate dozens of individual cries, evoking a babbling street, but the calls follow regular forms. Generally, the phrases descend in pitch (Dering's 'New mackerel, mackerel new'), or descend and return to their initial note, going down either gradually (Weelkes's 'Hot pudding pies, hot') or in a sharper V-shape (Gibbons's 'Hot codlings, hot').[38] Another type, appearing in all three pieces, was the repetition of the same note, occasionally punctuated with a leap (Dering's 'Plaice, plaice, plaice, new great plaice'). Though in practice street vendors used more varied tunes, the pieces direct us towards principles they may have applied. Most of the calls have a rhythmic style, blending notes of long and short duration, of which Dering's 'new sprats, sprats, sprats, two-pence a peck, two-pence a peck, two-pence a peck, at Milford Stairs' is a characterful example. Repetition was important too, perhaps with slight variations when a phrase returned. Most cries are short with simple melodies, allowing them to stick in the mind. The few studies of hawkers' calls in metropolises of today have found that street retailers still use a comparable set of techniques.[39]

Vendors may have developed more memorable tunes. In the second half of the eighteenth century, the singer, choirmaster, and composer William Savage wrote a batch of rounds, catches, and glees inspired by street cries, to be performed by several voices.[40] In the manuscript score, copied by one of Savage's pupils, beside each tune is a claim for its origins. Next to the opening of the four-voice round, 'Come buy my watercresses', the note reads, 'A cry in London. The first line.'[41] The sprightly melody, which rises then descends in each phrase, may have lingered in listeners' memories and become characteristic of such sellers. In a chapter on street cries in his 1832 book, *Music in Nature*, William Gardiner transcribed another cry of watercress, which though different recalls the brightness of Savage's version.[42] Gardiner also included the hawker's tune that lodged itself most deeply in English culture, despite its fleeting season. Cries historian Charles Hindley believed the call of 'One-a-penny, two-a-penny, hot cross buns!' had rung out 'Passion week after Passion week' for 'Century after Century'.[43] However old it really was, the nursery rhyme hummed to this day was well known by the time of Gardiner's book.

Hawkers probably worried less about tunefulness and more about manipulating their voice to get their message across. As Gardiner explained, certain criers picked a word for emphasis 'upon which he can pour out the whole of the voice' or added the 'common expletive, ho!' Some syllables were hard to shout loudly, such as the second half of 'turnips', leading some to cry 'turnopes' instead.[44] Another trick was the sudden leap in pitch, used to stress a word, syllable, or nonsense sound, like the riff on the milk seller's call, 'Mi-eau!'[45]

What was scribbled on the stave discloses just part of how hawkers, in London as elsewhere, alerted city dwellers to their presence. In the 1930s, Danish composer Vagn Holmboe, fascinated with Copenhagen's street vendors, invented notation for the unusual vocal manipulations within the 366 cries he collected.[46] In London, hawkers would have varied their tone and inflection, like a preacher stirring emotion in his congregation.[47] They may have combined cries with gestures, using their face or arms, and broken up calls with patter and jokes.[48] They would have adapted their cries to the neighbourhoods through which they walked, the ebb and flow of traffic, the buildings that loomed above, and the changing weather. For listening Londoners, the sound of the cry was determined by the street environment. To them, the hawker's call was not an isolated snippet, recreated at perfect pitch, but a sound that carried through the city, ringing over and over, as the vendor passed by. As a denizen of Belgravia denounced a crying watercress seller to *The Times* in 1864, 'As she walks very slowly along the pavement, she is seldom on the stage for less than seven or eight minutes at a time.'[49]

Declaring the seasons

More than disruptive noise, the shouts of hawkers were described as impossible to understand. This trope of incomprehensibility appeared throughout street selling's history and is linked to the notion that these traders were disreputable or uncivilized, as reflected in the brabbling fishwife of the seventeenth century and, later, Andrew Tuer's attempts to render in prose the accent of the 'peripatetic Cockney vendor'.[50] Mishearing was sometimes the product of mischief. When Lucy Broadwood listened to an old man selling brooms in Westminster, she managed to jot down the melody, but struggled to ascertain the words. After questioning the vendor on a subsequent meeting, she concluded that he used the same rhythmical chant 'into which he fits whatever words come into his head at the time'.[51] On occasions, the lack of understanding came from the very methods hawkers employed to make their calls distinct. In his 1839 book about metropolitan street characters, John Thomas Smith remembered an elderly vendor of cheesecakes who used 'a tone so whining and slovenly, that most people thought he said "All my teeth ache"'.[52]

While making such mix-ups, Londoners made sense of the cries. Since the 1960s, sound theorists such as R. Murray Schafer and Barry Truax have proposed ways to appreciate the significance of the various sounds we might hear in a specific environment. In their terms, the calls of hawkers were 'sound signals'. Standing out from the background hum, these 'acoustic warning devices' conveyed meaningful information, much like church bells, police whistles, or car horns in the present day. Such signals drew listeners into an 'acoustic community', united by the sounds its inhabitants heard and the significance they gave them. An outsider may have ignored some sounds or dismissed them as noisy.[53] Applying these ideas, historians have explored how cities of past centuries, such as London, comprised multiple acoustic communities, which straddled the political boundaries of parish, ward, and county.[54]

Within these communities, hawkers' calls carried meaning, despite their seemingly mangled language. Cries are in-between sounds: they use words, but do not have the clarity of speech; they are tuneful, but break the rules of learned music; they are raw exclamations—'cry' itself suggests an animalistic howl—but follow more audible arrangements than the sounds of the natural world.[55] Of course, many listeners understood what street vendors shouted. But the patterns of cries mattered as much as their content. Cries were repeated, as their brief melodies were sung again and again by a vendor at work and as the same calls returned after days, weeks, and months. Longtime residents may not have registered each single cry, but heard them as part of the mosaic of sensations that made up their neighbourhood.[56] The calls made most sense to those that heard them come and go within their everyday.

Cries were among the sounds that marked passing time in the city. Church bells tolled, chatter rose and subsided in houses and shops, carts trundled towards market, new weather augured the onset of a season, festival cheers marked a year rolling round—and the advertising calls of hawkers came and went.[57] As we have seen, different street sellers took to the streets as day turned to night, and one of the qualities of early street foods was their seasonality. These street selling patterns were expressed in the soundscape.

In John Gay's poem *Trivia*, the narrator claims that 'Experienc'd men, in'urd to city ways, | Need not the Kalendar to count their days', but could identify the weekday from the food being sold, the entertainments on offer, and the chores of servants. Most perceptibly of all, the poem continues:

> Successive Crys the Season's Change declare,
> And mark the Monthly Progress of the Year.
> Hark, how the Streets with treble Voices ring,
> To sell the bounteous Product of the Spring!
> Sweet-smelling Flow'rs, and Elders early Bud,
> With Nettle's tender Shoots, to clean the Blood:
> And when *June's* Thunder cools the sultry Skies,
> Ev'n *Sundays* are prophan'd by Mackrell Cries.

As the year moves on, the guide tells readers to listen out for walnuts, plums, and pears in autumn, along with the calls of rosemary and bay that meant Christmas was near.[58] Similarly, in William Marshall Craig's illustrated 1804 book of street characters, the accompanying text explains how the cry of 'Green Hastens' echoed from late June throughout pea season. One seller of hot loaves spent his summer calling several hours in the morning and after-noon, but paused for winter, when he took up muffins and a hand bell.[59] In the nineteenth century, passers-by and residents still listened intently to the coming and going of hawkers' cries, proof of which we find even in those letters that complained about the racket. One writer grumbled how his Sunday mornings were ruined by milkmen shouting from six in the morn-ing until eight, and the criers of watercress and fish who joined the follow-ing hour. Along with the oranges and other goods that were advertised all afternoon, the street was not quiet until evening.[60] By giving such details, the writers may have intended to add weight to their grievances, to show their complaints were not nebulous. But in doing so they also proved that they noticed when the cries were changing.

Later descriptions of calendar-like cries may draw on forerunners like *Trivia*, or at least betrayed a recognizable nostalgia. Gay's poem is a light-hearted reimagining of Virgil's *Georgics*, in which the routines of country life are translated to the eighteenth-century capital.[61] Reciting the cycle of cries was a means of mourning a London that was lost. According to an 1874 article in the journal *All the Year Round*, in a time when 'the great city is less picturesque than it used to be', the cries of hawkers 'remind us of the changes of the season, as pleasant recallers of old memories as the cry of the cuckoo, or the twitter of the April swallow'.[62] Wistful as such writing was, the changing cries were one of the many ways the soundscape structured life in the capital. Because they occupied the public spaces of the street, bargained face to face with suppliers and customers, and moved through the city as they cried, hawkers impressed the rhythms of their work on Londoners. In the late Victorian metropolis, the soundscape remained full of voices charged with meaning.

The end of the cries?

The calls of street vendors also marked longer stretches of time. Nineteenth-century writers who discussed these sounds were preoccupied about their disappearance. They typically compared the calls contained in poems, images, and music from as far back as the fifteenth century, with what they heard in the London of their own era. In his 1841 essay on street noises, Charles Knight described how the sounds of 'Cherry ripe' and 'Fair oranges' had gone, but the 'costardmonger' (a fruit seller in this case) remained rowdy and the milk vendor had merely changed her cry from 'Any milk here?' via 'Milk below' to 'Mio'.[63] Implying that the practice was a living tradition, Andrew Tuer wrote that 'many of the old cries, dying out elsewhere, may still be familiar, however, in the back streets of second and third rate neigh-bourhoods'.[64] In a section on 'the obsolete Cries of the Costermongers', Mayhew explained in a lengthy digression—'for the information of my younger readers'—the history of the salop stall, because that cry was no more.[65] With the losses came additions, which heralded new tastes, like the cries of 'Hokey Pokey', for ices sold by Italian vendors, and 'Taters all 'ot', for baked potatoes kept warm in a heated barrow.[66]

Representations of food hawkers had always articulated a feeling of loss. Though it has been argued that nostalgia did not become a theme of the Parisian Cries until the nineteenth century, in London it was there from the outset.[67] The English genre emerged in the turbulent decades either side of

1600. Around the time that street sellers were being licensed by the City's Common Council, they were symbolically brought into line in early versions of the Cries. The grid-like structure of the first printed images (such as Figure 6) shows hawkers locked into position, placed in individual cells and ordered in rows, so different to how, in reality, they roamed freely. Each figure has a cry written beneath them, but they were silenced in the medium of print.[68] In the same moment, Richard Dering and Orlando Gibbons both wrote musical Cries compositions for five voices, which energetically interact and conjure a lively atmosphere. But the pieces are artfully structured and never allowed to descend into formlessness. Gibbons builds his piece around the passage of a day and, at the end of each section, the voices unite in harmony. Considering equivalent pieces written in medieval Paris, musicologist Emma Dillon has suggested that such arrangements make listeners 'rehear the chaos and cacophony of the magnificent market within the tightly controlled framework of polyphony'.[69] By setting the competing calls within a musical or visual structure, the Cries genre reinterpreted disorder as something to be celebrated. The prints and songs praised another London, far from the unsettling present, a London where business thrived, and rich and poor assumed their rightful places. Three centuries later, the Folk Song Society's interest in preserving the last few cries expressed a different nostalgia. Stuck in the capital during the First World War, Lucy Broadwood and Juliet Williams began collecting the folk music of the city, remnants of a less dreadful past.[70]

By that time, those cries may have been less common. In the mid-nineteenth century, a letter published by Michael Bass, the member of Parliament behind the campaign against street music, explained vaguely how 'some years ago' new laws against the London cries had 'tranquilized our streets'.[71] The writer was presumably referring to the 1839 Metropolitan Police Act, which George Augustus Sala also called the 'most implacable foe to our cries'.[72] But while the Police Act introduced penalties for those who used horns or other instruments for advertisement, it did not include specific provisions for crying. Nor did the endpoint of Bass's crusade, the Street Music (Metropolis) Act of 1864, which aimed to speed up prosecutions against unwanted performers.[73] By the mid-Victorian period, hawkers' calls were no less of a nuisance, but other annoying sounds had risen to the fore.

If the use of cries was in decline, it may have been a symptom of a deeper sonic shift. Since the start of London's expansion in the sixteenth century, hawkers' calls were one of the many sounds with significance for urban listeners. Some of these sounds arrived and departed, and others changed subtly in meaning. But wood and stone were still the dominant materials, walking and horse-drawn transport were the main ways to travel, and calling voices, still audible over a distance, remained a normal means of passing on information.[74] From the middle of the nineteenth century, the culmination of long-term developments, like the quickening of traffic, and the uptake of technologies like steam power and electricity altered the sounds that signalled to Londoners on a regular basis. And for the listener, the airwaves became more congested.[75] This is not to say that sound mattered less: hearing was important to the modern metropolitan condition, for as straightforward a task as crossing a dangerous highway.[76] On busier and louder London streets, cries became harder to hear and follow.

Hawkers' calls did not simply fall silent. As we have seen, newspapers still printed objections about the disturbance they caused. The authors of these letters lived in well-heeled neighbourhoods or peaceful suburbs, like Kennington, West Brompton, Portland Place, and Stoke Newington.[77] Within those districts, possibly where the background noise was lower, cries still sounded loudly enough to cause offence. In the last decade of the nineteenth century, metropolitan authorities debated formal action. Local officials in St Giles in the Fields, St George Hanover Square, and Kensington all unsuccessfully petitioned the recently formed London County Council for powers to clamp down on street noise.[78] After several years of back and forth, the council's Local Government and Taxation Committee finally proposed a by-law concerning 'Street Shouting'. The committee stressed that this would not apply to costermongers and street sellers, but several council members worried that the exemption was not sufficiently clear, warning that the by-law risked 'placing a weapon in the hands of the police to suppress street sellers'. With most members not present, no decision was made.[79] In later meetings, when the issue was raised, responsibility was delegated to the metropolitan borough councils established in 1899.[80] Just as regulation of street sellers' obstruction was being devolved, crying became a local, not a London-wide problem.

Throughout the Victorian period and into the twentieth century, the street markets continued to vibrate with cries. In journalism and literature, the markets' sounds added to their carnivalesque character. On a Saturday night in the New Cut, Mayhew described the 'tumult of the thousand different cries of the eager dealers, all shouting at the top of their voices, at one and at the same time'. He recounted the calls in turn:

'So-old again,' roars one. 'Chestnuts all 'ot, a penny a score,' bawls another. 'An 'aypenny a skin, blacking,' squeaks a boy. 'Buy, buy, buy, buy, buy!' cries the butcher. 'Half-quire of paper for a penny,' bellows the street stationer. 'An 'aypenny a lot ing-uns.' 'Twopence a pound grapes.' 'Three a penny Yarmouth bloaters.' 'Who'll buy a bonnet for four-pence?' 'Pick 'em out cheap here! three pair for a halfpenny, bootlaces.' 'Now's your time! beautiful whelks, a penny a lot.' 'Here's ha'p'orths,' shouts the perambulating confectioner. 'Come and look at 'em! here's toasters!' bellows one with a Yarmouth bloater stuck on a toasting-fork. 'Penny a lot, fine russets,' calls the apple woman: and so the Babel goes on.[81]

As well as bringing to mind the music of the early Cries genre, Mayhew suggests that the sounds had taken on a new function. Rather than carrying through the city, as hawkers passed through street after street, the calls were restricted to certain places. Cries became sonic markers of areas like Whitecross Street, Leather Lane, and Mile End Road, where the working classes came to dine, buy supplies, and be entertained.

The idea of the cries also stayed embedded in London culture. Printed images in the Cries tradition, especially Francis Wheatley's drawings from the 1790s (see Figure 13), were widely circulated and translated into new forms, such as the series of cigarette cards issued by Faulkner and Player.[82] From the late nineteenth century, music hall stars performed songs that imitated cries, just as actors had inhabited the roles of street sellers way back on the Shakespearian stage.[83] *Pygmalion*, George Bernard Shaw's play that debuted in 1914 and became the musical *My Fair Lady*, deals with the classic Cries themes of class, gender, and sound. At the centre of the story is a professor of phonetics who attempts to reform the rough, uneducated speech of a Covent Garden flower girl in order to pass her off as a duchess.[84]

Since then, street sellers and their half-remembered voices have remained vessels for London myth. In the 1968 musical film *Oliver!* the titular hero wakes one morning in the comfortable house of his benefactor.[85] He is drawn to the window by the siren-like call of a flower seller, 'Who will buy my sweet red roses, two blooms for a penny?' Next we hear, from another direction, 'Will you buy any milk today, mistress?', the hawker's cry leaping in pitch. A fruit seller, a basket full of pottles on her hip, sings, 'Ripe straw-berries, ripe!' Their cries intersect, as they are joined by other traders, singing in unison, 'Who will buy?' In the number that follows, Oliver's verses are broken up by the cries of the various vendors, who pack the grand square, in a display that strikes him with wonder. The genre of Cries plainly influenced the film's director, Carol Reed, and the composer of the original stage musical, Lionel Bart, in creating the scene. The hawkers are dressed like street sellers drawn by artists such as Wheatley, Paul Sandby, and Marcellus Laroon. The songs are reminiscent of the street music captured by composers of the seventeenth and eighteenth centuries. Born in 1930, the son of a Jewish East End tailor, Bart's musicals stood out in the post-war period for using vernacular language and local accents, and bringing working class stories to the stage.[86] In adapting Charles Dickens's novel, Bart sanded the hard edges of realism and accentuated the sentimentality, which might explain something of the musical's enduring appeal. For its early audiences, the film may have captured a nostalgia for an older London, before the ravages of the two world wars. 'Who will buy?' was part of a centuries-old tradition: Londoners listened to the advertising calls of street sellers and imbued them with how they felt about their city.

Epilogue
The return of street food

Hawkers did not disappear from London's streets in an instant. In the first half of the twentieth century, their business seemed to be thriving. When in the 1930s researchers from the London School of Economics (LSE) published an updated version of Charles Booth's metropolitan survey, their findings on street sellers were strikingly familiar. Hawkers remained a diverse group of working people, women as well as men, some running kerbside shops most of the week, others scrabbling for stock money to deal a few cabbages from someone else's stall. They still gathered in the same streets in poor districts, where they served the inner-city population with food and the less quantifiable pleasures of gossip and buzz. About 30,000 Londoners were now making their living as costermongers, hawkers, pedlars, newspaper sellers, coffee stallkeepers, and sandwich board-carriers. To explain the high numbers, the researchers pointed to an influx of ex-soldiers using their post-war pay-outs to buy a stall or barrow, and increasing unemployment that pushed many towards irregular work.[1] That same decade, writer Mary Benedetta worked with photographer László Moholy-Nagy to produce *The Street Markets of London*, a book jointly inspired by the journalism of Henry Mayhew and the picturesque scenes of the Cries tradition. In the text, Benedetta described each market's personality, calling Portobello Road 'housewifely', Balham's Hildreth Street 'homely', and the New Cut 'unsavoury', and peopled her scenes with curious characters. Old Mrs Priddy, at her salad stall in East Street, Walworth, nibbles on a celery stalk, crying out between mouthfuls, 'Lettuces, twopence each, fresh and nice. Nice lettuce dear?' When asked about her taste for celery, Priddy promises, with a 'mischievous twinkle', that she only eats the top, perhaps the middle later on. Waiting beside her, next to the horseradish, is a glass of whisky.[2]

Beneath the customary bustle, however, food hawking had changed. Though Benedetta's book depicts a street trade apparently in rude health, moments of pensiveness break through. She notes how Leather Lane was once the liveliest street in the neighbourhood, but a new department store on Holborn Circus had diverted many of the market's visitors. 'In spite of everything it has kept its pride,' Benedetta wrote, 'like the old lady who rides through the streets in a dilapidated family coach, while her bearing makes all the people in the motorcars seem vulgar and stupid. And like the old lady it brings a lump to your throat, for there is something very sad about it.'[3] By then, the main difference was in how such markets were regulated. In 1911, the City finally registered all the street traders working within its bounds. In the regime's first year, 1,712 hawkers received badges and certificates.[4] Elsewhere, London's borough councils were handed the power to license street traders by a 1927 act of Parliament. Each hawker had to pay an annual fee of 5s. and between 6d. and 3s., depending on the market, to book a pitch for a week. Apart from in the City where no new badges were issued, bringing in licences did not automatically limit the extent of food hawking.[5] But what changed was the degree of top-down control. More so than at any other point in their metropolitan history, hawkers were able to be counted, traced, and fixed in position. A census of street sellers in the City listed them by police district and individual trading number, and stated each vendor's age and address. The grand old man was 83-year-old number 884, Thomas Exall of Minto Street, Bermondsey, who would have been a lad when Mayhew was doing his interviews.[6] In contrast to the shopping carnivals of the nineteenth century, the assigning of pitches made the street markets into more organized, containable affairs, operating with the oversight of the council. Away from the markets, the last few barrow-pushers and basket-toters were left unlicensed and exposed to prosecution, many of them resorting to hanging around at night at railway stations and dog tracks.[7] The LSE's *New Survey* warned that street trading had become a 'vested interest' in which it was 'extremely difficult for the stranger to gain a footing'.[8]

As for so much of London culture, the Second World War was a watershed. The glow of the interwar streets was extinguished by the devastation of the Blitz, the austerity of rationing, and the totalizing visions of post-war urban planning.[9] Though stalls eventually returned to many of the same streets, they faced much stiffer competition. From the late 1950s, film distributor the Rank Organisation produced hundreds of ten-minute documentaries, under the title *Look at Life*, which told stories of the extraordinary and everyday in British society. One of the films, narrated by the unmistakably voiced Sid James, compared London's last-remaining street markets with their flashy new rival—the supermarket. In glorious technicolour, we can see Petticoat Lane, Berwick Street, and Farringdon Road crowded with pedestrians, overflowing with useful wares, and staffed by charismatic stallholders, several of them caught in close-up mid-patter. Halfway through, the film cuts to the supermarkets, with their glass doors, brightly packaged goods in tins and clear plastic, and gleaming counters for fish and meat. 'A street market with a top hat on,' James calls the recent arrival. 'It's a bit more posh and a bit more modern. Everything is nice and clean and tidy and, when it comes to rain, you've got a roof over your loaf.'[10] The film does not take sides, but in sales of fresh food the supermarket quickly pulled away. In a 1983 photographic guide, updating Benedetta and Moholy-Nagy for the London of Ken Livingstone and Margaret Thatcher, Alec Forshaw and Theo Bergström commented how, in the 'supermarket age', many street markets had specialized into crafts, antiques, flowers, books, and fabrics. Just a few, like Brixton, Ridley Road, and Chapel Market, had kept up a broad retail business.[11] To this day, this handful of places remain linchpins of vibrant, local communities. Customers from every walk of life can pick up quality, affordable produce from stalls and shops run by long-standing tenants, alongside entrepreneurs and immigrants who see selling food as a chance to support themselves and their families.

Competition from supermarkets was just one factor in street trading's decline. As processes that began in the second half of the nineteenth century accelerated, the shape of London and the make-up of its population altered again. In the years leading up to the First World War, the number of people living in inner-city neighbourhoods, where hawkers had been so important, began to fall. By the 1980s, the population of the central boroughs almost halved, as the working classes joined the suburban exodus, industry moved deeper into Greater London and beyond, and offices and commerce filled the void. This continuing sprawl was made possible by further advances in transport. Receiving a jolt from the electrification of the tube, railways had started to make travel cheaper and faster within the metropolitan region. Along with international shipping and improvements in refrigeration, trains allowed food to pour in from previously unthinkable distances, ending forever the advantage of intensive, near-London industries like the fisheries, gardens, and dairies. By the interwar period, motor cars, buses, and lorries were unexceptional sights on the city's streets. On better-surfaced roads linked in a more complete network, they moved people and goods around at speed, but were a new hazard for walkers. Motorization certainly contributed to the demise of street culture. In the Edwardian capital, people still gathered in the open air, not just for buying and selling, but for political rallies, Bank Holiday fairs, and spontaneous celebrations, to flirt on weekends, cheer on a scrap, and play an impromptu game. Faster public and private transport, the trauma of two world wars, and the increasingly homebound nature of family life all shifted more urban activity indoors, a trend ingrained by mid-century.[12] As hawkers were being pushed off the highway, the Londoners they hoped would stop and buy were abandoning the streets for good.

What was this London where street selling had flourished? It was a city that was growing in a way that regularly made boundaries redundant, but retained a pulsating core of population and trade. It was a city with a peculiar economy, strongly seasonal, with petty commerce and services prominent, underpinned by an army of casual labourers ready to switch their job in a heartbeat. A city with a dynamic, specialized, and largely regional food supply, which overcame the challenges of perishability in the pre-railway age. A city where a medieval market system that adapted slowly was complemented by innumerable small shops and irregular retailers who made themselves indispensable. Where the streets were sites of business, conversation, and conflict as well as movement, and were filled with people and animals, causing hassle, irritation, and danger. Where governors and police, aware of the limitations of their power, were light-touch and pragmatic in their regulation of street trading and obstruction. Where people could use sounds to interpret their city, to place themselves in time, and think longingly of an imagined urban past. Between the late sixteenth and early twentieth centuries, London became in many ways more modern. Amenities like housing, roads, and hygiene undoubtedly improved. But I have tried to suggest that, for the majority of Londoners, for most of this stretch of the capital's history, the benefits of improvement were either out of reach or barely evident. Meanwhile, the process of modernization was halting, contradictory, and incomplete. Within this span of time, the most radical innovations, like the arrival of the railways and the strict management of street space, only appear late on, pointing forward to a modern era that arrived more conclusively after 1900. And features that we associate with modernity, such as frustration with nuisances and anxiety about women walking alone, distinguished the city for centuries. Street sellers help us appreciate how London lurched—instead of surged—towards its status as the world's pre-eminent metropolis.

Curating street food

In the last ten years or so, a new kind of street food has emerged. The financial crash of 2007–8 led eating out in London, a city whose culinary reputation had been rising since the start of the millennium, in a more casual direction. Diners sought out reasonably priced places to eat that also offered an intangible 'experience'. A few adventurous cooks, who had switched careers or might otherwise have worked in professional kitchens, started selling in the street. From vans with drop-down sides and gazebo-sheltered tables, these vendors prepared punchily flavoured dishes, served on disposable cardboard and plastic, to be scoffed standing up. Street food markets sprang up across the city, in empty car parks, pedestrianized streets, and buildings awaiting development. Nearby workers could select an unusual lunch from dozens of options, a kebab, a couscous salad, or fresh-cooked pasta delivering respite from a diet of pre-packed sandwiches. Weekend and night-time visitors could amble through the rows of stalls, each member of a party choosing whatever tempted their tastebuds, before washing it all down with booze from a pop-up bar. In time, smartly branded companies brought these markets under cover, fitting out warehouses with coloured lights, benches, and fully equipped kitchens, or constructing purpose-built food halls that melded fine dining with a festive vibe. Street food became a culinary category. Restaurants tried to mimic its playfulness and (to the English palate) original flavours: in 2017, trade magazine the *Caterer* projected that upcoming trends included lobster rolls, cheese toasties, and anything served in bowls. Manufacturers pumped out make-at-home street food lines for supermarket shelves, including spice mixes, street drinks, and meal kits for katsu curry and Caribbean jerk.[13]

The street food boom of the 2010s, it should be obvious, had little connection to London's older hawking history. Not only was it solely focused on cooked food, rather than the fish, fruit, milk, and greens for which street sellers used to be known, but the influences of this burgeoning industry were global. This new cuisine was drawn from across the world: gourmet burgers and slow-cooked meats from the United States; tacos, ceviche, and empanadas from Latin America; noodles and dumplings from China; steaming broths from southeast Asia; street snacks from India that broke the mould of the Brick Lane curry house. When these translations were made with sensitivity and care, they were welcome additions to the city's menu, reflecting the successes of immigration and openness to foreign cultures. Often they were truly delicious.

This globalization of British taste benefited from foreign food feeling closer than ever before. Long-haul holidays have become cheaper, allowing more tourists to explore faraway cultures and sample their food first hand. Gastronomic travel has also become possible from the comfort of a sofa, as the television genres of travelogue and cookery show have merged. Netflix created a street food version of its documentary series *Chef's Table*, applying the format of artfully shot profiles of world-famous cooks to hawkers in Bangkok, Singapore, Buenos Aires, and Lima. The portraits emphasize the talents and personal battles of individual vendors, instead of the everyday importance of hawkers to these cities and the structural problems they face. The late chef, writer, and presenter Anthony Bourdain was among the first to bring street food to the small screen, in a succession of series where he ate his way around the globe. On a visit to Vietnam in 2016, Bourdain folded his angular frame onto a low stool to slurp noodles with then President Barack Obama. The scene is sentimental and romanticizes the back-to-basics appeal of a six-dollar dinner at a hole-in-the-wall spot. But just as Donald Trump was mooting plans for a border wall with Mexico, the meal was a political statement. As Obama later wrote in eulogy about Bourdain, 'He taught us about food—but more importantly, about its ability to bring us together. To make us a little less afraid of the unknown.'[14]

London's present-day street food is not as open as the street food of the past. Compared to North America, where the wave of gourmet food trucks and stalls has been building for much longer, the British phenomenon is relatively under-researched.[15] For her 2017 PhD thesis, Paz Concha carried out a nine-month ethnography of the London 'street food scene', embedding herself in a business that ran regular markets, and taking orders and cooking side by side with traders. Exploring the idea of 'curation', more typically applied to industries like fashion and music, Concha described how these markets were put together. Organizers headhunted vendors that 'fitted' certain locations and embraced the same ethos; they sought to offer a diverse blend of cooking styles that appealed to knowledgeable 'foodies'; they built venues with charm, but encouraged particular uses of the space, through directional arrows and shared seating.[16] This curation makes today's street food distinctive in two specific ways. First, it is planned. Running these markets involves striking agreements with landowners or paying a rent, then making deliberate choices that control how cooking, selling, browsing, and eating take place. Second, these markets have an audience in mind. As Concha notes, those who run them talk about their industry as 'democratic, open and organically configured', but in practice it is exclusive. Those tapped to join the roster, like most of the clientele, tend to be from the same middle class, culturally astute, younger-skewing demographic as the organizers themselves. The food may not be excessively expensive, but it is served in a way that only feels accessible to savvy consumers with money to spare.[17]

When coronavirus forced the UK into lockdown in the spring of 2020, the onward march of street food was halted. Anticipated openings were shelved and regular markets shuttered. As the year progressed, one business running sites in Shoreditch, Canada Water, Canary Wharf, and Lewisham was pushed into liquidation.[18] At the time of writing, in late 2021, it is hard to say whether this way of eating out, at high-footfall locations where strangers' bodies are pressed together, will keep the same attraction. The crowds at Borough Market, its part-covered structure allowing it to rapidly reopen despite restrictions, suggest that enthusiasm lingers for eating tasty, interesting food while perched on the pavement. One property consultancy predicted the UK had potential for 173 new food halls, following the street food market model.[19] Fashionable street food and the thorny questions of cultural influence, curation, and social exclusivity it raises are not going anywhere soon.

Hawkers past and present

The pandemic has been disastrous for ordinary street vendors around the world. Even if they were not evicted from public spaces by police enforcing curfews, most of their business evaporated overnight, as cities emptied and residents stayed at home. Because like many of the world's 2 billion informal workers they are generally unregistered and unwaged, most hawkers missed out on emergency financial support.[20] India alone is home to at least

4 million street vendors who, in addition to selling clothes, household goods, cooked food, and drinks, are the chief distributors of fresh fruit and vegetables to the urban middle and working classes. When coronavirus struck and with transport shut down, they joined the mass on-foot tramp from cities back to rural villages. As the editors of a recent collection of street vending research concluded, this crisis has revealed how small-scale hawking is 'often an *essential* way that poor people facilitate and sustain their livelihoods, just as it is an *essential* mechanism through which many people around the world procure their food'.[21]

Sociologists, anthropologists, and political scientists have generated a rich body of scholarship on the experience of street vendors, especially in Africa, Asia, and Latin America. Their work shows us that in the large cities of these continents food hawkers continue to sell fresh food along with prepared dishes, trade from regular pitches and push around portable stalls, cry out to draw in customers, and have finely balanced relationships with police and politicians. When reading these studies, either focused investigations like John Cross on Mexico City and Rocío Rosales on Los Angeles or the wide-angled analysis carried out by Irene Tinker and Caroline Skinner, it is clear that context matters.[22] Considered from a global point of view, street vendors are varied people from all sorts of backgrounds, and their work is shaped by the politics and social tensions of the cities where they operate. Making direct comparisons with London's hawkers, living and working in another technological and material world, is not productive. But versions of the problems that street vendors deal with today were grappled with by their counterparts in England's capital. Why is hawking, like other kinds of casual labour, so rarely recognized as legitimate work? Are the risks of working on the street borne equally by women and men? How can street vendors coexist with competing uses of public space? Can city governors regulate street business flexibly and with fairness, giving opportunities to poorer workers while keeping local residents content? Should street work be valued or improved out of existence?

One thread of current research has related the modern street food trend to the work of street vendors who meet more humble needs, examining their entanglements. In Italy, for example, classic *cibo di strada*, such as pizza and deep-fried rice balls, has been repackaged by a younger generation as hip street food. One of the motivations was fear about the loss of traditions, though the movement has actually left behind purveyors unwilling or unable to adapt.[23] One of the stars of Netflix's *Street Food* was the septuagenarian

Bangkok street chef Jay Fai, who wears protective goggles and a beanie hat, as she cooks over the searing heat of a wok. In 2018, her crab omelette, drunken noodles, tom yum soup, and yellow curry won her a Michelin star, resulting in queues of food-obsessed diners from every continent joining the regulars at her restaurant that opens onto the street.[24] By the mid-1990s, after decades of trying, the government of Singapore relocated all of the city state's tens of thousands of licensed street vendors into permanent, covered, and more hygienic buildings known as hawker centres.[25] The aesthetic of these institutions, with their solid stalls and communal tables, has influenced the street food halls that have spread across the West. The form of street food varies enormously across the world, from the gastronomic, exclusive, and walled-off to the basic, democratic, and exposed to the elements and traffic, but it always retains some sense of the street. Sociologist Krishnendu Ray has argued that street food, conceived in this broad way, can maintain what he calls the 'liveliness' of cities. This liveliness, Ray says, is 'generated in the shared use of public space by different groups of people, not always in harmony but [in] some degree of managed conflict'. A lively city has an accessible, sensorily rich food system, with strong local traditions and balanced regulation of spaces and markets, that works in the interests of the majority.[26]

By these criteria, London has become less lively in the last hundred years. Whether we think of this as liveliness, conviviality, or a common public life, we know instinctively that shared, routine experiences in the city's open spaces have declined. Street trading is one of the activities that has been jettisoned. Cars have pushed walkers onto pavements, spare patches of ground have come under stricter control by state and private interests, and individualized entertainment has coaxed city people inside. In the retailing of fresh food, supermarkets are unquestionably dominant. We should not pine for the past capital: Londoners now are, on the whole, safer and healthier, the streets are mostly clean and well surfaced, and supermarkets feed us cheaply and efficiently. Nor should we fetishize street trading where it goes on. It is usually tough, poorly paid, and insecure work that few would rush to do. But we can acknowledge that aspects of city life have been lost. The London full of hawkers was messy and dangerous, where most residents struggled to find a reasonable, regular livelihood, but it was also changing in vigorous, unplanned ways, home to a mixture of people rubbing against each other, most of whom were aware of the effort and labour that kept them fed and clothed. The reason why street food cannot be successfully curated, why its energy is impossible to capture, is that it requires accepting the bad as well as the good. In the end, food hawkers take us to another central tension of living in a great metropolis. The thrill of fast-expanding cities is based on contradiction, awkwardness, annoyance, and difficulty. What makes such cities exciting is what makes them hard places to survive.

Notes

INTRODUCTION

1. Deposition of John Wymes, 2 May 1611: LMA, DL/C/0220, ff. 495v–496v; Deposition of Elizabeth Richards, 7 June 1611: LMA, DL/C/0220, ff. 607r–608r; Trial of Hugh Connor, May 1744: *OBPO*, t17440510-14; Mayhew, *London Labour*, vol. 1, pp. 39–40.
2. On the spread of street markets, see Kelley, *Cheap Street*, pp. 4–7.
3. Emma Weinbren, 'Street Food: The New Trends Shaping Food Culture', *Grocer*, 12 September 2018, <https://www.thegrocer.co.uk/trend-reports/street-food-the-new-trends-shaping-foodie-culture/571368.article>.
4. Imogen Watson, 'Walkers Unveils Two "Trending Tastes" Crisps Inspired by Street Food', *Drum*, 22 February 2019, <https://www.thedrum.com/news/2019/02/22/walkers-unveils-two-trending-tastes-crisps-inspired-street-food>.
5. For recent examples, see White, *London in the Nineteenth Century*, pp. 197–200; White, *Great and Monstrous Thing*, pp. 196–9.
6. For relatively recent, broad surveys, see Shesgreen, *Images of the Outcast*; Maniates and Freedman, 'Street Cries'.
7. On the disorderly associations, see Cockayne, *Hubbub*, pp. 80–2, 99–100, 107, 124; Griffiths, *Lost Londons*, pp. 123–34; Dorey, 'Unwholesome for Man's Body?', ch. 6. On hawking as a 'pauper profession', see Hitchcock, *Down and Out*, pp. 49–53.
8. Earle, *City Full of People*, pp. 114–22, 144–6; Erickson, 'Married Women's Occupations'; Hubbard, *City Women*, pp. 196–207; Reinke-Williams, *Women, Work and Sociability*, pp. 103–7. On women's movement, see Gowing, 'Freedom of the Streets'.
9. For this quote, see Winter, *London's Teeming Streets*, p. 101. On street markets specifically, see Jones, 'Redressing Reform Narratives'; Kelley, *Cheap Street*. On hawkers' political significance, see Brodie, '"Jaunty Individualists"'; Jankiewicz, 'Dangerous Class'. On their social and economic importance, see Green, 'Street Trading'.
10. On these questions, see Pennell, '"Great Quantities of Gooseberry Pye"'; Smith, 'Wholesale and Retail Markets'.
11. On gender and urban mobility, see van den Heuvel, 'Gender in the Streets'.
12. For recent works on the complex experience of poverty, see Harley, 'Consumption and Poverty'; Hitchcock and McClure, *Routledge History of Poverty*.
13. Calaresu and van den Heuvel, 'Introduction', p. 12.

14. Milliot, *Les Cris de Paris*; Boutin, *City of Noise*.
15. Brunelle, 'Policing the Monopolizing Women'; Montenach, *Espaces et pratiques du commerce alimentaire*, pp. 15–18.
16. For the landmark studies, see International Labour Office, 'Employment, Incomes and Equality'; Hart, 'Informal Income Opportunities'.
17. For a discussion of how hawking can variously be deemed a pre-modern, modern, or post-modern phenomenon, see Cross, 'Street Vendors, and Postmodernity'.
18. Finlay and Shearer, 'Population Growth and Suburban Expansion', p. 39; Harding, 'Population of London'; Schwarz, *London in the Age of Industrialisation*, pp. 2–3; White, *London in the Nineteenth Century*, pp. 90, 98.
19. Finlay and Shearer, 'Population Growth and Suburban Expansion', p. 45; White, *Great and Monstrous Thing*, p. 553; White, *London in the Nineteenth Century*, ch. 3.
20. White, *London in the Nineteenth Century*, p. 477.
21. Porter, *London: A Social History*, p. 159. On innovation despite the division, see Innes, 'Managing the Metropolis'.
22. For a discussion of such boundaries, see Jenner and Griffiths, 'Introduction'.
23. For example, see the timespan of Hitchcock and Shore, *Streets of London*.
24. For key works in this vein, see Ogborn, *Spaces of Modernity*; Nead, *Victorian Babylon*.
25. Gowing, 'Freedom of the Streets', p. 147; Jenner, 'Circulation and Disorder', p. 50.
26. Winter, *London's Teeming Streets*, p. 109; Kelley, *Cheap Street*, pp. 1–3.
27. For projects that have influenced this methodology, see Ågren, *Making a Living, Making a Difference*; Whittle and Hailwood, 'Gender Division of Labour'.
28. On the exceptions to this, such as the work of Jennifer Davis, as well as discussion of the 868 police court cases I have compiled as a sample, see Chapter 8.
29. On the latter approach, see Calaresu, 'Food Selling and Urban Space', p. 118.

CHAPTER I

1. *PP, Select Committee on Artizans' and Labourers' Dwellings*, qq. 1847–8, 2750–2; Sims, *How the Poor Live*, p. 42.
2. *PP, Her Majesty's Commissioners for Inquiring into the Housing of the Working Classes*, qq. 1492, 1497; Greenwood, 'London Courts and Alleys', pp. 184–5.
3. Mayhew, *London Labour*, vol. 1, pp. 47–8; Sims, *How the Poor Live*, pp. 4–6.
4. Lupton, *London and the Country Carbonadoed*, pp. 91–4.
5. Griffiths, *Lost Londons*, p. 124.
6. Ward, *London Spy Compleat*, pp. 40–2. On these two accounts, see Capp, *When Gossips Meet*, pp. 331–2.
7. On the anxieties about female mobility, see Chapter 7. On the queerness of the fishwife, see Hadshar, ' "[T]heir Tales Are Sweet" ', ch. 2.
8. Korda, 'Gender at Work', p. 121.
9. 'Billingsgate, n.', in *OED Online*.
10. Shesgreen, *Images of the Outcast*, pp. 182–3.

11. For an example of the former pose, see Luigi Schiavonetti, after Francis Wheatley, 'Milk Below Maids', 1793: Yale Center for British Art, Paul Mellon Collection, B2001.2.1680. On the milkmaid character in various guises, see Shesgreen, *Images of the Outcast*, pp. 108–10.

12. Gay, 'Trivia', p. 178.

13. Taithe, *Essential Mayhew*, pp. 4–5.

14. Mayhew, *London Labour*, vol. 1, pp. 2–3. On race and otherness in Mayhew, see Nord, 'Social Explorer as Anthropologist', pp. 131–3.

15. Stedman Jones, *Outcast London*, pp. 285–6. On the earlier outcast generation, see Green, *From Artisans to Paupers*, p. 250.

16. Mayhew, *London Labour*, vol. 1, p. 13.

17. Stedman Jones, ' "Cockney" and the Nation', pp. 294–6; Kelley, *Cheap Street*, pp. 169–78.

18. *Lloyd's Illustrated Newspaper*, 10 April 1892, p. 9.

19. On the case for the coster origins of the 'pearlies', see Kelley, *Cheap Street*, pp. 134–42. Stedman Jones is more sceptical of the costermonger–cockney connection, in ' "Cockney" and the Nation', p. 288.

20. Shesgreen, *Images of the Outcast*, p. 73.

21. Münch, 'Henry Mayhew and the Street Traders', pp. 65–6; Kelley, *Cheap Street*, p. 112; Taithe, *Essential Mayhew*, pp. 31–2.

22. Integrated Census Microdata (I-CeM) project, 1851 census, 1901 census. These figures are based on people classifiable as 'street sellers, pedlars and hawkers' under the HISCO occupation code 45220 within the census county of London (including parts of Middlesex, Surrey, and Kent).

23. For more details, see Appendix.

24. For recent assessments of the census as a source for women's work, including discussion of the historiography, see Higgs and Wilkinson, 'Women, Occupations and Work', pp. 28–32; You, 'Women's Labour Force Participation', p. 120.

25. *PP, Report from the Select Committee on the Fresh Fruit Trade*, q. 3075.

26. *Daily News*, 1 September 1865, p. 3; *Standard*, 15 August 1882, p. 3.

27. For the discussion of street trading in these works, see Clark, *Working Life of Women*, pp. 202–9, 220–1; Pinchbeck, *Women Workers and the Industrial Revolution*, pp. 297–300.

28. For the classic statement of 'separate spheres', see Davidoff and Hall, *Family Fortunes*. For criticism of the 'breadwinner' model, see Horrell and Humphries, 'Women's Labour Force Participation'.

29. Alexander, 'Women's Work'; Alexander, Davin, and Hostettler, 'Labouring Women'.

30. McIntosh, *Working Women*, pp. 250–1. For discussion of the problematic chronological models, see Vickery, 'Golden Age to Separate Spheres?'.

31. Earle, *City Full of People*, p. 116; Schwarz, *London in the Age of Industrialisation*, pp. 16–17, 22; Green, 'Street Trading', pp. 136–7; Kay, 'Retailing, Respectability and the Independent Woman', pp. 152–6.

32. Shepard, 'Crediting Women', pp. 12–14; Erickson, 'Married Women's Occupations', pp. 269, 276–7.

33. Shepard, *Accounting for Oneself*, p. 150.

34. Froide, *Never Married*, p. 3; Hill, *Women Alone*, p. 40.

35. In the sample of 858 street sellers, we can identify the age of 105. The mean age among the women is 31.4 and the median was 29. Among the men, the mean was 25.2 and the median was 20.

36. Booth, *Life and Labour*, 2nd ser., vol. 3, p. 259.

37. Trial of William Brister and others, December 1744: *OBPO*, t17441205-34; Trial of Aaron Levi, January 1796: *OBPO*, t17960113-89.

38. Trial of Charles Rapley, William Dorr, February 1790: *OBPO*, t17900224-85; Trial of Thomas Collop, Elizabeth Gordon, February 1768: *OBPO*, t17680224-24. On children's contributions to the household, see Cunningham, 'Employment and Unemployment of Children', pp. 131, 139; Earle, *City Full of People*, p. 57.

39. Davin, *Growing Up Poor*, p. 85; Humphries, *Childhood and Child Labour*, pp. 211–12.

40. *Standard*, 5 December 1895, p. 6. See also the examples of children interviewed by Mayhew, in *London Labour*, vol. 1, pp. 39–40, 89–90, 151–2. On children working at market stalls, see Davin, *Growing Up Poor*, pp. 189–90.

41. Booth, *Life and Labour*, 2nd ser., vol. 3, p. 259. For similar findings in an earlier period, see Earle, *City Full of People*, pp. 118–19.

42. *Ordinary's Account*, June 1715: *OBPO*, OA17150622.

43. For example, see Deposition of Jane Collett, 2 November 1620: LMA, DL/C/0227, ff. 180r–180v; Trial of Sarah Gould, September 1809: *OBPO*, t18090920-123.

44. Earle, *City Full of People*, pp. 46–8; Meldrum, *Domestic Service and Gender*, pp. 18–19; Green, *From Artisans to Paupers*, p. 3.

45. Tinker, *Street Foods*, pp. 159–60. For a discussion of this in historical context, see van den Heuvel, 'Selling in the Shadows', p. 144.

46. On the form of the *Account*, see Linebaugh, 'Ordinary of Newgate'.

47. *Ordinary's Account*, January 1716: *OBPO*, OA17160127.

48. *Ordinary's Account*, February 1760: *OBPO*, OA17600211.

49. Trial of Mary Evans, Ann Allen, September 1805: *OBPO*, t18050918-135; Trial of Catharine Smith, May 1744: *OBPO*, t17440510-7.

50. Atkins, 'Retail Milk Trade', p. 523; Hayes, *London Milk Trail*, p. 9.

51. Booth, *Life and Labour*, 2nd ser., vol. 3, pp. 175–8; Hayes, *London Milk Trail*, p. 30.

52. Trial of Margaret Griffiths, July 1808: *OBPO*, t18080713-46.

53. Thomson and Smith, *Street Life*, pp. 53–4; Armfelt, 'Italy in London', p. 185.

54. Integrated Census Microdata (I-CeM) project, 1881 census, 1901 census. In the latter survey, individuals classified as 'street sellers, pedlars, and hawkers', who had Italian origins and whose occupation mentioned ice cream, lived in 25 registration districts. On the continuing importance of the Holborn district, see Sponza, 'Italian "Penny Ice-Men"', pp. 20–1, 26, 31–2.

55. *Lloyd's Illustrated Newspaper*, 9 June 1889, p. 7.

56. George, *London Life*, p. 120; Lees, *Exiles of Erin*, pp. 92–5.

57. Lees, *Exiles of Erin*, pp. 46–8.

58. Mayhew, *London Labour*, vol. 1, pp. 104–5, 466–7.

59. *Ordinary's Account*, September 1731: OBPO, OA17310924; *Ordinary's Account*, March 1741: OBPO, OA17410318; *Ordinary's Account*, October 1753: OBPO, OA17531029.

60. Examination of Mary Boswell, 19 April 1744: *LL*, smdsset_103_57800. On this approach, see Crymble, 'A Comparative Approach to Identifying the Irish'.

61. Kelley, *Cheap Street*, pp. 116–20.

62. Endelman, *Jews of Georgian England*, pp. 171–2, 179–80; Endelman, *Jews of Britain*, pp. 41–2.

63. For an early reference, see Mansion House Justice Room, Minute Books: LMA, CLA/004/02/055, entries for 26 January 1790. For further discussion, see Chapter 5.

64. Endelman, *Jews of Britain*, pp. 90–2, 127–30.

65. *Lloyd's Illustrated Newspaper*, 28 June 1891, p. 10.

66. Deposition of Mary Risebrook, 17 July 1701: LMA, DL/C/0247, ff. 162r–163r. On worth statements at the church courts and this benchmark of poverty, see Shepard, *Accounting for Oneself*, pp. 126–7.

67. Trial of Mary Shepherd, February 1783: OBPO, t17830226-62.

68. Trial of John Weddal Guyer, January 1809: OBPO, t18090111-42.

69. Trial of Dorothy Green, December 1790: OBPO, t17901208-51.

70. For example, see Examination of Frances Lee, 27 July 1750: *LL*, WCCDEP358050286.

71. Greenwood, 'Mission Among City Savages', pp. 12–13, 15–16, 24.

72. J. A. Groom, *The Poor Watercress Sellers of London* (1871): LMA, LMA/4305/06/037.

73. Deposition of Elizabeth Charter, 26 April 1619: LMA, DL/C/0226, 2nd ser., ff. 3v–4r, 15r. On the 40s. threshold, see Shepard, *Accounting for Oneself*, pp. 96–104.

74. Trial of Elizabeth Knotmill, January 1757: OBPO, t17570114-17; Trial of Thomas Jones, January 1767: OBPO, t17670115-4; Trial of Jane Purton, April 1801: OBPO, t18010415-87; *Morning Post*, 30 September 1836, p. 4.

75. Inventory of Nicholas Spincser, 3 September 1694: LMA, CLC/313/K/C/009/MS19504/046/34; Will of Nicholas Spinster, 4 September 1694: LMA, CLC/313/K/C/006/MS25628/35/28.

76. Trial of Abraham Cohen, January 1782: OBPO, t17820109-10. For examples of eighteenth-century wages, see Boulton, 'Wage Labour', pp. 279–83; Stephenson, ' "Real" Wages?', p. 121.

77. Mayhew, *London Labour*, vol. 1, p. 55.

78. Statistical Society of London, 'Investigation into the State of the Poorer Classes in St. George's in the East', p. 210.

79. Booth, *Life and Labour*, 2nd ser., vol. 3, p. 270. For a similar figure, see London County Council Public Control Committee, *London Markets*, p. 25.

80. Booth, *Life and Labour*, 1st ser., vol. 1, pp. 33–5.

81. Mayhew, *London Labour*, vol. 1, pp. 54–5.

82. For a description of the sixteenth-century social structure, see Stow, *Survey*, vol. 2, pp. 207–8. On the middling sort's emergence, see Earle, 'Middling Sort', pp. 143–5. For a discussion of inter-class distinctions, see Shepard, 'Poverty, Labour and the Language of Social Description', p. 92.

83. Stedman Jones, *Outcast London*, pp. 55–6. On the eighteenth century, see Schwarz, *London in the Age of Industrialisation*, p. 57.

84. Shepard and Spicksley, 'Worth, Age, and Social Status', pp. 516, 519–20; Shepard, 'Poverty, Labour and the Language of Social Description', p. 92.

85. On the proportion of the population receiving relief, see Arkell, 'Incidence of Poverty', p. 46.

86. Court of Alderman, Repertory 22: LMA, COL/CA/01/01/024, ff. 172r, 176v.

87. Mayhew, *London Labour*, vol. 1, pp. 4–6.

88. Booth, *Life and Labour*, 2nd ser., vol. 3, p. 259.

89. Mayhew, *London Labour*, vol. 1, p. 47.

90. Integrated Census Microdata (I-CeM) project, 1851 census. The ten registration districts with the most 'street sellers, pedlars, and hawkers' were in order: St George Southwark, Whitechapel, St Giles, Bethnal Green, Westminster, Newington, Shoreditch, Lambeth, East London, and Holborn.

91. Integrated Census Microdata (I-CeM) project, 1901 census.

92. Harvey, Green, and Corfield, 'Continuity, Change, and Specialization', pp. 479–80.

93. Finlay and Shearer, 'Population Growth and Suburban Expansion', pp. 44–6.

94. Spence, *London in the 1690s*, pp. 45–8, 67–75.

95. Dyos and Reeder, 'Slums and Suburbs', p. 362; Schwarz, *London in the Age of Industrialisation*, pp. 7–8. On St Giles, see Crymble, 'Decline and Fall', pp. 9–10.

96. Wohl, *Eternal Slum*, pp. 2–3; Stedman Jones, *Outcast London*, p. 154. On the changing geography of poverty, see Green, *From Artisans to Paupers*, pp. 192–8.

97. Greenwood, 'Mission Among City Savages', pp. 13–14.

98. Mearns, *Bitter Cry*, pp. 4–6, 18–20.

99. *PP, Select Committee on Artizans' and Labourers' Dwellings Improvement*, qq. 1539–47. On the wider crisis, see Wohl, *Eternal Slum*, pp. xiv–xvii, 21.

100. Harding, 'Families and Housing', pp. 130–4; Baer, 'Housing the Poor and Mechanick Class', pp. 20–2. On the rebuilding, see McKellar, *Birth of Modern London*, pp. 155–7.

101. Boulton, *Neighbourhood and Society*, pp. 175–83; Hitchcock, *Down and Out*, pp. 10–11.

102. Trial of Thomas Baldwin, May 1774: *OBPO*, t17740518-44.

103. George, *London Life*, pp. 98–9. For discussion of cellars for retailing, see Chapter 5.

104. Trial of Mary Hatfield, Mary Hicks, May 1780: *OBPO*, t17800510-6; Trial of William Cunningham, October 1789: *OBPO*, t17891028-18; Trial of Mary Wootton, September 1806: *OBPO*, t18060917-19.

105. Trial of Mary Hobbs, December 1812: *OBPO*, t18121202-105.

106. On lodging houses, see McEwan, 'Lodging Exchange', p. 52; Crymble, 'Decline and Fall', pp. 14–17.

107. Trial of Augustin Doreice, July 1812: *OBPO*, t18120701-59.

108. Sims, *How the Poor Live*, pp. 39–43.

109. *PP, Select Committee on Artizans' and Labourers' Dwellings Improvement,* qq. 1820, 1849–52, 1991–2, 2054–5; *PP, Her Majesty's Commissioners for Inquiring into the Housing of the Working Classes*, qq. 3040–5, 9579–81, 11,653–4. On these restrictions, see Stedman Jones, *Outcast London*, pp. 184–5.

110. For descriptions of such facilities, see *PP, Select Committee on Artizans' and Labourers' Dwellings Improvement,* qq. 2765–6, 3638–9, 4529, 5550; *PP, Her Majesty's Commissioners Inquiring into the Housing of the Working Classes*, qq. 3814, 3963–6, 11,652, 11,661–2, 11,796–809.

111. *Report from the Select Committee on Artizans' and Labourers' Dwellings,* qq. 1200–4, 2057, 2063. On inner London's magnetism, see Stedman Jones, *Outcast London*, pp. 172–3, 208–9.

CHAPTER 2

1. Mayhew, *London Labour*, vol. 1, p. 7.

2. Deposition of Mary Risebrook, 17 July 1701: LMA, DL/C/0247, ff. 161r–163r; Trial of Francis Doyle, September 1784: *OBPO*, t17840915-53.

3. Will of Benjamin Wilkinson, 17 November 1739: LMA, DL/AM/PW/1739/105.

4. Schwarz, *London in the Age of Industrialisation*, pp. 23–4, 44–5, 50–1, 121.

5. For the classic analysis of casual labour, see Stedman Jones, *Outcast London*, pp. 26–9. On the preceding period, see Green, *From Artisans to Paupers*, pp. 5–6, 22, 27–8, 250–1.

6. *Ordinary's Account*, March 1713: *OBPO*, OA17130313.

7. Trial of George Staples, June 1780: *OBPO*, t17800628-37.

8. *Standard*, 23 January 1895, p. 7.

9. Trial of John Taylor, December 1731: *OBPO*, t17311208-42; Examination of Christopher Kennedy: *LL*, LMSLPS150970240; Trial of William Booth, September 1802: *OBPO*, t18020918-96. On demobilization and the labour market, see Schwarz, *London in the Age of Industrialisation*, p. 95.

10. Trial of Hannah Laws, September 1809: *OBPO*, t18090920-93.

11. Mayhew, *London Labour*, vol. 1, p. 71.

12. Hitchcock, *Down and Out*, ch. 3; Stedman Jones, *Outcast London*, p. 61.

13. *PP, Select Committee on the Fresh Fruit Trade*, q. 3569. For an earlier example, see *Ordinary's Account*, July 1752: *OBPO*, OA17520702.

14. Trial of Jane Nichols, October 1755: *OBPO*, t17551022-9; *OBPO*, February 1772, Trial of James Jennings and others, February 1772: *OBPO*, t17720219-36; Trial of Elizabeth White, January 1760: *OBPO*, t17600116-12.

15. Ågren, 'Conclusion', p. 209; Shepard, *Accounting for Oneself*, pp. 249–57.

16. Schwarz, *London in the Age of Industrialisation*, pp. 48–9. On the census and women's work, see Chapter 1.

17. Trial of Jeremiah Connell and others, October 1799: *OBPO*, t17991030-7; Trial of James Blundell, October 1767: *OBPO*, t17671021-18.

18. Stedman Jones, *Outcast London*, pp. 35–41; Green, *From Artisans to Paupers*, pp. 32–42.

19. Thomson and Smith, *Street Life*, pp. 91–2.

20. For example, see Petition of John Jones, October 1785: *LL*, LMSMPS508010037.

21. Trial of Stephen Collard, May 1736: *OBPO*, t17360505-21; Trial of Grace Tasker, December 1762: *OBPO*, t17621208-38; Trial of Ann Ball, February 1772: *OBPO*, t17720219-44; Trial of Thomas Thatcher, September 1808: *OBPO*, t18080914-48.

22. Mayhew, *London Labour*, vol. 1, pp. 91–2.

23. Deposition of Margaret Hart, 2 December 1601: LMA, DL/C/0216, ff. 292r–293v. For more physical help, see Trial of William Harper, April 1733: *OBPO*, t17330404-53.

24. Trial of Elizabeth Bradshaw, December 1739: *OBPO*, t17391205-52.

25. Trial of Dorothy Lloyd, October 1759: *OBPO*, t17591024-14. For another description of this practice, see Trial of Margaret Edwards, July 1760: *OBPO*, t17600709-20. On similar practices elsewhere, see Brunelle, 'Policing the Monopolizing Women', p. 30.

26. For bulk purchases in the nineteenth century, see Thomson and Smith, *Street Life*, p. 67.

27. Simonton, 'Widows and Wenches', p. 102. See also Froide, *Never Married*, pp. 102–15.

28. Trial of William Bullinbroke, December 1738: *OBPO*, t17381206-13. For another example, see Deposition of Elizabeth Dixon, 23 January 1672: LMA, DL/C/0236, ff. 327r–327v.

29. Meldrum, *Domestic Service and Gender*, pp. 14–17; Kent, 'Ubiquitous but Invisible', p. 113; Richardson, *Household Servants*, pp. 64–5; Hill, *Servants*, p. 253.

30. On the changing nature of nineteenth-century service, see Higgs, 'Domestic Servants and Households', p. 207; Schwarz, 'English Servants and Their Employers', p. 253; Erickson, 'What Shall We Do About the Servants?', pp. 281–3.

31. Mayhew, *London Labour*, vol. 1, pp. 33–4; Greenwood, 'Only a Coster', pp. 4–5.

32. For example, see Bridewell Hospital, Minutes of the Court of Governors: BMM, BCB 4, f. 242r; BCB 8, f. 46v.

33. Trial of Margaret Edwards, July 1760: *OBPO*, t17600709-20. On standard terms, see Kent, 'Ubiquitous but Invisible', pp. 123–4.

34. Hill, *Servants*, pp. 251–2; Mansell, 'Variety of Women's Experiences as Servants', p. 332.

35. Bridewell Hospital, Minutes of the Court of Governors: BMM, BCB 9, p. 817. For later examples, see St Dunstan in the West, Vestry Minute Books: LMA, P69/DUN2/B/001/MS03016/002, f. 187r; Middlesex Sessions, Sessions Papers, Petition of Churchwarden and Overseers of Saffron Hill, December 1762: *LL*, LMSMPS505170070; Examination of Elizabeth Birch, December 1765: *LL*, smdsset_120_59528; Examination of Susannah Lewis, August 1776: *LL*, GLBAEP103160112; Examination of Ann Sistram, May 1784: *LL*, GLBAEP103200131.

36. On the institution, see Snell, *Annals of the Labouring Poor*, pp. 278–87; Simonton, 'Apprenticeship'; Lane, *Apprenticeship*, ch. 4; Hindle, *On the Parish?*, pp. 191–223; Humphries, *Childhood and Child Labour*, pp. 295–304; Levene, 'Parish Apprenticeship'.

37. On the 'continuum' of pauper apprenticeship, see Hindle, *On the Parish?*, p. 223. For a more positive evaluation, see Humphries, *Childhood and Child Labour*, p. 305.

38. Examination of Mary Boswell, 19 April 1744: *LL*, smdsset_103_57800; Examination of Elizabeth Birch, December 1765: *LL*, smdsset_120_59528.

39. Middlesex Sessions, Sessions Papers, Petition of Frances Hall, October 1696: *LL*, LMSMPS500450015.

40. Greenwood, 'Only a Coster', pp. 4–5.

41. For examples of older servants, see Examination of Maudlin Owen, May 1751: *LL*, smdsset_94_56838; Examination of Anne Allen, January 1763: *LL*, smdsset_75_54989; Examination of William Tippett, February 1771: *LL*, WCCDEP358220241.

42. The first example I have found appears in Trial of Elizabeth Humphreys, July 1763: *OBPO*, t17630706-56.

43. Booth, *Life and Labour*, 2nd ser., vol. 3, pp. 178–9; Atkins, 'Retail Milk Trade', pp. 523–4, 536.

44. This continued in the nineteenth century, as described critically in Dodd, *Food of London*, pp. 292–3.

45. Trial of Eleanor Donovan, February 1797: *OBPO*, t17970215-52; Trial of John Davis, January 1816: *OBPO*, t18160110-10; Atkins, 'Retail Milk Trade', p. 523.

46. Will of Mary Wordsworth, 17 April 1787: TNA, PROB 11/1152/152.

47. Will of Benjamin Wilkinson, 17 November 1739: LMA, DL/AM/PW/1739/105.

48. Arkell, 'Probate Process', p. 11.

49. Will of William Smallwood, 14 January 1747: TNA, PROB 11/744/157; Will of John Lester, 27 October 1749: TNA, PROB 11/774/237.

50. On commonly cited estimates of worth for these social groups, see Shepard, *Accounting for Oneself*, pp. 102–3, 110–11.

51. In the database of street selling incidents and individuals before 1825, I only included a 'milkman' if he was specifically described as carrying or selling milk on the street.

52. Mary Norton was the first London 'milkwoman' whose will was proved at the Prerogative Court of Canterbury in 1761. See TNA, PROB 11/864/41.

53. Lupton, *London and the Country Carbonadoed*, pp. 91–4.

54. For the ballad, see Anon., 'Jolly Jack of All Trades'. On its tune, see Simpson, *British Broadside Ballad*, pp. 40–2.

55. *Ordinary's Account*, January 1742: *OBPO*, OA17420113.

56. Mayhew, *London Labour*, vol. 1, p. 91.

57. On overcoming these difficulties, see Whittle and Hailwood, 'Gender Division of Labour'. On occupational titles, see Shepard, *Accounting for Oneself*, p. 233.

58. Shepard, *Accounting for Oneself*, pp. 262, 267–70, 310.

59. In a sample of 868 cases of 'costermongers' appearing as defendants at police courts in the nineteenth century, only in 26 cases were the hawkers identifiable as women. For more discussion of this sample, see Chapter 8.

60. Taverner, 'Moral Marketplaces', p. 10. For women and men called hucksters, see Pennington, 'Taking It to the Streets'.

61. Deposition of Mary Knapp, 3 December 1695: LMA, DL/C/0244, f. 367r.

62. Shepard, *Accounting for Oneself*, pp. 269–70.

63. Middlesex Sessions, Sessions Papers, Petition of John Castle, April 1734: LMA, MJ/SP/1734/04/12.

64. For examples of the latter, see Trial of William Smithson, July 1766: *OBPO*, t17660702-10; Trial of Asher Levy, February 1795: *OBPO*, t17950218-17.

65. Cox, *Complete Tradesman*, pp. 22–8, 32–5.

66. 'Costermonger, n.', in *OED Online*.

67. St Dunstan in the West Precinct, Wardmote Inquest Presentments: LMA, CLC/W/JB/044/MS03018/001, f. 100r.

68. Trial of Richard Peers, February 1793: *OBPO*, t17930220-17; Trial of Thomas Williams, James Smith, January 1794: *OBPO*, t17940115-52.

69. *Morning Post*, 16 July 1850, p. 5; Mayhew, *London Labour*, vol. 1, pp. 101–2.

70. For an early group, the 'London General Dealers' Friendly Society', see *Lloyd's Illustrated Newspaper*, 27 October 1861, p. 7. On the 1867 act and Sunday clearances, see Chapter 8.

71. Register of Friendly Societies, Trade Unions, Rules and Amendments, Costermongers' Federation, 1899–1900: TNA, FS 7/25/1184.

72. Brodie, ' "Jaunty Individualists" ', pp. 147–8, 160–1. On friendly societies, see Green, *From Artisans to Paupers*, pp. 97–102; Ismay, *Trust Among Strangers*, p. 23.

73. For example, *Lloyd's Illustrated Newspaper*, 18 December 1898, p. 3.

74. For example, see Letter from Whitechapel and Spitalfields Costermongers' and Street Sellers' Union to Superintendent of Hammersmith Police Station, October 1905: TNA, MEPO 2/456.

75. On working class cultural institutions, see Ross, *Love & Toil*, p. 23.

76. Lucas, 'Coster-Land', p. 78.

77. *Standard*, 15 January 1884, p. 5.

78. *Daily News*, 11 September 1900, p. 7.

79. Lucas, 'Coster-Land', p. 76.

80. Court of Aldermen, Repertory 34: LMA, COL/CA/01/01/038, f. 242r; Repertory 42: LMA, COL/CA/01/01/046, ff. 214v–215r; Repertory 45: LMA, COL/CA/01/01/049, ff. 296v–297r.

81. Court of Aldermen, Repertory 74: LMA, COL/CA/01/01/078, f. 121v.

CHAPTER 3

1. Dodd, *Food of London*, pp. 117–22.

2. Burnett, *Plenty and Want*, pp. 91, 111–15; Muldrew, *Food, Energy and the Creation of Industriousness*, pp. 57–64, 83–102.

3. For examples of such street sellers, see Middlesex Sessions, Sessions Papers, Confession of John Howell, December 1709: *LL*, LMSMPS501100039; Trial of James Kitchiner, Ann Bedford, October 1799: *OBPO*, t17991030-73; *Daily News*, 25 December 1868, p. 6; *Standard*, 29 July 1886, p. 4; Mayhew, *London Labour*, vol. 1, pp. 175–80. On this division of foods, see also Kelley, *Cheap Street*, p. 53.

4. Within the 858 individual street sellers identified up to 1825, 329 sold fruit or nuts, 270 sold fish or shellfish, 130 sold milk, 94 sold vegetables or herbs, 55 sold preparations like cakes, muffins, pies, and sausages. Just 25 sold meat, poultry, or provisions.

5. McGrath, 'Marketing of Food, Fodder and Livestock', pp. 209–10; Everitt, 'Marketing of Agricultural Produce', p. 511; Webber, *Market Gardening*, pp. 49–51.

6. Hartlib, *Samuel Hartlib His Legacie*, pp. 22–3.

7. Trial of Mary Royston, September 1715: *OBPO*, t17150907-23. On the varieties of apples and cherries, see Webber, *Market Gardening*, pp. 52, 56.

8. Deposition of Susanna Stockdell, 13 July 1671: LMA, DL/C/0236, ff. 275v–276v.

9. Thick, *Neat House Gardens*, p. 23; Webber, *Market Gardening*, p. 42.

10. Thick, *Neat House Gardens*, pp. 42, 44, 51.

11. Middleton, *View of the Agriculture*, p. 267; Atkins, ' "Charmed Circle" ', pp. 62–4.

12. Thick, *Neat House Gardens*, pp. 101–7.

13. Kalm, *Kalm's Account*, pp. 8–9. On longer seasons, see also Thick, *Neat House Gardens*, pp. 107, 111–12.

14. Middleton, *View of the Agriculture*, p. 256.

15. Atkins, ' "Charmed Circle" ', pp. 53–4, 67–8.

16. Trial of Edward Fennell, April 1781: *OBPO*, t17810425-17.

17. Atkins, ' "Charmed Circle" ', p. 66.

18. Atkins, ' "Charmed Circle" ', pp. 64–5. On decline in the East End, see Matheson, 'Common Ground', pp. 85–6.

19. Burnett, *Plenty and Want*, p. 8; Webber, *Covent Garden*, p. 118.

20. On transport costs, see Wrigley, 'Urban Growth', p. 88.

21. *PP*, *Royal Commission on Market Rights*, vol. 2, qq. 3672–3; Dodd, *Food of London*, pp. 375–7.

22. Atkins, 'Growth of London's Railway Milk Trade', pp. 208–10, 224; Burnett, *Plenty and Want*, p. 8.

23. Booth, *Life and Labour*, 2nd ser., vol. 3, pp. 173–5; Atkins, 'Growth of London's Railway Milk Trade', p. 220.

24. Stow, *Survey*, vol. 1, p. 126.

25. Inventory of Richard Hickman, 25 September 1662: LMA, CLC/313/K/C/009/MS19504/003/045; Inventory of Thomas Butterfield, 22 October 1663: LMA, CLC/313/K/C/009/MS19504/004/044; Inventory of William Warr, 26 July 1665: DL/C/B/030/MS09174/014/023; Inventory of Ann Patchet, 5 January 1678: LMA, CLC/313/K/C/009/MS19504/023/01; Inventory of Nathaniel James, 29 October 1677: LMA, DL/AM/PI/01/1677/048; Inventory of Richard Gray, 12 December 1695: TNA, PROB 4/14804.

26. Almeroth-Williams, *City of Beasts*, pp. 72–5, 93.
27. Atkins, 'London's Intra-Urban Milk Supply', pp. 385–90; Atkins, 'Retail Milk Trade', pp. 528, 531.
28. Almeroth-Williams, *City of Beasts*, p. 74; Atkins, 'London's Intra-Urban Milk Supply', p. 388; Hetherington, 'Dairy-Farming in Islington', p. 176. For current figures, see AHDB, 'UK and EU Cow Numbers', accessed 31 December 2020, <https://ahdb.org.uk/dairy/uk-and-eu-cow-numbers>.
29. Atkins, 'London's Intra-Urban Milk Supply', pp. 383–5; Almeroth-Williams, *City of Beasts*, pp. 74–5, 82–3.
30. Middleton, *View of the Agriculture*, p. 333; Atkins, 'London's Intra-Urban Milk Supply', pp. 383–5. For comparison, see AHDB, 'UK Milk Yield', accessed 31 December 2020, <https://ahdb.org.uk/dairy/uk-milk-yield>.
31. The earliest London cowkeeper I have identified was John Allen in 1666, whose will is available at LMA, DW/PA/05/1666/001. The first milkman was Nicholas Spincser or Spencer in 1694, whose inventory was discussed in Chapter 1.
32. For a 'milkman' with his own cows, see Trial of Joseph Biley, May 1780: *OBPO*, t17800510-27.
33. Trial of Samuel Harrison, July 1719: *OBPO*, t17190708-16; Trial of Gabriel Lawrence, April 1726: *OBPO*, t17260420-64; Trial of Mary Thursel, October 1750: *OBPO*, t17501017-7; Trial of Terence Kane, May 1757: *OBPO*, t17570526-14; Trial of John Cloud, October 1786: *OBPO*, t17861025-117.
34. *Morning Post*, 19 September 1882, p. 2.
35. Court of Aldermen, Repertory 34: LMA, COL/CA/01/01/038, f. 37v.
36. Trusler, *London Adviser*, p. 138.
37. Mayhew, *London Labour*, vol. 1, p. 192.
38. Atkins, 'Retail Milk Trade', pp. 529–31.
39. Anon., *London Fishery*, pp. 16–17, 24–5; Griffiths, *Jurisdiction and Conservancy of the River of Thames*, p. 21.
40. Dodd, *Food of London*, pp. 351–2; Anon., 'London Commissariat', pp. 273–80.
41. McManus, 'Trade and Market in Fish', p. 181. *PP, Select Committee on Channel Fisheries*, qq. 1548–50; Anon., 'London Commissariat', pp. 273–4; Chaloner, 'Trends in Fish Consumption', pp. 104–6.
42. Alexander, *Retailing*, pp. 13–19; Burnett, *Plenty and Want*, p. 117.
43. On Westminster and Hungerford markets, see Smith, 'Market Place', pp. 118–23. On Shadwell, see London County Council Public Control Committee, *London Markets*, p. 18.
44. Stern, 'Fish Marketing', pp. 69–70.
45. Mayhew, *London Labour*, vol. 1, pp. 45–6, 62, 69.
46. Taverner, 'Consider the Oyster Seller', pp. 9–12.
47. Griffiths, *Jurisdiction and Conservancy of the River of Thames*, pp. 238–9; Smith, *Oyster*, pp. 32–3, 73.
48. *PP, Select Committee on Channel Fisheries*, qq. 1744, 2374–85, 2395–403, 2431–5; Dodd, *Food of London*, pp. 361–2.

49. PP, *Select Committee on Channel Fisheries*, qq. 1588, 1594, 1598, 1601, 1827. See also Chaloner, 'Trends in Fish Consumption', p. 97.

50. PP, *Select Committee on the Fresh Fruit Trade*, qq. 1850–3, 1859–60, 1867–74.

51. Mayhew, *London Labour*, vol. 1, pp. 63–4, 81.

52. Deposition of Catherine Pitts, 20 November 1671: LMA, DL/C/0236, ff. 308r–309r; Deposition of Anna Balleston, 7 February 1694: LMA, DL/C/0244, f. 166v–167r; Deposition of Anna Hill, 3 March 1731: LMA, DL/C/0268, f. 2r.

53. Trial of Elizabeth Rigby, September 1789: OBPO, t17890909-131; Trial of Nathaniel Nutt, September 1825: OBPO, t18250915-200.

54. Recently there has been a flurry of research on early modern conceptions of time. On work-time in particular, see Champion, *Fullness of Time*, p. 30; Hailwood, 'Time and Work'.

55. Mayhew, *London Labour*, vol. 1, p. 69.

56. Dodd, *Food of London*, pp. 342–4; Alexander, *Retailing*, pp. 13–18; Burnett, *Plenty and Want*, p. 117.

57. PP, *Royal Commission on Market Rights*, vol. 2, qq. 526, 1853, 1887.

58. Dodd, *Food of London*, pp. 346–8.

59. Orlando Gibbons, 'The Cries of London', in *Consort Songs*, edited by Brett, pp. 114–26.

60. Marcellus Laroon (after), 'Colly Molly Puffe', 'Hott Bak'd Wardens Hott', and 'Buy My Dutch Biskets', 1688: British Museum, L,85.45, L,85.27, L,85.18.

61. Anon., 'Cries of London'.

62. Rembrandt van Rijn, 'The Pancake Woman', 1635: Fitzwilliam Museum, Cambridge, 23.K.5–202.

63. For examples of these foods, see Trial of Elizabeth Williamson, Sarah Jackson, December 1744: OBPO, t17441205-23; *Ordinary's Account*, March 1732: OBPO, OA17320306; Middlesex Sessions, Sessions Papers, Petition of George Slater, May 1751: LL, LMSMPS504110012. The absence of pancakes did not mean they were not sold. Pancakes 'nice and brown' are also mentioned in a ballad. See Anon., 'Humours of Rag-Fair'. For descriptions that mention the drinks, see Trial of Stephen Jones, September 1740: OBPO, t17400903-31; Trial of Elizabeth Knotmill, January 1757: OBPO, t17570114-17.

64. *Ordinary's Account*, March 1732: OBPO, OA17320306; *Ordinary's Account*, October 1717: OBPO, OA17171002.

65. For example, see Trial of John Haywood, John Elrey, April 1768: OBPO, t17680413-19.

66. Woolley, *Cook's Guide*, pp. 47–8.

67. See Chapter 4. As ever in the world of hawking there were exceptions, as described in Mayhew, *London Labour*, vol. 1, p. 201.

68. Pennell, *Birth of the English Kitchen*, pp. 65–6.

69. Woolley, *Cook's Guide*, pp. 95–6.

70. Glasse, *Art of Cookery*, pp. 281–2.

71. On the growing availability of sugar, see Stobart, *Sugar and Spice*, pp. 48–9. On earlier consumption, see Thirsk, *Food in Early Modern England*, pp. 324–6.

72. McGrath, 'Marketing of Food, Fodder and Livestock', p. 208.

73. Houghton, *Husbandry and Trade Improv'd*, vol. 3, pp. 10–11.

74. Trial of John Hyams, December 1816: *OBPO*, t18161204-10; Mayhew, *London Labour*, vol. 1, pp. 7, 84, 89.

75. *Standard*, 1 April 1897, p. 3.

76. Torode, 'Trends in Fruit Consumption', pp. 126–8.

77. Mayhew, *London Labour*, vol. 1, pp. 159, 173–4, 180, 196.

78. Mayhew, *London Labour*, vol. 1, p. 159.

79. Mayhew, *London Labour*, vol. 1, pp. 165–6; Walton, *Fish and Chips*, pp. 23–4; Panayi, *Fish and Chips*, pp. 27–32.

80. Weir, 'Penny Licks and Hokey Pokey', p. 295. For earlier, non-Italian ice cream, see Mayhew, *London Labour*, vol. 1, pp. 206–7.

81. *Lloyd's Illustrated Newspaper*, 9 June 1889, p. 7; Thomson and Smith, *Street Life*, pp. 54–5.

82. Tuer, *Old London Street Cries*, pp. 58–60; Weir, 'Penny Licks and Hokey Pokey', pp. 297–9.

83. *Morning Post*, 9 June 1885, p. 5. On claims of insanitary conditions and poisoning, see Sponza, 'Italian "Penny Ice-Men"', pp. 36–8.

84. On the enduring importance of the three staples, see Muldrew, *Food, Energy and the Creation of Industriousness*. For examples of the many works emphasizing these exotics, see Shammas, *Pre-Industrial Consumer*; Walvin, *Fruits of Empire*; Stobart, *Sugar and Spice*.

85. Thirsk, *Food in Early Modern England*, pp. 34–5, 288–9; Muldrew, *Food, Energy and the Creation of Industriousness*, pp. 106–11; Gentilcore, *Food and Health*, pp. 115–31.

86. Lloyd, 'Dietary Advice and Fruit-Eating', pp. 565–8.

87. Hinds, *Calendar of State Papers Relating to English Affairs in the Archives of Venice*, pp. 315–28.

88. PP, *Select Committee on the Fresh Fruit Trade*, p. iii.

89. Woolgar, 'Meat and Dairy Products', pp. 100–1; Muldrew, *Food, Energy and the Creation of Industriousness*, pp. 102–5.

90. Houghton, *Husbandry and Trade Improv'd*, vol. 1, pp. 409–10.

91. Forsyth, 'Gingerbread', p. 28.

92. Eden, *State of the Poor*, pp. 105–6, 244; Trusler, *London Adviser*, p. 27.

93. Atkins, 'Retail Milk Trade', pp. 536–7; Burnett, *Plenty and Want*, p. 177.

94. Muldrew, *Food, Energy and the Creation of Industriousness*, pp. 105–6; Burnett, *Plenty and Want*, pp. 12–13.

95. Serjeantson and Woolgar, 'Fish Consumption', pp. 105, 122–3.

96. On fasting, see Thirsk, *Food in Early Modern England*, pp. 265, 270; Gentilcore, *Food and Health*, pp. 106–7.

97. 'Additional documents: (nos 150–55)', in Hitchcock, *Richard Hutton's Complaints Book*.

98. PP, *Select Committee on Channel Fisheries*, qq. 1704, 1825, 1829.

99. Burnett, *Plenty and Want*, pp. 54–5.

100. For examples of budgets, see Reeves, *Round About a Pound*, pp. 103–4. On improving living standards, see Burnett, *Plenty and Want*, pp. 8, 111–15, 183–6.
101. Burnett, *Plenty and Want*, p. 61; Davin, 'Loaves and Fishes', p. 169.
102. For example, see Griffin, 'Diets, Hunger and Living Standards'.
103. On the notion of two 'food worlds', see Thirsk, *Food in Early Modern England*, p. 159.
104. On York, see the essays by Ann Rycraft, Peter Brears, and Eileen White in White, *Feeding a City: York*. On the other cities, see Hamling and Richardson, *Day at Home*, p. 193; Sacks, *Widening Gate*, pp. 44–50, 351; Estabrook, *Urbane and Rustic England*, pp. 6, 77–82, 276–7; Scola, *Feeding the Victorian City*, pp. 71–9, 93–105, 120–30; Blackman, 'Food Supply of an Industrial Town'; Chaloner, 'Trends in Fish Consumption', pp. 107–9.

CHAPTER 4

1. For examples of these scenes, see Dickens, 'Streets—Morning', pp. 70–1; Mayhew, *London Labour*, vol. 1, pp. 64, 82, 145–9; Greenwood, 'South Coast Fishermen', pp. 326–7; One of the Crowd, 'Watercress Sellers'.
2. For hawkers as typical 'informal' figures, see Buchner and Hoffmann-Rehnitz, 'Irregular Economic Practices'; Kelley, *Cheap Street*, pp. 8–10.
3. London County Council Public Control Committee, *London Markets*, p. 7.
4. For the best introductions to this culture, see Davis, *Medieval Market Morality*; Waddell, *God, Duty and Community*.
5. On London's market system in the seventeenth and eighteenth centuries, see McGrath, 'Marketing of Food, Fodder and Livestock'; Archer, 'Hugh Alley, Law Enforcement and Market Regulation'; Harding, 'Shops, Markets and Retailers'; Taverner, 'Moral Marketplaces'. On markets in Southwark and Westminster and their regulation, see Boulton, *Neighbourhood and Society*, pp. 74–5; Merritt, *Social World of Early Modern Westminster*, pp. 230–5.
6. 5 & 6 Edward VI c. 14, in Pickering, *Statutes at Large*, pp. 377–81.
7. Corporation of London, *Lawes of the Market*.
8. Court of Common Council, Journal 25: LMA, COL/CC/01/01/026, ff. 150v–152r.
9. Taverner, 'Moral Marketplaces', pp. 10–11.
10. For examples of such orders, see Court of Aldermen, Repertory 28: LMA, COL/CA/01/01/031, f. 124v; Company of Fishmongers, Minute Book of the Court of Assistants: GL, Ms 5770/2, pp. 489–90.
11. Court of Aldermen, Repertory 34: LMA, COL/CA/01/01/038, f. 10r.
12. Court of Aldermen, Repertory 74: LMA, COL/CA/01/01/078, f. 273r.
13. Taverner, 'Moral Marketplaces', pp. 12–13.
14. Archer, Barron, and Harding, *Hugh Alley's Caveat*, p. 55.
15. Court of Aldermen, Repertory 74: LMA, COL/CA/01/01/078, ff. 89r–91v, 271v–274v.

16. 'William III, 1698: An Act for Makeing Billingsgate a Free Market', in Raithby, *Statutes of the Realm: Volume 7*, pp. 513–14; Order of the Lord Mayor Concerning Billingsgate, December 1699: LMA, CLA/010/AD/01/002.

17. Smith, 'Market Place', pp. 27–8, 37.

18. Webber, *Covent Garden*, pp. 36–9, 93, 98–9; Sheppard, *Survey of London: Volume 35*.

19. Smith, 'Wholesale and Retail Markets', pp. 41–2.

20. Mayhew, *London Labour*, vol. 1, p. 82; *PP, Select Committee on the Fresh Fruit Trade*, qq. 1115–17, 1124, 3113–16.

21. *PP, Royal Commission on Market Rights*, vol. 2, qq. 3903–7, 3915–17.

22. The quotation is from Shaw and Wild, 'Retail Patterns', p. 282. For other arguments about change only coming later, see Jeffreys, *Retail Trading*, p. 5; Shaw, 'Role of Retailing', pp. 171, 174–7. Those arguing for earlier changes include Davis, *History of Shopping*, pp. 74, 203–4; Alexander, *Retailing*, pp. 231–4, 236–8.

23. For example, see Cox, *Complete Tradesman*; Stobart, *Sugar and Spice*.

24. Webber, *Covent Garden*, ch. 12.

25. Dickens, 'Streets—Morning', pp. 70–1.

26. Harding, 'Shops, Markets and Retailers'.

27. Dodd, *Food of London*, pp. 348–50; Webber, *Covent Garden*, p. 114; Smith, 'Market Place', p. 45.

28. *PP, Select Committee on Channel Fisheries*, q. 1765; *PP, Royal Commission on Market Rights*, vol. 2, qq. 3662, 3668, 3671; Greenwood, 'Bummarees', pp. 82–3.

29. *Daily News*, 8 May 1868, p. 7. For similar cases, see *Standard*, 18 December 1828, p. 4; *Morning Post*, 23 February 1832, p. 4; *Standard*, 4 July 1844, p. 3; *Daily News*, 1 September 1866, p. 6; *Lloyd's Illustrated Newspaper*, 26 October 1884, p. 2.

30. *PP, Royal Commission on Market Rights*, vol. 2, q. 1607.

31. *PP, Royal Commission on Market Rights*, vol. 2, qq. 3554–7.

32. Middleton, *View of the Agriculture*, p. 268.

33. *PP, Royal Commission on Market Rights*, vol. 2, q. 3562.

34. Society of Arts, 'Proceedings of the Society: Food Committee', 1867, pp. 92–4.

35. Trusler, *London Adviser*, p. 31.

36. Middleton, *View of the Agriculture*, pp. 331–2, 335. On the adulteration of milk, see Chapter 8.

37. Trial of William Dorsett, January 1801: *OBPO*, t18010114-83.

38. For example, see *PP, Royal Commission on Market Rights*, vol. 2, qq. 3672–8, 3691–4.

39. For this quote and similar arguments, see Houghton, *Husbandry and Trade Improv'd*, vol. 3, pp. 7–8, 77–8.

40. Anon., *London Fishery*, pp. 28–9.

41. This transition was not painless. For a summary of work on the moral economy and food riots, see Bohstedt, *Politics of Provisions*. On London, see Taverner, 'Moral Marketplaces'.

42. On this problem in relation to hawkers, see Kelley, *Cheap Street*, p. 52.

43. Trial of Mary Royston, September 1715: *OBPO*, t17150907-23; Deposition of John Wymes, 2 May 1611: LMA, DL/C/0220, ff. 495v–496v; Trial of John Hart, February 1813: *OBPO*, t18130217-108; Trial of David Bryan, September 1822:

OBPO, t18220911-235; Trial of Eleanor M'Intire, September 1799: *OBPO*, t17990911-22;Trial of John Franks, December 1794: *OBPO*, t17941208-62;Trial of William Figgins, June 1783: *OBPO*, t17830604-61; Trial of Sarah Metyard, Sarah Morgan, July 1762: *OBPO*, t17620714-30.

44. One of the Crowd, 'Watercress Sellers', pp. 36–7.
45. Mayhew, *London Labour*, vol. 1, pp. 66, 81.
46. Court of Aldermen, Repertory 74: LMA, COL/CA/01/01/078, f. 90r.
47. Trial of James Cannon, George Williams, May 1723: *OBPO*, t17230530-22;Trial of Thomas Thatcher, September 1808: *OBPO*, t18080914-48.
48. Society of Arts, 'Proceedings of the Society: Food Committee', 1868, p. 123.
49. London County Council Public Control Committee, *London Markets*, p. 24. The geographical trend was similar in 1901, as described in London County Council Public Control Department, *Street Markets*, p. 3.
50. Mayhew, *London Labour*, vol. 1, pp. 8, 75–6, 92–3.
51. Trial of Bridget King, December 1767: *OBPO*, t17671209-3; Trial of John Butler, Cornelius Foggerty, January 1808: *OBPO*, t18080113-34; Trial of John Taylor, December 1731: *OBPO*, t17311208-42;Trial of Sarah Goodye, September 1779: *OBPO*, t17790915-64; Deposition of John Wymes, 2 May 1611: LMA, DL/C/220, ff. 495v–496v;Trial of Sarah Dyall, January 1748: *OBPO*, t17480115-5; Trial of Mary Lovet, Winifred Cox, February 1759: *OBPO*, t17590228-4;Trial of John Okey, April 1781: *OBPO*, t17810425-4; Trial of Eleanor M'Intire, September 1799: *OBPO*, t17990911-22; Trial of John Franks, February 1798: *OBPO*, t17980214-72.
52. Trial of William Darby, September 1823: *OBPO*, t18230910-1. For other 'gentle' examples, see Deposition of Susanna Stockdell, 13 July 1671: LMA, DL/C/0236, ff. 275v–276v; *Ordinary's Account*, December 1744: *OBPO*, OA17441224.
53. Pepys, *Diary*, vol. 1, p. 318; vol. 9, pp. 364–5.
54. On early market provision, see Smith, 'Wholesale and Retail Markets', pp. 35–6. On the East End, see Power, 'Shadwell', pp. 42–3; Spence, *London in the 1690s*, p. 128.
55. Smith, 'Wholesale and Retail Markets', p. 36.
56. Smith, 'Wholesale and Retail Markets', pp. 45–6.
57. London County Council Public Control Committee, *London Markets*, p. 7.
58. Booth, *Life and Labour*, 2nd ser., vol. 3, p. 260.
59. *PP, Royal Commission on Market Rights*, vol. 2, q. 1439.
60. Stedman Jones, *Outcast London*, p. 173.
61. Burnett, *England Eats Out*, pp. 27–8, 32–5.
62. On cheap luxuries, see Spufford, *Great Reclothing*, pp. 114–15; Styles, *Dress of the People*, p. 245; Cox, *Retailing and the Language of Goods*, pp. 141–57.
63. Roche, *Sophie in London*, pp. 165–6.
64. For a court case in which a hawker at Green Park explained her business, see Trial of John Briant, September 1797: *OBPO*, t17970920-12.
65. Carlin, 'Fast Food and Urban Living', p. 51; Pennell, ' "Great Quantities of Gooseberry Pye" ', pp. 230–1; Burnett, *Plenty and Want*, pp. 42–3.

66. Reeves, *Round About a Pound*, pp. 59, 105–6. On this problem, see Burnett, *England Eats Out*, pp. 27–8.
67. Ross, *Love & Toil*, pp. 49–50; Davin, 'Loaves and Fishes', pp. 170–1.
68. On this cultural shift and lower-class eating venues, see Burnett, 'Eating in the Open Air', p. 28; Burnett, *England Eats Out*, pp. 32–5; Assael, *London Restaurant*, p. 179; Rich, *Bourgeois Consumption*, p. 155.
69. For an example of this omission, see Burnett, *England Eats Out*, p. 9. For more inclusive works, see Pennell, ' "Great Quantities of Gooseberry Pie" ', p. 235; Assael, *London Restaurant*, pp. 38–42.
70. On the sociological arguments in this area, see Warde and Martens, *Eating Out*, p. 16.

CHAPTER 5

1. Kostof, *City Assembled*, ch. 4.
2. Nevola, *Street Life*, esp. ch. 2; Laitinen and Cohen, 'Cultural History of Early Modern European Streets', pp. 1–2.
3. On the ideal of free movement, see Sennett, *Flesh and Stone*, p. 323. On street improvements as 'markers of urban modernity', see Ogborn, *Spaces of Modernity*, pp. 75–6; Corfield, 'Walking the City Streets', p. 150. On this complex process, see Hitchcock and Shore, 'Introduction'.
4. On Regent Street, see White, *London in the Nineteenth Century*, pp. 23–6; McWilliam, *London's West End*, pp. 26–8. On the pleasure district's development, see McWilliam, *London's West End*, pp. 32–3, 107, 111–13.
5. Gowing, 'Freedom of the Streets', p. 147; Jenner, 'Circulation and Disorder', p. 50.
6. Winter, *London's Teeming Streets*, pp. x–xi; Dyos, 'Urban Transformation', p. 259. On the contradictions of London's modernity, see Nead, *Victorian Babylon*, pp. 3, 5.
7. Trial of Jane Metcalfe, January 1807: OBPO, t18070114-19.
8. Trial of Priscilla Davis, October 1753: OBPO, t17531024-46; Trial of Matthew Pennell, September 1822: OBPO, t18220911-56.
9. On the openness of houses, see Harding, 'Space, Property, and Propriety', pp. 559–61.
10. Vickery, 'Englishman's Home Is His Castle?', pp. 153–4. On early modern doorways, see Gowing, 'Freedom of the Streets', p. 136; Flather, *Gender and Space*, p. 45.
11. Trial of Ann Parsons, October 1729: OBPO, t17291015-16.
12. Lord Mayor's Waiting Book: LMA, CLA/004/01/01/001, f. 101v.
13. Thomson and Smith, *Street Life*, pp. 90–1.
14. Clark, *English Alehouse*, pp. 132–3; Girouard, *Victorian Pubs*, pp. 6, 10–11; Hailwood, *Alehouses and Good Fellowship*, p. 20.
15. Clark, *English Alehouse*, p. 138; Hailwood, *Alehouses and Good Fellowship*, p. 21.
16. Girouard, *Victorian Pubs*, pp. 4–5; Jennings, *Local*, pp. 109–11.
17. Girouard, *Victorian Pubs*, p. 5; Flather, *Gender and Space*, pp. 110–21; Jennings, *Local*, pp. 112–13; Hailwood, *Alehouses and Good Fellowship*, pp. 179–81.

18. For examples of the extremes, see Trial of Katherine Dennis, August 1723: *OBPO*, t17230828-19; Trial of Bridget King, December 1767: *OBPO*, t17671209-3; Trial of Mary Ann Sullivan, July 1779: *OBPO*, t17790707-38.
19. Mayhew, *London Labour*, vol. 1, pp. 169–70.
20. Trial of Peter Noakes, January 1732: *OBPO*, t17320114-41; Trial of John Bird, George Bird, February 1820: *OBPO*, t18200217-85; Bridewell Hospital, Minutes of the Court of Governors: BMM, BCB 14, p. 48.
21. St Botolph Aldgate, Vestry Minute and Memoranda Book: LMA, P69/BOT2/B/001/MS09236, f. 42r; St Clement Danes, Vestry Minutes: *LL*, WCCDMV362110141; St Clement Danes, Vestry Minutes: *LL*, WCCDMV362090073; St Martin-in-the-Fields, Vestry Minute Books: WAC, F2006, p. 205.
22. Harding, *Dead and the Living*, pp. 52–5, 86–9; Barnes, *Root & Branch*, pp. 6–7.
23. St Dunstan in the West, Vestry Minute Books: LMA, P69/DUN2/B/001/MS03016/001, pp. 337, 433. The apple seller may have been the 'Aplewoman' Elizabeth Moore, who was paying the same rate in February 1649.
24. Trial of Elizabeth Burgis, January 1727: *OBPO*, t17270113-18; Trial of William Stephens, May 1736: *OBPO*, t17360505-33; Trial of John Donnoly and others, October 1766: *OBPO*, t17661022-6. On the theatre, see Sheppard, *Survey of London: Volume 35*.
25. Mayhew, *London Labour*, vol. 1, pp. 177–8; Adcock, 'Leaving the London Theatres', p. 13.
26. This included new constructions, like Regent's Park. See Trial of James Needham, September 1822: *OBPO*, t18220911-55.
27. The fullest accounts of the institution are in Saunders, *The Royal Exchange*.
28. Cornhill Wardmote Books: LMA, CLC/W/HF/001/MS04069/001, ff. 118v, 125r, 127r, 128v, 157r, 160r, 182r, 185v–186r; CLC/W/HF/001/MS040609/002/001, f. 24r.
29. Mercers' Company Archives, Gresham Repertories, 1669–76, ff. 77v, 99v; Order of the Committee for Gresham Affairs, 24 March 1692: LMA, CLA/062/04/016; Mercers' Company Archives, Gresham Repertories, 1678–1722, f. 285r. Thanks to Sarah Birt for these references.
30. Trial of William Cox and others, July 1767: *OBPO*, t17670715-19; Guildhall Justice Room, Minute Books: LMA, CLA/005/01/007, entries for 16 March 1779; Mansion House Justice Room, Minute Books: LMA, CLA/004/02/006, entries for 6 April 1785; CLA/004/02/055, entries for 26 January 1790; Trial of Hyam Moses, January 1813: *OBPO*, t18130113-107.
31. Gerhold, *London Bridge*, pp. 12, 100–3.
32. Court of Aldermen, Repertory 33: LMA, COL/CA/01/01/037, f. 66v. See also Bridewell Royal Hospital, Minutes of the Court of Governors: *LL*, BBBRMG202020394; Gerhold, *London Bridge*, p. 68.
33. Bridewell Hospital, Minutes of the Court of Governors: BMM, BCB 15, p. 257; Bridewell Royal Hospital, Minutes of the Court of Governors: *LL*,

BBBRMG2020010334; St Bride Fleet Street, Vestry Minute Books: LMA, P69/BRI/B/001/MS06554/002, f. 218r; P69/BRI/B/001/MS06554/003, f. 41r.

34. Ward, *London Spy Compleat*, pp. 130–1.

35. Dyos and Aldcroft, *British Transport*, pp. 217–18.

36. *Standard*, 16 November 1877, p. 2.

37. Trial of Sarah Dyall, January 1748: *OBPO*, t17480115-5; Book of Fines for Breach of City Ordinances: LMA, COL/CHD/CM/10/001, f. 255.

38. Trial of Mary Stafford, September 1806: *OBPO*, t18060917-120. On corners, see Nevola, *Street Life*, pp. 188–204.

39. Trial of John Franks, February 1798: *OBPO*, t17980214-72.

40. Guildhall Justice Room, Minute Books: LMA, CLA/005/01/044, entries for 25 March 1790; Trial of Aaron Levi, January 1796: *OBPO*, t17960113-89; Ritson, *Digest of the Proceedings of the Court Leet*, p. 16.

41. Mayhew, *London Labour*, vol. 1, p. 96.

42. Malvery, 'Gilding the Gutter', pp. 135, 144–5.

43. Westminster Court of Burgesses, Minute Books: WAC, WCB 2, pp. 140–1; Deposition of William Barnes, 1609: LMA, DL/C/0219, ff. 2r–2v.

44. McWilliam, 'Fancy Repositories', pp. 95–6.

45. Walsh, 'Shop Design', pp. 160, 162–4; Cox and Walsh, '"Their Shops Are Dens"', pp. 79–81; Morrison, *English Shops*, pp. 22–5, 42; Garrioch, 'House Names, Shop Signs', p. 35.

46. Morrison, *English Shops*, pp. 45–56.

47. On West End department stores, see McWilliam, *London's West End*, pp. 288–90.

48. On food shop design, see Morrison, *English Shops*, pp. 41–2, 56, 83.

49. Cox and Walsh, '"Their Shops Are Dens"', pp. 77–9; Morrison, *English Shops*, pp. 26–7; Walsh, 'Stalls, Bulks, Shops', pp. 37–8.

50. For example, see Deposition of Isabelle Leonard, 14 May 1618: LMA, DL/C/0225, f. 277v; Trial of Ann Owen, September 1745: *OBPO*, t17450911-36.

51. On early modern cellars, see Schofield, *London Surveys of Ralph Treswell*, pp. 26–30; Wallis, 'Consumption, Retailing, and Medicine', p. 36. For examples of fruit and milk cellars, see Deposition of Elizabeth Derrick, 19 November 1695: LMA, DL/C/0244, f. 357r; Trial of John Linch, October 1734: *OBPO*, t17341016-22; Deposition of Mary Brooks, 17 February 1760: LMA, DL/C/0276, f. 453r; Trial of Mary Edgers, Ann Higgins, September 1771: *OBPO*, t17710911-43.

52. Trial of John England, William Craftow, May 1725: *OBPO*, t17250513-24.

53. On the most basic forms of stall, see Mayhew, *London Labour*, vol. 1, p. 99.

54. Lucas, 'Coster-Land', p. 76; Kelley, 'London's Street Markets', pp. 196–8.

55. Mayhew, *London Labour*, vol. 1, pp. 149–50.

56. *Morning Post*, 4 July 1860, p. 7.

57. For an example of a hawker with scales, see Trial of Margaret Coates, February 1825: *OBPO*, t18250217-183.

58. Mayhew, *London Labour*, vol. 1, pp. 151–2; Thomson and Smith, *Street Life*, p. 68.

59. For examples of bills, see Trial of Mary Lynch, September 1815: *OBPO*, t18150913-16; Trial of Samuel Hyllier, December 1823: *OBPO*, t18231203-190. For tokens, see Trial of Mary Cavenaugh, January 1812: *OBPO*, t18120115-131.

60. Trusler, *London Adviser*, p. 27. On alternative ways of counting, see Thomas, 'Numeracy', pp. 119–20.

61. Trial of Thomas Hobson, Robert Green, April 1773: *OBPO*, t17730421-47.

62. Sala, *Gaslight and Daylight*, pp. 259–60.

63. Doré and Jerrold, *London: A Pilgrimage*, pp. 157–8.

64. Adcock, 'Saturday Night in London', pp. 378–9. On reading such literary flourishes, see Walkowitz, *Nights Out*, p. 144. On the analogy between British slums and foreign cultures, Nord, 'Social Explorer as Anthropologist', p. 122.

65. On market architecture, see Schmiechen and Carls, *British Market Hall*, pp. 105–22; Morrison, *English Shops*, ch. 6.

66. Kelley, *Cheap Street*, pp. 97–102; Kelley, 'London's Street Markets', pp. 193, 196, 198–201.

67. London County Council Public Control Committee, *London Markets*, pp. 24–5.

68. London County Council Public Control Committee, *London Markets*, pp. 70–3.

69. London County Council Public Control Committee, *London Markets*, pp. 37, 41, 51.

70. London County Council Public Control Committee, *London Markets*, p. 24.

71. See also the calculations in Mayhew, *London Labour*, vol. 1, p. 11; Society of Arts, 'Proceedings of the Society: Food Committee', 1867, p. 92.

72. Metropolitan Police Report on Hammersmith Costermongers, 12 March 1885: TNA, HO 45/9960/X2772/50.

73. Stern, 'Baroness's Market', pp. 356–7; Jones, 'Redressing Reform Narratives', pp. 73–4; Kelley, *Cheap Street*, pp. 28–31.

74. Doré and Jerrold, *London: A Pilgrimage*, pp. 151–2.

75. For a discussion of the factors, see Kelley, *Cheap Street*, pp. 31–2.

76. On Cawston's schemes, see London County Council Public Control Department, *Street Markets*, p. 26; Jones, 'Redressing Reform Narratives', pp. 75–8. For other failed examples, see Kelley, *Cheap Street*, pp. 32–3; Kelley, 'London's Street Markets', pp. 203–6.

77. Farringdon Without, St Dunstan in the West Precinct, Register of Presentments of the Wardmote Inquest: LMA, CLC/W/JB/044/MS03018/001, ff. 94r, 95v, 97r, 100r, 101v, 104v, 107r–107v, 111v, 122v, 123v, 103v, 170v, 171v, 175v, 176v. For more on this hotspot, see Taverner, 'Selling Food in the Streets', pp. 110–12.

78. Trial of Thomas Cash and others, April 1718: *OBPO*, t17180423-49; Trial of Grace Long, January 1734: *OBPO*, t17340116-42; Trial of Elizabeth Whitney, Mary Nash, February 1740: *OBPO*, t17400227-2; City of London Sessions, Sessions Papers, Examination and Confession of Eleanor Price, April 1718: *LL*, LMSLPS150290021.

CHAPTER 6

1. Mayhew, *London Labour*, vol. 1, pp. 27, 167, 173–4.

2. For an illustration of a similar design, see Doré and Jerrold, *London: A Pilgrimage*, p. 114.

3. For descriptions of kettles, basins, and fires used for salop, see Trial of Joseph Levy, May 1784: *OBPO*, t17840526-43; Trial of Edmund Law, Thomas Webb, January 1823: *OBPO*, t18230115-97.

4. This argument is forcefully put forward in Edgerton, *Shock of the Old*, pp. 20–1, 65–6.

5. Bichard, *Baskets in Europe*, p. 59.

6. For example, see Inventory of Thomas Balleston, 8 April 1702: LMA, CLC/313/K/C/010/MS19504/054/11.

7. Trial of Elizabeth White, January 1760: *OBPO*, t17600116-12.

8. Trial of John Bravo, February 1796: *OBPO*, t17960217-57.

9. 'Strawberries', in Craig, *Itinerant Traders*.

10. On this 'urban pastoral' theme, see Shesgreen, *Images of the Outcast*, pp. 177–9; Barrell, *Dark Side of the Landscape*, p. 51.

11. Trial of Eleanor M'Intire, September 1799: *OBPO*, t17990911-22; Trial of John Smith, September 1801: *OBPO*, t18010916-132.

12. Pottles, nineteenth century: Museum of English Rural Life, University of Reading, 51/9 and 51/10. On the pottle, see Bichard, *Baskets in Europe*, p. 80.

13. Bichard, *Baskets in Europe*, pp. 65–6.

14. For example, see Verdicts and Presentments of Leet Juries for Guildable Manor, Southwark: LMA, CLA/043/01/010, 1661–2 book, f. 13v.

15. On these various basket types, see Mayhew, *London Labour*, vol. 1, p. 27.

16. On back baskets, see Bichard, *Baskets in Europe*, pp. 93–4, 159–62. For examples of these images, see Marcellus Laroon (after), 'Buy My Flounders', 1688: British Museum, 1972,U.370.24; 'Hot Loaves', in Craig, *Itinerant Traders*.

17. For a discussion of such images, see Jane Whittle, 'Why Do Women Carry Things on Their Heads?', *Women's Work in Rural England, 1500–1700*, 23 February 2016, <https://earlymodernwomenswork.wordpress.com/2016/02/23/why-do-women-carry-things-on-their-heads/>.

18. Trial of Thomas Jones, James Rigby, September 1781: *OBPO*, t17810912-50; Trial of Mary Derby, December 1780: *OBPO*, t17801206-20; Trial of John Saunders, John Nixon, July 1814: *OBPO*, t18140706-120.

19. Edgar Scamell, Photograph of Hawker Selling Muffins in London, 1895: Victoria and Albert Museum, E.3608-2000.

20. For early studies, see Maloiy et al., 'Energetic Cost of Carrying Loads'; Charteris, Scott, and Nottroot, '"Free-Ride" Hypothesis'; Heglund et al., 'Energy-Saving Gait Mechanics'.

21. Lloyd et al., 'No "Free Ride" for African Women'.

22. See marginal note by Gregory King in Laslett, *Earliest Classics*, p. 213.

23. Dodd, *Food of London*, pp. 379–80.

24. On the importance of carrying, see Amato, *On Foot*, pp. 48–9.

25. Ingold, 'Culture on the Ground', p. 325; Amato, *On Foot*, p. 8.

26. Lord Mayor's Charge Books: LMA, CLA/004/01/02/001, f. 190v.

27. Marcellus Laroon (after), 'Twelve Pence a Peck Oysters', 1688: British Museum, L,85.23.

28. Trial of John Harris, December 1712: *OBPO*, t17121210-28.

29. For an early example, see Trial of John Bew, September 1748: *OBPO*, t17480907-2. For later incidents, see Mansion House Justice Room, Minute Books: LMA, CLA/004/02/001, entries for 26 November 1784; Trial of Hannah Hill, September 1809: *OBPO*, t18090920-98; Trial of Mary Corbett, May 1820: *OBPO*, t18200517-93.

30. Matthies, 'Medieval Wheelbarrow', pp. 356–7; Lewis, 'Origins of the Wheelbarrow', pp. 472–5.

31. For example, see the probate inventories of a Middlesex victualler and a St Pancras brewer: Inventory of John Devon, 20 December 1684: LMA, CLC/313/K/C/009/MS19504/031/26; Inventory of Edward Reynolds, 12 November 1688: LMA, CLC/313/K/C/009/MS19504/038/41-42.

32. In addition to Rowlandson's potato vendor, see Jacopo Amigoni, 'Golden Pippins', *c.*1732–9: British Museum, 1873,0809.29; 'Baking or Boiling Apples', in Craig, *Itinerant Traders*.

33. Matthies, 'Medieval Wheelbarrow', p. 360.

34. Paul Sandby, 'A Pudding, a Pudding, a Hot Pudding', 1760: British Museum, 1904,0819.566. The hawker also has straps on his barrow.

35. Mayhew, *London Labour*, vol. 1, p. 27. For another photograph, see Lucas, 'Coster-Land', p. 78.

36. Malvery, 'Gilding the Gutter', p. 144.

37. As depicted in Giovanni Vendramini, after Francis Wheatley, 'Hot Spice Gingerbread Smoking Hot', 1796: Yale Center for British Art, Paul Mellon Collection, B2001.2.1690.

38. Kelley, *Cheap Street*, pp. 95–7.

39. *Ordinary's Account*, January 1742: *OBPO*, OA17420113.

40. Trial of Catharine Bulkley, May 1792: *OBPO*, t17920523-60; Trial of Sarah Blackall, July 1803: *OBPO*, t18030706-20; Trial of Mary Corbett, May 1820: *OBPO*, t18200517-93.

41. Mayhew, *London Labour*, vol. 1, p. 30.

42. One of the Crowd, 'Covent Garden Market', pp. 75–6.

43. Greenwood, 'Mission Among City Savages', pp. 23–4; Thomson and Smith, *Street Life*, pp. 58–9.

44. Lucas, 'Coster-Land', p. 78.

45. Mayhew, *London Labour*, vol. 1, p. 30; Booth, *Life and Labour*, 2nd ser., vol. 3, p. 270.

46. Mayhew, *London Labour*, vol. 1, pp. 26–7.

47. Almeroth-Williams, *City of Beasts*, pp. 46–50; Turvey, 'Horse Traction', p. 41.

48. For example, see Trial of John Pinchen, October 1756: *OBPO*, t17561020-18; Trial of Edward Warne, April 1781: *OBPO*, t17810425-41; Trial of William Appleton, June 1802: *OBPO*, t18020602-12.

49. Marcellus Laroon (after), 'Lilly White Vinegar 3 Pence a Quart', 1688: British Museum, L,85.13.

50. The 1696–7 act of Parliament that introduced licensing for hawkers and pedlars required payments for every horse or animal. On the act, see Chapter 8.

51. Trial of Andrew Welch, May 1766: *OBPO*, t17660514-40. Welch's is the earliest incidental description I have found of a hawker with a donkey.

52. Trial of Thomas Collop, Elizabeth Gordon, February 1768: *OBPO*, t17680224-24; Trial of John Roe, October 1768: *OBPO*, t17681019-39.

53. For example, see Trial of Joseph Herbert, Thomas Holdsworth, September 1787: *OBPO*, t17870912-5; Trial of Thomas Williams, James Smith, January 1794: *OBPO*, t17940115-52.

54. Trial of Robert Hill, May 1814: *OBPO*, t18140525-68; Trial of John Jones, John Merriman, May 1819: *OBPO*, t18190526-69; Malvery, 'Gilding the Gutter', pp. 146–7.

55. Mayhew, *London Labour*, vol. 1, pp. 27–9.

56. Mayhew, *London Labour*, vol. 1, pp. 29, 92.

57. Trial of John Jones, John Merriman, May 1819: *OBPO*, t18190526-69.

58. Lucas, 'Coster-Land', p. 75.

59. *Morning Post*, 7 May 1844, p. 6; One of the Crowd, 'Working Dogs', pp. 116–17. For an earlier case in which a costermonger's dog was stolen, see *Morning Post*, 3 April 1833, p. 4.

60. *Morning Post*, 2 October 1833, p. 4.

61. *Daily News*, 29 May 1854, p. 6; *Daily News*, 31 August 1897, p. 3; *Daily News*, 10 August 1900, p. 7.

62. Donald, ' "Beastly Sights" ', p. 517; Adelman, *Civilised by Beasts*, pp. 39–47. For a useful summary of these debates, see Almeroth-Williams, *City of Beasts*, pp. 216–18.

63. *Standard*, 20 June 1837, p. 4.

64. Malvery, 'Gilding the Gutter', pp. 146–7.

65. *Morning Post*, 10 August 1864, p. 3. For other reports, see *Standard*, 8 August 1864, p. 6; *Daily News*, 10 August 1864, p. 2; *Penny Illustrated Paper*, 20 August 1864, pp. 1–2.

66. *Daily News*, 7 May 1874, p. 3; *Daily News*, 30 August 1887, p. 7; *Pall Mall Gazette*, 31 August 1893, p. 11.

67. Hawkers' barrows changed in shape again, taking on a more regular, rectangle shape with four evenly sized wheels. They were probably pushed a shorter distance and were no longer pulled by donkeys. See Forshaw and Bergström, *Markets of London*, pp. 32–3.

CHAPTER 7

1. Raines, *Marcellus Laroon*, pp. 7–9. On Laroon's use of clothing, see Shesgreen, *Images of the Outcast*, pp. 49, 57.

2. Styles, *Dress of the People*, pp. 67–9.

3. Mayhew, *London Labour*, vol. 1, p. 51.

4. On Ward, Gay, and other eighteenth-century writers, see Ogborn, *Spaces of Modernity*, pp. 111–14; Stenton, 'Spatial Stories', pp. 68–9. On nineteenth-century walkers, see Nord, 'City as Theater', p. 188; Womack, 'Walking as

Labour', p. 137. For a discussion of women's street lives specifically, see Nord, *Walking the Victorian Streets*, pp. 3–4.

5. Ingold, 'Culture on the Ground', p. 323.

6. Mayhew, *London Labour*, vol. 1, p. 72.

7. Mayhew, *London Labour*, vol. 1, pp. 68–9.

8. Lucas, 'Coster-Land', pp. 75–7.

9. Trial of Barney White, October 1824: *OBPO*, t18241028-161.

10. Swift, 'Description of a City Shower'.

11. Smollett, *Expedition of Humphrey Clinker*, p. 122.

12. Society of Arts, 'Traction on Roads', p. 689. On the general problem of street mud, see also Mayhew, *London Labour*, vol. 2, pp. 185, 200; Turvey, 'Street Mud', p. 134; Jackson, *Dirty Old London*, pp. 27–8.

13. Mayhew, *London Labour*, vol. 2, pp. 189–92.

14. Grew, *Shoes and Pattens*, pp. 91–101; Buck, *Dress in Eighteenth-Century England*, pp. 131–2.

15. Gay, 'Trivia', p. 176. On gender and walking, see Riello, 'Material Culture of Walking', pp. 49–51.

16. Marcellus Laroon (after), 'Hot Bak'd Wardens Hott', 1688: British Museum, L,85.27; Paul Sandby, 'A Girl with a Basket of Oranges', c.1759: Yale Center for British Art, Paul Mellon Collection, B1975.3.223.

17. Evelyn, *Fumifugium*, address to the reader; Jenner, 'Politics of London Air', p. 540. On early street conditions, see also Cockayne, *Hubbub*, pp. 162–3, 182–3.

18. McKellar, *Birth of Modern London*, p. 219. On the damage, see Porter, *The Great Fire of London*, pp. 71–2, 127–8.

19. 'Charles II, 1662: An Act for Repairing the High Wayes and Sewers', in Raithby, *Statutes of the Realm: Volume 5*, pp. 351–7.

20. Major post-Fire acts that touched on the streets included 18 & 19 Charles II c. 8; 22 Charles II c. 11; 2 William & Mary session 2 c. 8. On the parts of rebuilding focused on widening streets, stopping encroachments, and improving drainage, see Reddaway, *Rebuilding of London*, pp. 286–94.

21. 2 George III c. 21. On the act, see Sheppard, *Local Government*, pp. 132–3; Cockayne, *Hubbub*, pp. 204–5.

22. Ogborn, *Spaces of Modernity*, pp. 91–6, 103–4.

23. Spranger, *Proposal or Plan*, preface; Hanway, *Letter to Mr John Spranger*, p. 47; Massie, *Essay on the Many Advantages*, pp. 98–9.

24. Whitworth, *Plan for the More Easy and Speedy Execution*, pp. 10–11, 14–16. See also Cockayne, *Hubbub*, pp. 181–3. On paving in Marylebone, see Sheppard, *Local Government*, pp. 132–4.

25. Turvey, 'Street Mud', pp. 131, 133, 140; Winter, *London's Teeming Streets*, pp. 36–7.

26. Turvey, 'Street Mud', p. 146; Winter, *London's Teeming Streets*, pp. 37–8.

27. Turvey, 'Street Mud', p. 137.

28. Society of Arts, 'Traction on Roads', pp. 701–3.

29. Winter, *London's Teeming Streets*, p. 42; Turvey, 'Street Mud', pp. 141–3; Jackson, *Dirty Old London*, p. 44.

30. The meanings of these four periods vary, but they offer a structure for analysis. When a time is stated, I have designated 4 a.m. to 12 p.m. as morning, 12 p.m. to 6 p.m. as afternoon, 6 p.m. to 10 p.m. as evening, and 10 p.m. to 4 a.m. as night. The 175 incidents divide into 46 in the morning, 48 in the afternoon, 47 in the evening, and 34 at night.

31. For example, see Trial of James Ballentine, January 1764: *OBPO*, t17640113-40. On the nineteenth century, see Booth, *Life and Labour*, 2nd ser., vol. 3, pp. 180–1.

32. Doré and Jerrold, *London: A Pilgrimage*, p. 114.

33. Mayhew, *London Labour*, vol. 1, pp. 180–1.

34. Trial of Mary Harwood, October 1740: *OBPO*, t17401015-65; Trial of Stephen Jones, September 1740: *OBPO*, t17400903-31.

35. Wilson, 'Midnight London', pp. 126–8.

36. For example, see Bridewell Hospital, Minutes of the Court of Governors: BMM, BCB 7, f. 133r; Trial of Mary Marlow, September 1742: *OBPO*, t17420909-7; Trial of Samuel Lawrence, October 1756: *OBPO*, t17561020-20; Trial of Simon Clark, February 1771: *OBPO*, t17710220-14.

37. Falkus, 'Lighting in the Dark Ages', pp. 249–50.

38. For example, see Bridewell Hospital, Minutes of the Court of Governors: BMM, BCB 7, f. 133r; BMM, BCB 8, f. 63r.

39. Koslofsky, *Evening's Empire*, pp. 2–3. For a similar argument, see Ekirch, *At Day's Close*, pp. 324–9.

40. Nead, *Victorian Babylon*, pp. 85–6.

41. Falkus, 'Lighting in the Dark Ages', pp. 253, 255–7, 260–1. On candles, lanterns, and oil lamps, see Beer, 'Early History of London Street-Lighting', pp. 312–13.

42. Beer, 'Early History of London Street-Lighting', pp. 323–4; Sheppard, *Local Government*, p. 140.

43. Turnbull, 'Lighting', pp. 322–5; O'Dea, *Social History of Lighting*, pp. 21–3; Nead, *Victorian Babylon*, p. 88; White, *London in the Nineteenth Century*, pp. 21–2, 60–1.

44. Spranger, *Proposal or Plan*, preface. See also Hanway, *Letter to Mr John Spranger*, p. 34.

45. Beer, 'Early History of London Street-Lighting', p. 314.

46. Trial of Thomas Bulker, January 1736: *OBPO*, t17360115-9.

47. On Sandby's critique of Hogarth, see Quilley, 'Analysis of Deceit', p. 44.

48. Trial of Benjamin M'Cowl, George Brace, July 1787: *OBPO*, t17870711-7.

49. Sala, *Gaslight and Daylight*, p. 259.

50. Kelley, *Cheap Street*, pp. 87–90.

51. *Morning Post*, 8 September 1873, p. 6.

52. Trial of Peter Noakes, January 1732: *OBPO*, t17320114-41; Trial of William Flemming, September 1732: *OBPO*, t17320906-67.

53. *Morning Post*, 6 November 1855, p. 7.

54. Trial of John Lee, January 1722: *OBPO*, t17220112-23.

55. Spence, *Accidents and Violent Death*, pp. 110–16.

56. Society of Arts, 'Traction on Roads', pp. 699–700. For later estimates, see Winter, *London's Teeming Streets*, p. 48.

57. Gay, 'Trivia', p. 197.

58. Sala, 'Locomotion in London', pp. 454, 456–7.

59. Ward, *London Spy Compleat*, p. 157.

60. Dickens, 'Dangers of the Streets', p. 154.

61. White, *London in the Nineteenth Century*, p. 62.

62. Winter, *London's Teeming Streets*, pp. 45–9.

63. Dyos and Aldcroft, *British Transport*, pp. 219–20; Winter, *London's Teeming Streets*, p. 40.

64. Statement of Acts and History of the Case of King Street Costermongers for Hammersmith Borough Council, 2 February 1906: TNA, HO 45/10329/134628/5.

65. Jenner, 'Circulation and Disorder', p. 53.

66. *Standard*, 12 August 1857, p. 8; *Daily News*, 15 October 1858, p. 7; *Lloyd's Illustrated Newspaper*, 25 January 1874, p. 4.

67. *Morning Post*, 3 August 1894, p. 2.

68. Dyos and Aldcroft, *British Transport*, pp. 217–18; Nead, *Victorian Babylon*, p. 36.

69. Turvey, 'Horse Traction', p. 57; Dyos and Aldcroft, *British Transport*, p. 213.

70. Winter, *London's Teeming Streets*, pp. x–xi, 194, 203; Dyos and Aldcroft, *British Transport*, pp. 299, 334–5.

71. Deposition of Margaret Taylor, 22 January 1672: LMA, DL/C/0236, ff. 326r–327v.

72. For examples of stall thefts, see Trial of Joseph Markham, April 1743: *OBPO*, t17430413-21; Trial of William Perry, December 1787: *OBPO*, t17871212-20; Trial of Joseph Nettlefold, September 1821: *OBPO*, t18210912-127. For barrows, see Mansion House Justice Room, Minute Books: LMA, CLA/004/02/057, entries for 20 March 1790; *Morning Post*, 4 August 1853, p. 8; *Lloyd's Illustrated Newspaper*, 19 October 1890, p. 8.

73. Trial of Mary Swinhy, Jane Biller, September 1742: *OBPO*, t17420909-33; Trial of John Gutteridge, April 1822: *OBPO*, t18220417-157; Trial of Hannah Lyons, December 1823: *OBPO*, t18231203-174.

74. For example, see *Standard*, 27 July 1858, p. 7; *Standard*, 28 August 1883, p. 6.

75. *Standard*, 27 July 1889, p. 6.

76. On this discourse, see Rendell, 'Displaying Sexuality', p. 87; Walkowitz, 'Going Public', pp. 19–20; Wilson, *Sphinx in the City*, p. 46; Winter, *London's Teeming Streets*, pp. 181–2; Nead, *Victorian Babylon*, pp. 62–6; Nord, *Walking the Victorian Streets*, pp. 15, 181–5. On department store controversies in particular, see Rappaport, *Shopping for Pleasure*, pp. 46–7.

77. Gowing, 'Freedom of the Streets', p. 147. On the movement of eighteenth-century women, see Shoemaker, 'Gendered Spaces'; Corfield, 'Walking the City Streets', p. 134.

78. 'Aniseed Robin n.', in *Green's Dictionary of Slang*.

79. Depositions of Christopher Sumner and Susanna Stockdell, 13 July 1671: LMA, DL/C/0236, ff. 274v–276v.

80. On this use of language, see Gowing, *Domestic Dangers*, pp. 59–110.

81. Shoemaker, 'Public Spaces, Private Disputes?'

82. Trial of Grace Long, January 1734: *OBPO*, t17340116-42. On the particular associations of this kind of hawker, see Taverner, 'Consider the Oyster Seller'. On the area's crime rate, see Griffiths, *Lost Londons*, pp. 84–5.

83. City of London Sessions, Sessions Papers, Examination of Diana Pushee, 13 August 1753: *LL*, LMSLPS150640067; Examination of John Hussey, 13 August 1753: *LL*, LMSLPS150640070.

84. Depositions of William Barnes and Elizabeth Smith, 1609: LMA, DL/C/0219, ff. 2r–3v. Gowing uses this particular case as an example of restrictions on women's mobility, in Gowing, 'Freedom of the Streets', pp. 143–5.

85. Guildhall Justice Room, Minute Books: LMA, CLA/005/01/044, entries for 25 March 1790.

86. *Lloyd's Illustrated Newspaper*, 30 January 1887, p. 4.

CHAPTER 8

1. On the form of these courts, see Griffiths, *Lost Londons*, pp. 19–20; Beattie, *Policing and Punishment*, pp. 92–5; Gray, *Crime, Prosecution and Social Relations*, pp. 17–18, 23–4; Davis, 'Poor Man's System of Justice', p. 311.

2. Bridewell Hospital, Minutes of the Court of Governors: BMM, BCB 8, f. 63r; Lord Mayor's Charge Books: LMA, CLA/004/01/02/002, f. 113r; *Lloyd's Illustrated Newspaper*, 27 September 1863, p. 12.

3. Griffiths, *Lost Londons*, pp. 125–33; Dorey, 'Unwholesome for Man's Body?', ch. 6; Reinke-Williams, *Women, Work and Sociability*, pp. 104–7.

4. Smith, 'Market Place', pp. 76–8; Winter, *London's Teeming Streets*, pp. 107–9; Inwood, 'Policing London's Morals', pp. 131–9; Kelley, *Cheap Street*, pp. 23–7.

5. For two key works on stability and the sense of crisis, see Archer, *Pursuit of Stability*; Griffiths, *Lost Londons*.

6. Court of Common Council, Journal 25: LMA, COL/CC/01/01/026, ff. 150v–152r; Journal 26: LMA, COL/CC/01/01/027, ff. 6r–7r.

7. Archer, *Pursuit of Stability*, pp. 6–7.

8. Court of Aldermen, Repertory 21: LMA, COL/CA/01/01/023, ff. 73r, 115r; Repertory 22: LMA, COL/CA/01/01/024, ff. 172r, 176v; Repertory 28: LMA, COL/CA/01/01/031, f. 159r; Court of Common Council, Journal 27: LMA, COL/CC/01/01/028, f. 205r.

9. Court of Common Council, Journal 28: LMA, COL/CC/01/01/029/01, ff. 300r–302r. On the fishmongers' encouragement, see Remembrancia, Volume 3: LMA, COL/RMD/PA/01/003, ff. 42r–42v.

10. Only six identifiable street sellers appeared in the period 1617–27 and one of these was probably not selling food. See Bridewell Hospital, Minutes of the Court of Governors: BMM, BCB 6, ff. 128r, 231r, 298r, 350r, 421r.

11. Court of Aldermen, Repertory 30: LMA, COL/CA/01/01/033, f. 310v; Court of Common Council, Journal 29: LMA, COL/CC/01/01/030, f. 187r.

12. Court of Aldermen, Repertory 74: LMA, COL/CA/01/01/078, f. 121v; Repertory 74: LMA, COL/CA/01/01/078, f. 170v.

13. City of London Sessions, Session Minute Books, Gaol Delivery, Oyer and Terminer, and Peace, July 1681: LMA, CLA/047/LJ/04/052, f. 47v; Court of Aldermen, Repertory 86: LMA, COL/CA/01/01/090, ff. 170v, 186v, 201v–202r; Repertory 91: LMA, COL/CA/01/01/095, f. 32v.

14. Bromley, 'Street Vending and Public Policy', pp. 14–15; Roever and Skinner, 'Street Vendors and Cities', pp. 362, 364.

15. Stern, *Porters of London*, pp. 43–5, 84–8; Bennett, *Worshipful Company of Carmen*, pp. 23–4, 82–4; Jenner, 'Circulation and Disorder', pp. 41–2, 50.

16. 'William III, 1696–7: An Act for Licensing Hawkers and Pedlars', in Raithby, *Statutes of the Realm: Volume 7*, pp. 266–9. On the act, see Spufford, *Great Reclothing*, pp. 6–10, 13–16.

17. *PP, Select Committee of the House of Lords, on the Traffic Regulation (Metropolis) Bill*, qq. 97–107, 287–9.

18. 30 & 31 Victoria c. 134: Metropolitan Streets Act 1867.

19. *Lloyd's Illustrated Newspaper*, 3 November 1867, p. 12; *Morning Post*, 2 November 1867, p. 7.

20. *Daily News*, 2 November 1867, p. 3; *Reynold's Newspaper*, 10 November 1867, p. 8; *Lloyd's Illustrated Newspaper*, 17 November 1867, p. 6.

21. *Daily News*, 8 November 1867, p. 3; *Standard*, 8 November 1867, p. 2.

22. *Standard*, 4 November 1867, p. 4; *Reynold's Newspaper*, 10 November 1867, p. 4.

23. 31 & 32 Victoria c. 5: Metropolitan Streets Act Amendment Act 1867.

24. Metropolitan Police, Report on the History of Costermonger Regulation, 1910: TNA, MEPO 2/1199.

25. Bridewell Hospital, Minutes of the Court of Governors: BMM, BCB 4, ff. 147v, 230r, 240r, 242r, 345r, 366v, 378r, 403v, 416r, 418v; BCB 5, ff. 101v, 108v, 128r, 163r–164r, 351v.

26. On the numbers in the court books, see Griffiths, *Lost Londons*, pp. 19–21; Dabhoiwala, 'Summary Justice', pp. 796–9, 806. The last entry for a hawker arrested simply for food selling appears in 1676, in Bridewell Hospital, Minutes of the Court of Governors: BMM, BCB 13, p. 324.

27. Beattie, *Policing and Punishment*, pp. 92–5.

28. In the first extant charge book, which covers just under three years, only eighteen identifiable hawkers were charged. See Lord Mayor's Charge Books: LMA, CLA/004/01/02/001, ff. 116v–117r, 139v, 190v, 233v. The next decade, mayor William Ashurst dealt with 216 offences each year, as quantified in Beattie, *Policing and Punishment*, p. 96.

29. Gray, *Crime, Prosecution and Social Relations*, pp. 19–20. For similar courts beyond the City, see Mehta, 'Summary Justice', p. 57.

30. Like the mayor's charge books, the records of these sittings are incomplete. To give reasonable coverage, I have examined the records from the Mansion House November 1784–April 1785 (LMA, CLA/004/02/001–006), January–July 1790 (LMA, CLA/004/02/055–060), November 1800–September 1803 (LMA, CLA/004/02/066–072), August 1819–August 1821 (LMA, CLA/004/02/073) and from the Guildhall all remaining records May 1752–June 1781 (LMA,

CLA/005/01/001–013) and March 1790–April 1791 (LMA, CLA/005/01/ 044–047). On the volume of business, see Gray, *Crime, Prosecution and Social Relations*, pp. 167–8.

31. On the earlier structures of officeholding, see Beattie, *Policing and Punishment*, pp. 114–16, 158–9, 163–5. On these mid-eighteenth-century innovations, see Beattie, *Policing and Punishment*, pp. 172–97; Emsley, *English Police*, pp. 19–20; Reynolds, *Before the Bobbies*, pp. 16–25.

32. Emsley, *English Police*, pp. 20–1; Reynolds, *Before the Bobbies*, pp. 85–6.

33. Emsley, *English Police*, pp. 26, 60; Reynolds, *Before the Bobbies*, p. 149.

34. Reynolds, *Before the Bobbies*, pp. 85–6; Gray, *Crime, Policing and Punishment*, pp. 206–7; Davis, 'Poor Man's System of Justice', pp. 311–12.

35. Davis, 'Poor Man's System of Justice', p. 312. The sample was created by using keyword search for 'police' and 'costermonger' on *British Library Newspapers*. To tighten the parameters, I only used reports from four newspapers: the *Morning Post*, *Standard*, *Daily News*, and *Lloyd's Illustrated*. As well as providing the highest number of results, these four papers offer a reasonable diversity of political orientations and publication types (weekly or daily).

36. Of the 868 cases identified, the first charge mentioned in 266 was a personal crime (such as assault, murder, or rape) and in 252 it was a property crime (the likes of burglary, theft, or robbery). Of the remainder, 110 cases involved some form of general disorder (including drunkenness, gambling, and swearing), 96 involved street obstruction, 48 involved animal cruelty, 32 involved improper weights and measures, 16 involved selling unfit food, 12 involved Sunday trading, and 7 involved causing a nuisance (usually noise). The remaining few dozen concerned miscellaneous offences like counterfeiting coins and neglecting children.

37. Mayhew, *London Labour*, vol. 1, p. 16.

38. Out of the sample of 868 police court proceedings, 55 had assaulting a police officer as the first charge listed. For an example of police violence against hawkers, see *Times*, 21 November 1867, p. 9.

39. Inwood, 'Policing London's Morals', pp. 129–31, 142–4; Davis, *Law Breaking and Law Enforcement*, pp. 185–9.

40. On the early history of officeholders and arrest, see Miller, 'Touch of the State'.

41. Beattie, *Policing and Punishment*, pp. 24–31; King, 'Summary Courts and Social Relations', pp. 126–7; Dabhoiwala, 'Summary Justice'; Gray, *Crime, Prosecution and Social Relations*, pp. 167–9.

42. Lord Mayor's Charge Books: LMA, CLA/004/01/02/005, entries for 10 October 1732. For similar leniency elsewhere, see Mansion House Justice Room, Minute Books: LMA, CLA/004/02/057, entries for 24 March 1790; CLA/004/02/071, entries for 18 April 1803.

43. *Times*, 2 December 1867, p. 11.

44. Colquhoun, *Treatise on the Police*, pp. vii–viii.

45. Mayhew, *London Labour*, vol. 1, pp. 2–3.

46. Bridewell Hospital, Minutes of the Court of Governors: BMM, BCB 4, f. 345r.

47. Bridewell Hospital, Minutes of the Court of Governors: BMM, BCB 5, f. 108v; Griffiths, 'Meanings of Nightwalking', pp. 222–3.

48. Dabhoiwala, 'Pattern of Sexual Immorality', pp. 92–4; Henderson, *Disorderly Women*, pp. 14–18; Taverner, 'Consider the Oyster Seller', pp. 10–14.

49. On the similar profile of sex workers to those in earlier periods, see Walkowitz, *Prostitution and Victorian Society*, pp. 15–16, 23–5.

50. Middleton, *View of the Agriculture*, pp. 336–7.

51. On investigations into milk adulteration and the extent of the problem, see Atkins, 'Sophistication Detected', pp. 319–23; Wohl, *Endangered Lives*, pp. 21–2, 52–4.

52. *Morning Post*, 15 October 1857, pp. 7–8; *Daily News*, 24 August 1871, p. 2.

53. *Daily News*, 9 September 1897, p. 3.

54. Mayhew, *London Labour*, vol. 1, p. 61.

55. *Lloyd's Illustrated Newspaper*, 15 October 1882, p. 1.

56. *Morning Post*, 16 July 1842, p. 7.

57. Middlesex Sessions, Sessions Book 560: LMA, MJ/SB/B/0055, pp. 72–3; Sessions Book 575: MJ/SB/B/0056, pp. 46–7; Sessions Book 653: MJ/SB/B/0064, pp. 57–8, Sessions Book 729: MJ/SB/B/0072, pp. 65–6. See also City of London Sessions, Sessions Papers, Presentment of the Grand Jury, May 1716: *LL*, LMSLPS150270027.

58. Lord Mayor's Charge Books: LMA, CLA/004/01/02/002, f. 51r.

59. On the campaign, see Shoemaker, 'Reforming the City'; Hitchcock and Shoemaker, *London Lives*, pp. 34–42, 58–60, 107–21.

60. *Morning Post*, 15 December 1875, p. 7; *Daily News*, 16 April 1878, p. 3.

61. Mayhew, *London Labour*, vol. 1, p. 196. For details of the game, see Trial of James Dorset, George Manners, January 1813: *OBPO*, t18130113-62.

62. Bridewell Hospital, Minutes of the Court of Governors: BMM, BCB 6, f. 421r; BCB 7, f. 133r; BCB 15, p. 257; *LL*, BBBRMG202020098.

63. Parker, *English Sabbath*, pp. 118–19; Capp, *England's Culture Wars*, pp. 100–9. For examples of complaints, see City of London Sessions, Sessions Papers, Presentment of the Grand Jury, December 1692: *LL*, LMSLPS150030163; Presentment of the Grand Jury, April 1787: *LL*, LMSLPS150980043. See also Smith, 'Market Place', p. 164.

64. For example, see St Clement Danes, Vestry Minutes: *LL*, WCCDMV362090073. See also the discussion of churchyards in Chapter 5.

65. *PP, Select Committee of the House of Lords on Unnecessary Trading on Sunday in the Metropolis*, qq. 1293–6.

66. Inwood, 'Policing London's Morals', p. 134. For an alternative view, see Green, 'Street Trading', pp. 141–4. For evidence from Police Commissioner Richard Mayne, see *PP, Select Committee of the House of Lords on Unnecessary Trading on Sunday in the Metropolis*, qq. 1395–6, 1434, 1441, 1449.

67. Harrison, 'Sunday Trading Riots', pp. 220–5; White, *London in the Nineteenth Century*, pp. 369–70.

68. *Standard*, 5 April 1869, p. 7.

69. *Daily News*, 18 December 1871, p. 2; *Lloyd's Illustrated Newspaper*, 31 December 1871, p. 2.

70. *Daily News*, 19 January 1872, p. 3.

71. *Lloyd's Illustrated Newspaper*, 18 February 1872, p. 7.

72. *Lloyd's Illustrated Newspaper*, 5 May 1872, p. 7.

73. *Daily News*, 8 June 1872, p. 6.

74. *Lloyd's Illustrated Newspaper*, 28 July 1872, p. 8.

75. Taverner, 'Moral Marketplaces', p. 12.

76. On obstructions by traders in Southwark, see Taverner, 'Selling Food in the Streets', pp. 183–4.

77. 57 George III c. 29: Metropolitan Paving Act 1817.

78. 2 & 3 Victoria c. 47: Metropolitan Police Act 1839.

79. St Dunstan in the West Precinct, Register of Presentments of the Wardmote Inquest: LMA, CLC/W/JB/044/MS03018/001, f. 95v; Mansion House Justice Room, Minute Books: LMA, CLA/004/02/006, entries for 6 April 1785.

80. Statistical Society of London, 'Police of the Metropolis', pp. 97, 101–2.

81. For example, see the orders in St Bride Fleet Street, Vestry Minute Books: LMA, P69/BRI/B/001/MS06554/004, f. 40r; St Clement Danes, Vestry Minutes: *LL*, WCCDMV362070300; Middlesex Sessions, Sessions Papers, Order of the Middlesex Justices on Wheelbarrows and Other Abuses, 11 October 1716: *LL*, LMSMPS501570078.

82. See Guildhall Justice Room, Minute Books: LMA, CLA/005/01/004, entries for 15 December 1775; Mansion House Justice Room, Minute Books: LMA, CLA/004/02/001, entries for 22 and 25 November 1784.

83. Middlesex Sessions, Sessions Papers, Report of High Constable John Mills, 8 September 1716: *LL*, LMSMPS501550039.

84. Mayhew, *London Labour*, vol. 1, p. 20.

85. *PP, Select Committee on the London (City) Traffic Regulation Bill*, appendix 1, pp. 47–8.

86. *Lloyd's Illustrated Newspaper*, 5 July 1885, p. 3; *Morning Post*, 21 August 1889, p. 6; *Daily News*, 29 September 1892, p. 7.

87. *PP, Royal Commission on London Traffic. Volume 1*, pp. 86–8.

88. Cavert, *Smoke of London*, p. 79; Skelton, *Sanitation*, pp. 162–3.

89. *Lloyd's Illustrated Newspaper*, 13 June 1875, p. 4.

90. Mayhew, *London Labour*, vol. 1, pp. 58–9.

91. Metropolitan Police Orders, 17 April 1882: TNA, MEPO 2/199.

92. Instructions to the Street Keeper of Newington Vestry, 15 December 1885: TNA, HO 45/9513/18010.

93. Report on the History of Costermonger Regulation, 1910: TNA, MEPO 2/1199. On these proposals, see Letter from Town Clerk of the City of Westminster to the Commissioner of Police, 24 July 1908: TNA, MEPO 2/1199.

94. On the clearances, see *Morning Post*, 11 February 1852, p. 8; *Morning Post*, 28 July 1852, p. 7.

95. For example, see Letter from Metropolitan Police to Home Secretary, 12 January 1900: TNA, HO 45/9734/A53794; Metropolitan Police, Reports from Acting Superintendent of Hammersmith Station, 1 April 1901 and 6 June 1903: TNA, MEPO, 2/456.
96. *PP, Royal Commission on Market Rights*, vol. 2, qq. 3688–90.
97. *PP, Royal Commission on Market Rights*, vol. 2, qq. 3575–86.
98. *PP, Royal Commission on Market Rights*, vol. 2, qq. 3790–9, 3866–7, 3889–99.
99. Metropolitan Police, Police Notice, Regulations for Costermongers, 28 December 1869: TNA, MEPO 2/1199.
100. Metropolitan Police, Draft Regulations for Costermongers, 1869: TNA, MEPO 2/9424.
101. London County Council Public Control Committee, *London Markets*, p. 19.
102. London County Council Public Control Department, *Street Markets*, p. 3.
103. *PP, Report of the Committee on Street Trading*, pp. 13–15.
104. London School of Economics, *New Survey*, pp. 298–9.
105. For an example of how this process operates, see Hummel, 'Disobedient Markets', p. 1532.

CHAPTER 9

1. *Pall Mall Gazette*, 15 July 1876, pp. 4–5.
2. For a recent study of other kinds of criers, see Jensen, *Ballad-Singer*, ch. 3.
3. Jonson, *Epicœne, or The Silent Woman*, act 1, scene 1.
4. *Spectator*, 18 December 1711.
5. Swift, *Journal to Stella*, vol. 2, p. 581.
6. Smollett, *Expedition of Humphrey Clinker*, p. 120.
7. Bailey, 'Breaking the Sound Barrier', pp. 23–4.
8. For example, see Smith, 'What Means This Noise?', p. 25; Sterne, 'Sonic Imaginations', p. 9.
9. Anon., 'Common Cries of London Town'.
10. Anon., 'Excellent New Ditty'.
11. On the untuneful characterization of hawkers' sounds on stage, see Korda, 'Gender at Work', p. 133; Korda, *Labors Lost*, pp. 144–5.
12. Marsh, *Music and Society*, pp. 44–6.
13. Garrioch, 'Sounds of the City', pp. 24–5.
14. *Spectator*, 18 December 1711.
15. *St James's Chronicle*, 3–6 May 1788, p. 2.
16. On the link between the famous image and the Cries, see Shesgreen, 'William Hogarth's "Enraged Musician"'.
17. *Times*, 2 May 1856, p. 9.
18. *Examiner*, 14 November 1857, p. 10.
19. For example, see *Standard*, 17 December 1879, p. 3; *Daily News*, 8 September 1882, p. 3.

20. Sterne, *Audible Past*, pp. 22–3, 62–3.

21. Picker, 'Aural Anxieties and the Advent of Modernity', pp. 603, 607–8; Picker, *Victorian Soundscapes*, p. 6.

22. On interpreting the street music campaign, see Picker, 'Soundproof Study'; Picker, *Victorian Soundscapes*, pp. 44–5.

23. This is an old argument, appearing for example in Schafer, *Soundscape*, pp. 66–7. For a recent version, see Sharma, 'Food Cries, Historical City Sounds'.

24. Smith, *Acoustic World*, pp. 57–60.

25. Garrioch, 'Sounds of the City', p. 21.

26. Picker, *Victorian Soundscapes*, p. 4.

27. Mayhew, *London Labour*, vol. 1, pp. 45, 51–2.

28. This translates as, 'We buy mattresses, drums, fridges...or any old metal that you're selling!' See Kirk Semple, 'Who's That Voice Asking for Scrap Metal in Mexico? A 10-Year-Old Girl', *New York Times*, 12 October 2016, <https://www.nytimes.com/2016/10/13/world/what-in-the-world/whos-that-voice-asking-for-scrap-metal-in-mexico-a-10-year-old-girl.html>.

29. Anon., 'Cries of London'.

30. For introductions to the broadside ballad, see Watt, *Cheap Print and Popular Piety*; Fumerton, *Unsettled*; Marsh, *Music and Society*.

31. On crying as advertisement, see Smith, *Acoustic World*, pp. 63–4.

32. Tuer, *Old London Street Cries*, p. 64.

33. Hindley, *History of the Cries*, pp. 20–2. However, the claim should be treated sceptically, because Mayhew, one of Hindley's sources, describes hawkers using both versions. See Mayhew, *London Labour*, vol. 1, pp. 51–2.

34. On evaluating street music and using such ethnographic evidence, see Watt, 'Street Music in London in the Nineteenth Century', pp. 9–10. An important study of older Cries music was published soon after. See Bridge, *Old Cryes*.

35. Williams, Broadwood, and Gilchrist, 'London Street Cries'.

36. Gilchrist, 'Note on the "Lavender" and Some Other Cries', pp. 75–6. On Parisian cries, see Boutin, *City of Noise*, p. 59.

37. For copies of the scores, see Brett, *Consort Songs*. For recordings available on streaming platforms, see Fretwork with Paul Nicholson and Red Byrd, *Cries and Fancies: Fantasias, In Nomines and the Cries of London* (London: Virgin Classics, 1989).

38. The V-shape was also suggested in Gilchrist, 'Note on the "Lavender" and Some Other Cries', pp. 75–6.

39. See Rasmussen, 'Sales and Survival', pp. 319–20; Hajar, 'Street Cries in English and Indonesian', pp. 60–1.

40. On Savage's biography, see Burrows, 'Savage, William'. For an introduction to catches and glees, see Price, *Music from the Canterbury Catch Club*.

41. William Savage, 'Come Buy My Watercresses', from 'Odes, Duets, and Other Vocal Compositions': British Library, Add Ms 31814, f. 63v.

42. Gardiner, *Music of Nature*, p. 312.

43. Gardiner, *Music of Nature*, pp. 319–21; Hindley, *History of the Cries*, pp. 212–14, 218–20.
44. Gardiner, *Music of Nature*, pp. 318–19.
45. For examples of these, see William Savage, 'Hot Loaves', from 'Odes, Duets, and Other Vocal Compositions': British Library, Add Ms 31814, f. 63v; Gardiner, *Music of Nature*, p. 312.
46. Kreutzfeldt, 'Street Cries and the Urban Refrain', pp. 68–74.
47. Schafer, *Soundscape*, p. 64; Garrioch, 'Sounds of the City', p. 8. On such techniques in preaching, see Hunt, *Art of Hearing*, pp. 84–91.
48. On performances in the street markets, see Sims, 'Kerbstone London', p. 380; Kelley, *Cheap Street*, pp. 159–60.
49. *Times*, 2 November 1864, p. 5.
50. Tuer, *Old London Street Cries*, pp. 30–1.
51. Williams, Broadwood, and Gilchrist, 'London Street Cries', pp. 57–8.
52. Smith, *Cries of London*, pp. 7–9.
53. Truax, *Acoustic Communication*, pp. 58–61; Schafer, *Soundscape*, pp. 9–10.
54. Garrioch, 'Sounds of the City', p. 14; Smith, *Acoustic World*, pp. 46, 52–6.
55. On this 'sonic continuum', see Truax, *Acoustic Communication*, pp. 43–7. For an application of this model to street cries, see Smith, *Acoustic World*, pp. 67–8.
56. Sound scholar Jacob Kreutzfelt persuasively linked street cries to Deleuze and Guattari's notion of the 'refrain', in 'Street Cries and the Urban Refrain', p. 68.
57. On the well-established connection between time and the acoustic community, see Truax, *Acoustic Communication*, pp. 65–9; Corbin, 'Identity, Bells', pp. 190–2; Smith, *Acoustic World*, pp. 46–7; Garrioch, 'Sounds of the City', pp. 10–14.
58. Gay, 'Trivia', p. 189.
59. 'Green Hastens', in Craig, *Itinerant Traders*.
60. *Standard*, 16 December 1879, p. 2.
61. On Gay's reference points, see Braund, 'Walking the Streets of Rome'.
62. Anon., 'London Street Cries'.
63. Knight, 'Street Noises', pp. 133–4, 137.
64. Tuer, *Old London Street Cries*, pp. 61–2.
65. Mayhew, *London Labour*, vol. 1, p. 8.
66. Tuer, *Old London Street Cries*, pp. 58–60. On the link between sound and socio-economic change, see Wilson, 'Plagues, Fairs, and Street Cries'.
67. Boutin, *City of Noise*, pp. 129–30; Karlin, *Street Songs*, p. 144.
68. On this grid structure, see Shesgreen, *Images of the Outcast*, pp. 28–31.
69. Dillon, *Sense of Sound*, p. 90.
70. Val, *In Search of Song*, p. 139.
71. Bass, *Street Music in the Metropolis*, pp. 76–8.
72. Sala, 'Cries of London', pp. 132–5.
73. Food sellers were still mentioned by the MP's correspondents, in Bass, *Street Music in the Metropolis*, pp. 16–17, 105–8. On the campaign's lack of success, even against organ grinders, see Picker, *Victorian Soundscapes*, p. 77.

74. On such continuities in towns across Europe, see Garrioch, 'Sounds of the City', p. 25.
75. On hi-fi and lo-fi soundscapes, see Schafer, *Soundscape*, p. 71; Truax, *Acoustic Communication*, p. 57.
76. For discussions of sound and urban modernity, see Thompson, *Soundscape of Modernity*; Bailey, 'Breaking the Sound Barrier'; Boutin, *City of Noise*.
77. *Pall Mall Gazette*, 15 July 1876, pp. 4–5; *Standard*, 16 December 1879, p. 2; *Standard*, 17 December 1879, p. 3; *Pall Mall Gazette*, 21 March 1895, p. 4.
78. *Daily News*, 7 December 1892, p. 3; *Standard*, 7 December 1892, p. 3; *Standard*, 11 January 1893, p. 6.
79. *Standard*, 29 June 1898, p. 3. This inaction prompted some anger in the newspapers. See *Standard*, 4 July 1898, p. 2; *Morning Post*, 28 July 1898, p. 2.
80. *Standard*, 30 June 1900, p. 3; *Standard*, 20 October 1900, p. 3; *Times*, 10 December 1903, p. 8; *Times*, 3 June 1910, p. 10.
81. Mayhew, *London Labour*, vol. 1, pp. 9–10.
82. The Gentle Author, 'The Cries of London', *British Library*, accessed 27 May 2020, <https://www.bl.uk/romantics-and-victorians/articles/the-cries-of-london>.
83. Kelley, *Cheap Street*, p. 178. On the 'Cryes of Rome' in a 1607 play, see Bretz, 'Sung Silence'.
84. Shaw, *Pygmalion*.
85. *Oliver!*, directed by Carol Reed (Romulus Films, 1968).
86. *Times*, 5 April 1999, p. 23; Taylor, 'Lionel Bart', pp. 483–4, 487–90.

EPILOGUE

1. London School of Economics, *New Survey*, ch. 13.
2. For these specific sections, see Benedetta, *Street Markets*, pp. 61–5, 105, 113–15.
3. Benedetta, *Street Markets*, p. 9.
4. City of London Police, General Order for Street Traders, 26 August 1912: LMA, CLA/048/AD/07/023.
5. London School of Economics, *New Survey*, pp. 298–9; Kelley, *Cheap Street*, pp. 39–40.
6. City of London Police, Summary of Returns of Street Traders, February 1930: LMA, CLA/048/AD/07/031.
7. London School of Economics, *New Survey*, pp. 310–12; Benedetta, *Street Markets*, p. 179.
8. London School of Economics, *New Survey*, pp. 299–300.
9. On this chronology, see Kelley, *Cheap Street*, pp. 3–4, 6; White, *London in the Twentieth Century*, pp. 247–8.
10. A recently published DVD version is available at Rank Organisation, *Look at Life. Volume 7: Business and Industry* (Network, 2015).
11. Forshaw and Bergström, *Markets of London*, pp. 31–2.
12. On these factors, see White, *London in the Twentieth Century*, pp. 12–16, 30–2, 197–9, 308–18.

13. Richard McComb, 'Streets Ahead: The Latest Trends in Street Food', *Caterer*, 9 June 2017, <https://www.thecaterer.com/products/food-drink/streets-ahead-the-latest-trends-in-street-food>; Emma Weinbren, 'Street Food: The New Trends Shaping Foodie Culture', *Grocer*, 12 September 2018, <https://www.thegrocer.co.uk/trend-reports/street-food-the-new-trends-shaping-foodie-culture/571368.article>.

14. Barack Obama (@BarackObama), 8 June 2018, *Twitter*, <https://twitter.com/BarackObama/status/1005117568913412098?s=20>.

15. For example, see Agyeman, Matthews, and Sobel, *Food Trucks, Cultural Identity, and Social Justice*.

16. Concha, 'Curation of the Street Food Scene', pp. 215–16; Concha, 'Curators of Markets, Designers of Place', pp. 72, 75.

17. Concha, 'Curation of the Street Food Scene', pp. 242, 246. On the related issue of gentrification in 'food quarters' like Borough Market, see Parham, *Market Place*, pp. 3–4.

18. James McAllister, 'Jonathan Downey Liquidates Street Food Businesses', *Big Hospitality*, 16 October 2020, <https://www.bighospitality.co.uk/Article/2020/10/16/Jonathan-Downey-liquidates-street-food-businesses-operating-company-Dinerama-Hawker-House-Giant-Robot-and-Model-Market>. See also Sophie Witts, 'Market Halls' Future at "Real Risk" as It Launches CVA Proposals', *Caterer*, 1 June 2021, <https://www.thecaterer.com/news/market-halls-london-cva-proposal-reopening>.

19. P-Three, 'F-Hubs: The New Generation of Food Halls', accessed 26 September 2021, <https://www.p-three.co.uk/f-hubs-2021-report>.

20. International Labour Organization, 'ILO Monitor: COVID-19 and the World of Work'.

21. Allison, Ray, and Rohel, 'Mobilizing the Streets', pp. 2–4.

22. These are just highlights of a deep seam of work that have been influential for this present study. See Cross, *Informal Politics*; Rosales, *Fruteros*; Tinker, *Street Foods*; Roever and Skinner, 'Street Vendors and Cities'.

23. Parasecoli, 'Eating on the Go'.

24. Jay Fai's success has not prevented trouble for Bangkok's hawkers. For example, see Rina Chandran, 'Bangkok Street Vendors: From Michelin Star to Fighting Eviction', *Reuters*, 17 September 2018, <https://www.reuters.com/article/us-thailand-rights-lawmaking-idUSKCN1LX23V>.

25. Bhowmik, 'Street Vendors in Asia', p. 2259; Bender, 'Dipping in the Common Sauce Pot', pp. 79–81.

26. Krishnendu Ray, 'Re-thinking Street Food', *SOAS Food Studies Centre*, 17 January 2019, <https://www.soas.ac.uk/foodstudies/forum/lectures/17jan2019-re-thinking-street-food.html>.

Appendix: Identifying street sellers, 1600–1825

To present a more rounded picture of street selling before the nineteenth century, I used a variety of sources to build a dataset of individual street sellers and street selling incidents. This approach was first developed in my 2019 PhD thesis, covering the period 1600–1750, and was extended up to 1825 for the present study. Its methodology was influenced by several ongoing projects on the themes of gender and work (most notably in the UK, the *Forms of Labour* project at the University of Exeter), and digital humanities projects such as *London Lives*. The aim was to create an 'archive' of information about hawkers, taking different forms of evidence and placing them in a structure suitable for quantitative and qualitative analysis.

The 858 individual street sellers and 443 acts of street selling were drawn from two bodies of material. The first consisted of incidental descriptions found in depositions to the diocese of London's consistory court, witness statements in Old Bailey trials, biographies in the *Ordinary of Newgate's Account*, and the working papers of the Middlesex and City of London sessions. The second set of sources were produced when hawkers were being regulated by metropolitan authorities. These included the minutes of Bridewell's court of governors, summary proceedings held by the mayor and City aldermen, an early seventeenth-century book of fines, and records of local bodies such as wards and parishes. For each of the individuals we have at least their name and what they were selling. The incidents of street selling can all be linked to a specific year.

Because of the nature of the sources involved, the dataset is inevitably uneven. Of the individuals, 102 (11.9 per cent) come from the years up to 1675, 240 (28.0 per cent) from 1676–1750, and 516 (60.1 per cent) from 1751–1825. Of the incidents, 55 (12.4 per cent) derive from the first third of the sample period, 124 (28.0 per cent) from the second, and 264 (59.6 per cent) from the third. Most of this imbalance is due to the presence of the Old Bailey records, which only begin towards the end of the seventeenth century and expand dramatically in volume thereafter. This also contributes to the different weighting of sources within each stretch of time. Of the street selling individuals in the first third of the period, exactly half (51) were identified at Bridewell prison. In that segment, records of parishes, wards, and the church courts are also prominent. The proportion of individuals identified from Old Bailey trials rises from 39.6 per cent (95) in the second third of the period to 94.6 per cent (488) in the final third.

Using this approach requires flexibility as well as awareness of the material's limitations. The diversity of sources is a strength, but also limits the opportunities for robust statistical analysis. When I quote figures, as I do throughout the book, I stress that they need to be read with care and only provide broad indications of patterns. Building the sample, I had to exercise judgement, for example when locating parishes of residence and how exactly hawkers were trading (for men in particular, I did not include any individuals merely described as a 'milkman', a title that was potentially misleading). I also had to take the descriptions within these records at face value, knowing that we lack corroborating evidence for most of the details provided. Despite these considerations, this is the largest collection of references so far compiled about irregular food selling in London. It provides the foundation for a richer, long-term history of hawkers and hawking.

Bibliography

ARCHIVAL SOURCES

Bethlem Museum of the Mind, Beckenham (BMM)
BCB 4–15: Bridewell Hospital, Minutes of the Court of Governors, 1598–1689

British Library
Add Ms 31814: Odes, Duets, and Other Vocal Compositions, Chiefly in Full Score, Followed, at f. 79, by Some Violin Pieces by William Savage. At the End, f. 95, is a Miscellaneous Collection of Pieces for Organ and Pianoforte, Chiefly Transcribed by R. J. S. Stevens

Guildhall Library, London (GL)
Ms 5570/1–6: Company of Fishmongers, Minute Books of the Court of Assistants, 1592–1752

London Metropolitan Archives (LMA)
CLA/004/01/01/001: Lord Mayor's Waiting Book 1, 1624–6
CLA/004/01/02: Lord Mayor's Charge Books
CLA/004/02: Mansion House Justice Room, Minute Books
CLA/005/01: Guildhall Justice Room, Minute Books
CLA/010/AD/01/002: Order of the Lord Mayor Concerning Billingsgate, December 1699
CLA/043/01/009–015: Verdicts and Presentments of Leet Juries for Guildable Manor, Great Liberty Manor, and King's Manor in Southwark, 1631–1786
CLA/047/LJ/04: City of London Sessions, Session Minute Books, Gaol Delivery, Oyer and Terminer, and Peace
CLA/047/LJ/13: City of London Sessions, Sessions Papers, Gaol Delivery and Peace
CLA/048/AD/07/023: City of London Police, General Orders for Street Traders, 1912–19
CLA/048/AD/07/031: City of London Police, Returns of Street Traders, 1929–30
CLA/062/04/016: Order of a Committee for Gresham Affairs, 24 March 1692
CLC/313/K/C/006/MS25628: St Paul's Cathedral, Dean and Chapter, Peculiar Court, Original Wills
CLC/313/K/C/009/MS19504: St Paul's Cathedral, Dean and Chapter, Peculiar Court, Inventories of the Goods, Chattels, Ready Money and Debts of Deceased Persons

CLC/W/HF/001/MS04069/001–003: Cornhill, Wardmote and Wardmote Inquest Minute and Account Books, 1571–1800

CLC/W/JB/044/MS03018/001: Farringdon Without, St Dunstan in the West Precinct, Register of Presentments of the Wardmote Inquest, 1558–1823

COL/CA/01/01: Court of Aldermen, Repertories

COL/CA/05/01: Court of Aldermen, Papers

COL/CC/01/01: Court of Common Council, Journals

COL/CHD/CM/10/001: Book of Fines for Breach of City Ordinances, 1517–1628

COL/RMD/PA/01: Corporation of London, Remembrancia

DL/AM/PI/01: Diocese of London, Archdeaconry of Middlesex, Probate Inventories

DL/AM/PW: Diocese of London, Archdeaconry of Middlesex, Original Wills

DL/C: Diocese of London, Consistory Court, Depositions Books

DL/C/A/003/MS09189/001: Diocese of London, Consistory Court, Examination or Deposition Books, Chiefly Relating to Libel Actions, 1622–4

DL/C/B/030/MS09174: Diocese of London, Commissary Court of London, Inventories and Declarations

DW/PA/05: Diocese of Winchester, Archdeaconry Court of Surrey, Original Wills

DW/PC/05: Diocese of Winchester, Commissary Court of Surrey, Original Wills

LMA/4305/06/037: J. A. Groom, *The Poor Watercress Sellers of London* (1871)

MJ/SB/B: Middlesex Sessions of the Peace, Sessions Books

MJ/SP: Middlesex Sessions of the Peace, Sessions Papers

P69/BOT2/B/001/MS09236: St Botolph Aldgate, Vestry Minute and Memoranda Book, 1583–1640

P69/BRI/B/001/MS06554/001–005: St Bride Fleet Street, Vestry Minute Books, 1644–1767

P69/DUN2/B/001/MS03016/001–002: St Dunstan in the West, Vestry Minute Books, 1558–1749

Mercers' Company Archives, London

Gresham Repertories, 1669–76

Gresham Repertories, 1678–1722

The National Archives, Kew (TNA)

FS 7/25/1184: Register of Friendly Societies, Trade Unions, Rules, and Amendments, Costermongers' Federation, 1899–1900

HO 45/9513/18010: Home Office, Registered Papers on Police Regulations for Costermongers, 1869–89

HO 45/9734/A53794: Home Office, Registered Papers on Street Trading at Broadway, Wimbledon, 1892–1900

HO 45/9960/X2772: Home Office, Registered Papers on Obstruction by Costermongers in Hammersmith, 1884–5

HO 45/10329/134628: Home Office, Registered Papers on Costermongers in King Street, Hammersmith, 1905–6

MEPO 2/199: Metropolitan Police, Office of the Commissioner, Correspondence and Papers on Pedlars, Hawkers, and Costermongers, 1882–9

MEPO 2/456: Metropolitan Police, Office of the Commissioner, Correspondence and Papers on Costermongers in King Street, Hammersmith, 1891–1902

MEPO 2/1199: Metropolitan Police, Office of the Commissioner, Correspondence and Papers on Costermonger Regulations, 1908–12

MEPO 2/9424: Metropolitan Police, Office of the Commissioner, Correspondence and Papers on Regulations for Costermongers, 1924–52

PROB 4: Prerogative Court of Canterbury and Other Probate Jurisdictions, Engrossed Inventories Exhibited from 1660

PROB 11: Prerogative Court of Canterbury and Related Probate Jurisdictions, Will Registers

Westminster Archives Centre (WAC)

F2003–2007: St Martin-in-the-Fields, Vestry Minute Books, 1651–1778

WCB 1–4: Westminster Court of Burgesses, Minute Books, 1610–1714

DIGITAL RESOURCES

17th and 18th Century Burney Newspapers Collection. <https://www.gale.com/intl/c/17th-and-18th-century-burney-newspapers-collection>.

British Library Newspapers. <https://www.gale.com/intl/primary-sources/british-library-newspapers>.

EEBO: Early English Books Online. <https://about.proquest.com/en/products-services/eebo>.

Fumerton, Patricia, dir. *English Broadside Ballad Archive,* <https://ebba.english.ucsb.edu>. (abbreviated as *EBBA*)

Historical Texts. <https://historicaltexts.jisc.ac.uk>.

Hitchcock, Tim, Robert Shoemaker, Clive Emsley, Sharon Howard, Jamie McLaughlin, et al. *The Old Bailey Proceedings Online, 1674–1913* (version 8.0, March 2018). <www.oldbaileyonline.org>. (abbreviated as *OBPO*)

Hitchcock, Tim, Robert Shoemaker, Sharon Howard, Jamie McLaughlin, et al. *London Lives, 1690–1800* (version 2.0, March 2018). <www.londonlives.org>. (abbreviated as *LL*)

Green, Jonathon, *Green's Dictionary of Slang.* <https://greensdictofslang.com/>.

OED Online. <https://www.oed.com>.

The Times Digital Archive. <https://www.gale.com/intl/c/the-times-digital-archive>.

Schürer, Kevin, and Edward Higgs, dirs. *Integrated Census Microdata (I-CeM) Project.* <http://icem.data-archive.ac.uk/>.

UK Parliamentary Papers. <https://parlipapers.proquest.com/parlipapers>.

PARLIAMENTARY PAPERS (*PP*)

Report from the Select Committee on Channel Fisheries (1833). Cd. 676.

Report from the Select Committee on the Fresh Fruit Trade; Together with Minutes of Evidence, and Appendix (1839). Cd. 398.

Report from the Select Committee of the House of Lords, Appointed to Consider of the Bill, Intituled 'An Act to Prevent Unnecessary Trading on Sunday in the Metropolis'; and to Report Thereon to the House; Together with the Minutes of Evidence (1850). Cd. 441.

Special Report from the Select Committee on the London (City) Traffic Regulation Bill; Together with the Proceedings of the Committee, Minutes of Evidence and Appendix (1866). Cd. 174.

Report from the Select Committee of the House of Lords, on the Traffic Regulation (Metropolis) Bill [H.L.], Together with the Proceedings of the Committee, Minutes of Evidence, and Index (1867). Cd. 186.

Report from the Select Committee on Artizans' and Labourers' Dwellings Improvement; Together with the Proceedings of the Committee, Minutes of Evidence, and Appendix (1881). Cd. 358.

First Report of Her Majesty's Commissioners for Inquiring into the Housing of the Working Classes (1885). Cd. 4402.

First Report of the Royal Commission on Market Rights and Tolls. 3 vols (1888–9). Cd. 5550.

Royal Commission on London Traffic. Volume 1. Report of the Royal Commission Appointed to Inquire into and Report Upon the Means of Locomotion and Transport in London (1905). Cd. 2597.

Report of the Committee Appointed by the Secretary of State for the Home Department to Consider the Question of the Regulation of Street Trading in the Metropolitan Police District (1922). Cd. 1624.

ILLUSTRATIONS NOT PICTURED

Amigoni, Jacopo (after). 'Golden Pippins', *c.*1732–9: British Museum, 1873,0809.29.

Craig, William Marshall. *The Itinerant Traders of London in Their Ordinary Costume* (1804): British Library, 10349.h.13.

Laroon, Marcellus (after). 'Buy My Dutch Biskets', 1688: British Museum, L,85.18.

Laroon, Marcellus (after). 'Buy My Flounders', 1688: British Museum, L,85.24.

Laroon, Marcellus (after). 'Colly Molly Puffe', 1688: British Museum, L,85.45.

Laroon, Marcellus (after). 'Hott Bak'd Wardens Hott', 1688: British Museum, L,85.27.

Laroon, Marcellus (after). 'Lilly White Vinegar 3 Pence a Quart', 1688: British Museum, L,85.13.

Laroon, Marcellus (after). 'Twelve Pence a Peck Oysters', 1688: British Museum, L,85.23.

Rijn, Rembrandt van. 'The Pancake Woman', 1635: Fitzwilliam Museum, Cambridge, 23.K.5–202.

Sandby, Paul. 'A Girl with a Basket of Oranges', *c.*1759: Yale Center for British Art, Paul Mellon Collection, B1975.3.223.

Sandby, Paul. 'A Pudding, a Pudding, a Hot Pudding', 1760: British Museum, 1904,0819.566.

Scamell, Edgar, Photograph of Hawker Selling Muffins in London, 1895: Victoria and Albert Museum, E.3608–2000.

Schiavonetti, Luigi, after Francis Wheatley, 'Milk Below Maids', 1793: Yale Center for British Art, Paul Mellon Collection, B2001.2.1680.

Vendramini, Giovanni, after Francis Wheatley. 'Hot Spice Gingerbread Smoaking Hot', 1796: Yale Center for British Art, Paul Mellon Collection, B2001.2.1690.

PUBLISHED WORKS

Adcock, A. St John. 'Leaving the London Theatres'. In *Living London*, edited by George R. Sims (London: Cassell and Company, 1902), vol. 2: pp. 9–14.

Adcock, A. St John. 'Saturday Night in London'. In *Living London*, edited by George R. Sims (London: Cassell and Company, 1902), vol. 2: pp. 378–84.

Adelman, Juliana. *Civilised by Beasts: Animals and Urban Change in Nineteenth-Century Dublin* (Manchester: Manchester University Press, 2020).

Ågren, Maria. 'Conclusion'. In *Making a Living, Making a Difference: Gender and Work in Early Modern European Society*, edited by Maria Ågren (Oxford: Oxford University Press, 2017), pp. 204–20.

Ågren, Maria, ed. *Making a Living, Making a Difference: Gender and Work in Early Modern European Society* (Oxford: Oxford University Press, 2017).

Agyeman, Julian, Caitlin Matthews, and Hannah Sobel, eds. *Food Trucks, Cultural Identity, and Social Justice: From Loncheras to Lobsta Love* (Cambridge, MA: MIT Press, 2017).

Alexander, David. *Retailing in England During the Industrial Revolution* (London: Athlone Press, 1970).

Alexander, Sally. 'Women's Work in Nineteenth-Century London: A Study of the Years 1820–50'. In *The Rights and Wrongs of Women*, edited by Juliet Mitchell and Ann Oakley (Harmondsworth: Penguin, 1976), pp. 59–111.

Alexander, Sally, Anna Davin, and Eve Hostettler. 'Labouring Women: A Reply to Eric Hobsbawm'. *History Workshop Journal* 8, no. 1 (1979): pp. 174–82. <https://doi.org/10.1093/hwj/8.1.174>.

Allison, Noah, Krishnendu Ray, and Jaclyn Rohel. 'Mobilizing the Streets: The Role of Food Vendors in Urban Life'. *Food, Culture & Society* 24, no. 1 (2021): pp. 2–15. <https://doi.org/10.1080/15528014.2020.1860454>.

Almeroth-Williams, Thomas. *City of Beasts: How Animals Shaped Georgian London* (Manchester: Manchester University Press, 2019).

Amato, Joseph. *On Foot: A History of Walking* (New York: New York University Press, 2004).

Anon. 'The Common Cries of London Town, Some Go Up Street, Some Go Down. With Turners Dish of Stuff, or a Gallymausery' (1662): National Library of Scotland, Crawford.EB.841(1), EBBA 33383.

Anon. 'The Cries of London' (1728–63?): British Library, Roxburghe 3.466–7, C.20.f.9.466–467, EBBA 31167.

Anon. 'An Excellent New Ditty; Or, Which Proveth That Women the Best Warriers Be, For They Made the Devill From Earth for to Flee' (1601–40?): British Library, Roxburghe 1.108–9, C.20.f.7.108–109, EBBA 30071.

Anon. 'The Humours of Rag-Fair: Or, the Countryman's Description of Their Several Trades and Callings' (1756–90?): British Library, Roxburghe 3.550–1, C.20.f.9.550–551, EBBA 31251.

Anon. 'Jolly Jack of All Trades, Or, The Cries of London City' (1685–8?): Pepys Library, Magdalene College, Cambridge, Pepys 4.263, EBBA 21924.

Anon. 'The London Commissariat'. *Quarterly Review* 95 (1854): pp. 271–308.

Anon. *The London Fishery Laid Open: Or the Arts of the Fishermen and Fishmongers Set in a True Light. With Some Further Considerations, Arising from the Good Effect the Public Has Received by the Act of Parliament Passed to Prevent the Forestalling and Monopolising of Fish, and the Act for Amending the Same; and Shewing Also How This Evil May Effectually Be Cured* (London, 1759).

Anon. 'London Street Cries', *All the Year Round*, New Series 11, no. 14 (1874): pp. 372–5.

Archer, Ian. 'Hugh Alley, Law Enforcement and Market Regulation in the Later Sixteenth Century'. In *Hugh Alley's Caveat: The Markets of London in 1598*, edited by Ian Archer, Caroline Barron, and Vanessa Harding (London: London Topographical Society, 1988), pp. 15–29.

Archer, Ian W. *The Pursuit of Stability* (Cambridge: Cambridge University Press, 2002).

Archer, Ian W., Caroline Barron, and Vanessa Harding, eds. *Hugh Alley's Caveat: The Markets of London in 1598. Folger Ms V. a. 318* (London: London Topographical Society, 1988).

Arkell, Tom. 'The Incidence of Poverty in England in the Later Seventeenth Century'. *Social History* 12, no. 1 (1987): pp. 23–47. <https://doi.org/10.1080/03071028708567670>.

Arkell, Tom. 'The Probate Process'. In *When Death Do Us Part: Understanding and Interpreting the Probate Records of Early Modern England*, edited by Nesta Evans and Nigel Goose (Oxford: Leopard's Head Press, 2000), pp. 3–13.

Armfelt, Count E. 'Italy in London'. In *Living London*, edited by George R. Sims (London: Cassell and Company, 1902), vol. 1: pp. 183–9.

Assael, Brenda. *The London Restaurant, 1840–1914* (Oxford: Oxford University Press, 2018).

Atkins, P. J. 'The Growth of London's Railway Milk Trade, c.1845–1914'. *Journal of Transport History* 4, no. 4 (1978): pp. 208–26.

Atkins, P. J. 'London's Intra-Urban Milk Supply, circa 1790–1914'. *Transactions of the Institute of British Geographers* 2, no. 3 (1977): pp. 383–99. <https://doi.org/10.2307/621838>.

Atkins, P. J. 'The Retail Milk Trade in London, c.1790–1914'. *Economic History Review* 33, no. 4 (1980): pp. 522–37. <https://doi.org/10.2307/2594801>.

Atkins, P. J. 'Sophistication Detected: Or, the Adulteration of the Milk Supply, 1850–1914'. *Social History* 16, no. 3 (1991): pp. 317–39. <http://www.jstor.org/stable/4285958>.

Atkins, Peter. 'The "Charmed Circle"'. In *Animal Cities: Beastly Urban Histories*, edited by Peter Atkins (Abingdon: Routledge, 2016), pp. 53–76.

Baer, William C. 'Housing the Poor and Mechanick Class in Seventeenth-Century London'. *London Journal* 25, no. 2 (November 2000): pp. 13–39. <https://doi.org/10.1179/ldn.2000.25.2.13>.

Bailey, Peter. 'Breaking the Sound Barrier'. In *Hearing History: A Reader*, edited by Mark M. Smith (Athens, GA: University of Georgia Press, 2004), pp. 23–35.

Barnes, Melvyn. *Root & Branch: A History of the Worshipful Company of Gardeners of London* (London: The Worshipful Company of Gardeners of London, 1994).

Barrell, John. *The Dark Side of the Landscape: The Rural Poor in English Painting 1730–1840* (Cambridge: Cambridge University Press, 1983).

Bass, Michael T. *Street Music in the Metropolis: Correspondence and Observations on the Existing Law, and Proposed Amendments* (London: John Murray, 1864).

Beattie, J. M. *Policing and Punishment in London, 1660–1750: Urban Crime and the Limits of Terror* (Oxford: Oxford University Press, 2002).

Beer, E. S. de. 'The Early History of London Street-Lighting'. *History* 25 (1941): pp. 311–24. <https://doi.org/10.1111/j.1468-229X.1941.tb00748.x>.

Bender, Daniel E. 'Dipping in the Common Sauce Pot: Satay Vending and Good Taste Politics in Colonial and Post-Colonial Singapore'. *Food, Culture & Society* 24, no. 1 (2021): pp. 66–83. <https://doi.org/10.1080/15528014.2020.1859921>.

Benedetta, Mary. *The Street Markets of London* (London: John Miles, 1936).

Bennett, Eric. *The Worshipful Company of Carmen of London* (London: Simpkin Marshall, 1952).

Bhowmik, Sharit K. 'Street Vendors in Asia: A Review'. *Economic and Political Weekly* 40, nos 22/23 (2005): pp. 2256–64.

Bichard, Maurice. *Baskets in Europe* (Abingdon: Fyfield Wick Editions, 2008).

Blackman, Janet. 'The Food Supply of an Industrial Town'. *Business History* 5, no. 2 (1963): pp. 83–97. <https://doi.org/10.1080/00076796300000002>.

Bohstedt, John. *The Politics of Provisions: Food Riots, Moral Economy, and Market Transition in England, c. 1550–1850* (Farnham: Ashgate, 2010).

Booth, Charles, ed. *Life and Labour of the People in London*. 17 vols (London: Macmillan, 1902–3).

Boulton, Jeremy. *Neighbourhood and Society: A London Suburb in the Seventeenth Century* (Cambridge: Cambridge University Press, 1987).

Boulton, Jeremy. 'Wage Labour in Seventeenth-Century London'. *Economic History Review* 49, no. 2 (1996): pp. 268–90. <https://doi.org/10.2307/2597916>.

Boutin, Aimée. *City of Noise: Sound and Nineteenth-Century Paris* (Urbana, IL: University of Illinois Press, 2015).

Braund, Susanna Morton. 'Walking the Streets of Rome'. In *Walking the Streets of Eighteenth-Century London: John Gay's Trivia (1716)*, edited by Clare Brant and Susan E. Whyman (Oxford: Oxford University Press, 2007), pp. 149–66.

Brett, Phillip, ed. *Consort Songs*, Musica Britannica 22 (London: Stainer and Bell, 1967).

Bretz, Andrew. 'Sung Silence: Complicity, Dramaturgy, and Song in Heywood's Rape of Lucrece'. *Early Theatre* 19, no. 2 (2016): pp. 101–18. <https://www.jstor. org/stable/90018449>.

Bridge, Frederick. *The Old Cryes of London* (London: Novello and Company, 1921).

Brodie, Marc. ' "Jaunty Individualists" or Labour Activists? Costermongers, Trade Unions, and the Politics of the Poor'. *Labour History Review* 66, no. 2 (2001): pp. 147–64. <https://doi.org/10.3828/lhr.66.2.147>.

Bromley, Ray. 'Street Vending and Public Policy: A Global Review'. *International Journal of Sociology and Social Policy* 20, nos 1/2 (2000): pp. 1–28. <https://doi. org/10.1108/01443330010789052>.

Brunelle, Gayle K. 'Policing the Monopolizing Women of Early Modern Nantes'. *Journal of Women's History* 19, no. 2 (2007): pp. 10–35. <https://doi.org/10.1353/ jowh.2007.0034>.

Buchner, Thomas, and Phillip R. Hoffmann-Rehnitz. 'Introduction: Irregular Economic Practices as a Topic of Modern (Urban) History—Problems and Possibilities'. In *Shadow Economies and Irregular Work in Urban Europe: 16th to Early 20th Centuries*, edited by Thomas Buchner and Phillip R. Hoffmann-Rehnitz (Münster: LIT, 2011), pp. 3–36.

Buck, Anne. *Dress in Eighteenth-Century England* (London: Batsford, 1979).

Burnett, John. 'Eating in the Open Air in England, 1830–1914'. In *Eating Out in Europe: Picnics, Gourmet Dining and Snacks since the Late Eighteenth Century*, edited by Marc Jacobs and Peter Scholliers (Oxford: Berg, 2003), pp. 21–37.

Burnett, John. *England Eats Out: A Social History of Eating Out in England from 1830 to the Present* (Harlow: Pearson, 2004).

Burnett, John. *Plenty and Want: A Social History of Food in England from 1815 to the Present Day* (Abingdon: Routledge, 1989).

Burrows, Donald. 'Savage, William'. *Grove Music Online. Oxford Music Online* (Oxford: Oxford University Press, 2001). <https://doi.org/10.1093/gmo/ 9781561592630.article.24647>.

Calaresu, Melissa. 'Food Selling and Urban Space in Early Modern Naples'. In *Food Hawkers: Selling in the Streets from Antiquity to the Present*, edited by Melissa Calaresu and Danielle van den Heuvel (Abingdon: Routledge, 2016), pp. 107–34.

Calaresu, Melissa, and Danielle van den Heuvel, 'Introduction: Food Hawkers from Representation to Reality'. In *Food Hawkers: Selling in the Streets from Antiquity to the Present*, edited by Melissa Calaresu and Danielle van den Heuvel (Abingdon: Routledge, 2016), pp. 1–18.

Capp, Bernard. *England's Culture Wars: Puritan Reformation and Its Enemies in the Interregnum, 1649–1660* (Oxford: Oxford University Press, 2012).

Capp, Bernard. *When Gossips Meet: Women, Family and Neighbourhood in Early Modern England* (Oxford: Oxford University Press, 2003).

Carlin, Martha. 'Fast Food and Urban Living in Medieval England'. In *Food and Eating in Medieval Europe*, edited by Martha Carlin and Joel T. Rosenthal (London: Hambledon, 1998), pp. 27–51.

Cavert, William M. *The Smoke of London: Energy and Environment in the Early Modern City* (Cambridge: Cambridge University Press, 2016).

Chaloner, W. 'Trends in Fish Consumption'. In *Our Changing Fare: Two Hundred Years of British Food Habits*, edited by T. C. Barker, J. C. McKenzie, and John Yudkin (London: Macgibbon and Kee, 1966), pp. 94–114.

Champion, Matthew. *The Fullness of Time: Temporalities of the Fifteenth-Century Low Countries* (Chicago: University of Chicago Press, 2017).

Charteris, J., P. A. Scott, and J. W. Nottroot. 'The "Free-Ride" Hypothesis: A Second Look at the Efficiency of African Women Headload Carriers'. *South African Journal of Science* 85, no. 1 (1989): pp. 68–71.

Clark, Alice. *Working Life of Women in the Seventeenth Century* (London: Routledge, 1992).

Clark, Peter. *The English Alehouse: A Social History, 1200–1830* (London: Longman, 1983).

Cockayne, Emily. *Hubbub: Filth, Noise & Stench in England 1660–1770* (New Haven: Yale University Press, 2007).

Colquhoun, P. *A Treatise on the Police of the Metropolis*. 5th edn (London, 1797).

Concha, Paz. 'The Curation of the Street Food Scene in London' (PhD, London School of Economics, 2017).

Concha, Paz. 'Curators of Markets, Designers of Place: The Case of the Street Food Scene in London'. *Design Issues* 35, no. 4 (2019): pp. 69–78. <https://doi.org/10.1162/desi_a_00566>.

Corbin, Alain. 'Identity, Bells, and the Nineteenth-Century French Village'. In *Hearing History: A Reader*, edited by Mark M. Smith (Athens, GA: University of Georgia Press, 2004), pp. 184–201.

Corfield, Penelope J. 'Walking the City Streets: The Urban Odyssey in Eighteenth-Century England'. *Journal of Urban History* 16, no. 2 (1990): pp. 132–74. <https://doi.org/10.1177/009614429001600202>.

Corporation of London. *The Lawes of the Market* (London, 1595).

Cox, Nancy. *The Complete Tradesman: A Study of Retailing, 1550–1820* (Aldershot: Ashgate, 2000).

Cox, Nancy. *Retailing and the Language of Goods, 1550–1820* (Farnham: Ashgate, 2015).

Cox, Nancy, and Claire Walsh. ' "Their Shops Are Dens, the Buyer Is Their Prey": Shop Design and Sale Techniques'. In *The Complete Tradesman: A Study of Retailing, 1550–1820* (Aldershot: Ashgate, 2000), pp. 76–115.

Cross, John. 'Street Vendors, and Postmodernity: Conflict and Compromise in the Global Economy'. *International Journal of Sociology and Social Policy* 20, nos 1/2 (2002): pp. 29–51. <https://doi.org/10.1108/01443330010789061>.

Cross, John C. *Informal Politics: Street Vendors and the State in Mexico City* (Stanford, CA: Stanford University Press, 1998).

Crymble, Adam. 'A Comparative Approach to Identifying the Irish in Long Eighteenth-Century London'. *Historical Methods* 48, no. 3 (2015): pp. 141–52. <https://doi.org/10.1080/01615440.2015.1007194>.

Crymble, Adam. 'The Decline and Fall of an Early Modern Slum: London's St Giles "Rookery", c.1550–1850'. *Urban History* 49, no. 2 (2021): pp. 1–25. <https://doi.org/10.1017/S0963926821000183>.

Cunningham, Hugh. 'The Employment and Unemployment of Children in England c.1680–1851'. *Past and Present* 126, no. 1 (1990): pp. 115–50. <https://doi.org/10.1093/past/126.1.115>.

Dabhoiwala, Faramerz. 'The Pattern of Sexual Immorality in Seventeenth- and Eighteenth-Century London'. In *Londinopolis: Essays in the Cultural and Social History of Early Modern London*, edited by Paul Griffiths and Mark S. R. Jenner (Manchester: Manchester University Press, 2000), pp. 86–106.

Dabhoiwala, Faramerz. 'Summary Justice in Early Modern London'. *English Historical Review* 121, no. 492 (2006): pp. 796–822. <https://doi.org/10.1093/ehr/cel107>.

Davidoff, Leonore, and Catherine Hall. *Family Fortunes: Men and Women of the English Middle Class 1780–1850* (Abingdon: Routledge, 2019).

Davin, Anna. *Growing Up Poor: Home, School and Street in London 1870–1914* (London: Rivers Oram Press, 1996).

Davin, Anna. 'Loaves and Fishes: Food in Poor Households in Late Nineteenth-Century London'. *History Workshop Journal* 41 (1996): pp. 167–92. <http://www.jstor.org/stable/4289435>.

Davis, Dorothy. *A History of Shopping* (London: Routledge and Kegan Paul, 1966).

Davis, James. *Medieval Market Morality: Life, Law and Ethics in the English Marketplace, 1200–1500* (Cambridge: Cambridge University Press, 2012).

Davis, Jennifer. 'A Poor Man's System of Justice: The London Police Courts in the Second Half of the Nineteenth Century'. *Historical Journal* 27, no. 2 (1984): pp. 309–35. <http://www.jstor.org/stable/2639178>.

Davis, Jennifer Sandra. 'Law Breaking and Law Enforcement: The Creation of a Criminal Class in Mid-Victorian London' (PhD, Boston College, 1985).

Dickens, Charles. 'The Dangers of the Streets'. *All the Year Round* 15 (24 February 1866): pp. 154–7.

Dickens, Charles. 'The Streets—Morning'. In *Sketches by Boz*, edited by Dennis Walder (London: Penguin, 1995), pp. 69–74.

Dillon, Emma. *The Sense of Sound: Musical Meaning in France, 1260–1330* (New York: Oxford University Press, 2012).

Dodd, George. *The Food of London: A Sketch of the Chief Varieties, Sources of Supply, Probable Quantities, Modes of Arrival, Processes of Manufacture, Suspected Adulteration, and Machinery of Distribution of the Food for a Community of Two Millions and a Half* (London: Longman, Brown, Green and Longmans, 1856).

Donald, Diana. '"Beastly Sights": The Treatment of Animals as a Moral Theme in Representations of London c.1820–1850'. *Art History* 22, no. 4 (1999): pp. 514–44. <https://doi.org/10.1111/1467-8365.00174>.

Doré, Gustave, and Blanchard Jerrold. *London: A Pilgrimage* (London: Grant and Co., 1872).

Dorey, Margaret A. 'Unwholesome for Man's Body?: Concerns about Food Quality and Regulation in London C1600–C1740' (PhD, University of Western Australia, 2011).

Dyos, H. J. 'Urban Transformation: A Note on the Objects of Street Improvement in Regency and Early Victorian London'. *International Review of Social History* 2, no. 2 (1957): pp. 259–65. <https://www.jstor.org/stable/44581363>.

Dyos, H. J., and D. H. Aldcroft. *British Transport: An Economic Survey from the Seventeenth Century to the Twentieth* (Leicester: Leicester University Press, 1971).

Dyos, H. J., and D. A. Reeder. 'Slums and Suburbs'. In *The Victorian City: Images and Realities*, edited by H. J. Dyos and Michael Wolff (London: Routledge and Kegan Paul, 1973), pp. 359–86.

Earle, Peter. *A City Full of People: Men and Women of London 1650–1750* (London: Methuen, 1994).

Earle, Peter. 'The Middling Sort in London'. In *The Middling Sort of People: Culture, Society and Politics in England, 1550–1800*, edited by Jonathan Barry and Christopher Brooks (Basingstoke: Macmillan, 1994), pp. 141–58.

Eden, Frederick. *The State of the Poor: A History of the Labouring Classes in England, with Parochial Reports*, edited by A. G. L. Rogers (London: George Routledge and Sons, 1928).

Edgerton, David. *The Shock of the Old: Technology and Global History since 1900* (London: Profile Books, 2019).

Ekirch, A. Roger. *At Day's Close: A History of Nighttime* (London: Weidenfeld and Nicolson, 2005).

Emsley, Clive. *The English Police: A Political and Social History* (Harlow: Pearson, 1996).

Endelman, Todd. *The Jews of Georgian England, 1714–1830: Tradition and Change in a Liberal Society* (Philadelphia: Jewish Publication Society of America, 1979).

Endelman, Todd M. *The Jews of Britain, 1656–2000* (Berkeley: University of California Press, 2002).

Erickson, Amy Louise. 'Married Women's Occupations in Eighteenth-Century London'. *Continuity and Change* 23, no. 2 (2008): pp. 267–307. <https://doi.org/10.1017/S0268416008006772>.

Erickson, Amy Louise. 'What Shall We Do About the Servants?' *History Workshop Journal*, 67 (2009): pp. 277–86. <http://www.jstor.org/stable/40646229>.

Estabrook, Carl B. *Urbane and Rustic England: Cultural Ties and Social Spheres in the Provinces 1660–1780* (Manchester: Manchester University Press, 1998).

Evelyn, John. *Fumifugium: Or the Inconveniencie of the Aer and Smoak of London Dissipated. Together with Some Remedies Humbly Proposed by J.E. Esq; to His Sacred Majestie and to the Parliament Now Assembled* (London, 1661).

Everitt, Alan. 'The Marketing of Agricultural Produce'. In *The Agrarian History of England and Wales. Volume IV 1500–1640*, edited by Joan Thirsk (Cambridge: Cambridge University Press, 1967), pp. 466–592.

Falkus, Malcolm. 'Lighting in the Dark Ages of English Economic History: Town Streets before the Industrial Revolution', edited by D. C. Coleman and D. H. John (London: Weidenfeld and Nicolson, 1976), pp. 248–73.

Finlay, Roger, and Beatrice Shearer. 'Population Growth and Suburban Expansion'. In *London 1500–1700: The Making of the Metropolis*, edited by A. L. Beier and Roger Finlay (Harlow: Longman, 1986), pp. 37–57.

Flather, Amanda. *Gender and Space in Early Modern England* (Woodbridge: Boydell Press for the Royal Historical Society, 2007).

Forshaw, Alec, and Theo Bergström. *The Markets of London* (Harmondsworth: Penguin, 1983).

Forsyth, Hazel. 'Gingerbread'. In *London Eats Out: 500 Years of Capital Dining* (London: Philip Wilson, 1999), pp. 28–9.

Froide, Amy M. *Never Married: Singlewomen in Early Modern England* (Oxford: Oxford University Press, 2005).

Fumerton, Patricia. *Unsettled: The Culture of Mobility and the Working Poor in Early Modern England* (Chicago: University of Chicago Press, 2006).

Gardiner, William. *The Music of Nature; Or, An Attempt to Prove That What Is Passionate and Pleasing in the Art of Singing, Speaking, and Performing Upon Musical Instruments Is Derived from the Sounds of the Animated World* (London: Longman, Rees, Orme, Brown, Green, and Longman, 1832).

Garrioch, David. 'House Names, Shop Signs and Social Organization in Western European Cities, 1500–1900'. *Urban History* 21, no. 1 (1994): pp. 20–48. <https://www.jstor.org/stable/44612627>.

Garrioch, David. 'Sounds of the City: The Soundscape of Early Modern European Towns'. *Urban History* 30, no. 1 (2003): pp. 5–25. <https://doi.org/10.1017/S0963926803001019>.

Gay, John. 'Trivia: Or, the Art of Walking the Streets of London'. In *Walking the Streets of Eighteenth-Century London: John Gay's Trivia (1716)*, edited by Clare Brant and Susan E. Whyman (Oxford: Oxford University Press, 2007), pp. 169–215.

Gentilcore, David. *Food and Health in Early Modern Europe: Diet, Medicine and Society, 1450–1800* (London: Bloomsbury, 2016).

George, M. Dorothy. *London Life in the Eighteenth Century* (Harmondsworth: Penguin, 1966).

Gerhold, Dorian. *London Bridge and Its Houses, c.1209–1761* (London: London Topographical Society, 2019).

Gilchrist, A. G. 'A Note on the "Lavender" and Some Other Cries'. *Journal of the Folk-Song Society* 6, no. 22 (1919): pp. 73–7. <https://www.jstor.org/stable/4434065>.

Girouard, Mark. *Victorian Pubs* (New Haven: Yale University Press, 1984).

Glasse, Hannah. *The Art of Cookery, Made Plain and Easy* (London, 1788).

Gowing, Laura. *Domestic Dangers: Women, Words, and Sex in Early Modern London* (Oxford: Clarendon Press, 1996).

Gowing, Laura. '"The Freedom of the Streets": Women and Social Space, 1560–1640'. In *Londinopolis: Essays in the Cultural and Social History of Early Modern London*, edited by Paul Griffiths and Mark S. R. Jenner (Manchester: Manchester University Press, 2000), pp. 130–51.

Gray, Drew. *Crime, Policing and Punishment in England, 1660–1914* (London: Bloomsbury, 2016).

Gray, Drew D. *Crime, Prosecution and Social Relations: The Summary Courts of London in the Late Eighteenth Century* (Basingstoke: Palgrave Macmillan, 2009).

Green, David R. *From Artisans to Paupers: Economic Change and Poverty in the London, 1790–1870* (Aldershot: Scolar Press, 1995).

Green, David R. 'Street Trading in London: A Case Study of Casual Labour, 1830–60'. In *The Structure of Nineteenth Century Cities*, edited by James H. Johnson and Colin G. Pooley (Beckenham: Croom Helm, 1982), pp. 129–51.

Greenwood, James. 'Bummarees'. In *Low-Life Deeps: An Account of the Strange Fish to Be Found There* (London: Chatto and Windus, 1876), pp. 79–85.

Greenwood, James. 'London Courts and Alleys'. In *In Strange Company: Being the Experiences of a Roving Correspondent* (London: Henry S. King and Co., 1873), pp. 178–87.

Greenwood, James. 'A Mission Among City Savages'. In *In Strange Company: Being the Experiences of a Roving Correspondent* (London: Henry S. King and Co., 1873), pp. 12–32.

Greenwood, James. 'Only a Coster'. *Railway Review* 1a, no. 9 (10 September 1880): pp. 4–6.

Greenwood, James. 'The South Coast Fishermen'. In *The Wilds of London* (London: Chatto and Windus, 1874), pp. 326–39.

Grew, Francis, and Margrethe de Neergaard. *Shoes and Pattens: Medieval Finds from Excavations in London* (London: Her Majesty's Stationery Office, 1988).

Griffin, Emma. 'Diets, Hunger and Living Standards During the British Industrial Revolution'. *Past & Present* 239, no. 1 (2018): pp. 71–111. <https://doi.org/10.1093/pastj/gtx061>.

Griffiths, Paul. *Lost Londons: Change, Crime, and Control in the Capital, 1550–1660* (Cambridge: Cambridge University Press, 2008).

Griffiths, Paul. 'Meanings of Nightwalking in Early Modern England'. *Seventeenth Century* 13, no. 2 (1998): pp. 212–38. <https://doi.org/10.1080/0268117X.1998.10555448>.

Griffiths, Roger. *An Essay to Prove That the Jurisdiction and Conservancy of the River of Thames, &c. Is Committed to the Lord Mayor, and City of London, Both in Point of Right and Usage, By Prescription, Charters, Acts of Parliament, Decrees, Upon Hearing before the King, Letters-Patents, &c. &c. To Which Is Added. A Brief Description of Those Fish, with Their Seasons, Spawning-Times, &c. That Are Caught in the Thames, or Sold in London. With Some Few Observations on the Nature, Element, Cloathing, Numbers, Passage, Wars, and Sensation, &c. Peculiar to Fish in General. And, Also, of the Water Carriage on the River Thames, to the Several Parts of the Kingdom; with a List of the Keys, Wharfs, and Docks, Adjoining to the Same* (London, 1746).

Hadshar, Rose. '"[T]heir Tales Are Sweet": A Queer Social History of Fishwives in Early Modern London' (MA by Research, University of York, 2016).

Hailwood, Mark. *Alehouses and Good Fellowship in Early Modern England* (Woodbridge: Boydell and Brewer, 2014).

Hailwood, Mark. 'Time and Work in Rural England, 1500–1700'. *Past & Present* 248, no. 1 (2020): pp. 87–121. <https://doi.org/10.1093/pastj/gtz065>.

Hajar, Andi. 'Street Cries in English and Indonesian with Special Reference to Makassarese'. *International Journal of Humanities and Innovation* 2, no. 2 (2019): pp. 59–64. <https://doi.org/10.33750/ijhi.v2i2.41>.

Hamling, Tara, and Catherine Richardson. *A Day at Home in Early Modern England: Material Culture and Domestic Life, 1500–1700* (New Haven: Yale University Press, 2017).

Hanway, J. *A Letter to Mr John Spranger, On His Excellent Proposal For Paving, Cleansing, and Lighting the Streets of Westminster, and the Parishes in Middlesex* (London, 1754).

Harding, Vanessa. *The Dead and the Living in Paris and London, 1500–1670* (Cambridge: Cambridge University Press, 2002).

Harding, Vanessa. 'Families and Housing in Seventeenth-Century London'. *Parergon* 24, no. 2 (2007): pp. 115–38. <https://doi.org/10.1353/pgn.2008.0015>.

Harding, Vanessa. 'The Population of London, 1550–1700: A Review of the Published Evidence'. *London Journal* 15, no. 2 (1990): pp. 111–28. <https://doi.org/10.1179/ldn.1990.15.2.111>.

Harding, Vanessa. 'Shops, Markets and Retailers in London's Cheapside, *c.*1500–1700'. In *Buyers & Sellers: Retail Circuits and Practices in Medieval and Early Modern Europe*, edited by Bruno Blondé, Peter Stabel, Jon Stobart, and Ilja van Damme (Turnhout: Brepols, 2006), pp. 155–70.

Harding, Vanessa. 'Space, Property, and Propriety in Urban England'. *Journal of Interdisciplinary History* 32, no. 4 (2002): pp. 549–69. <https://www.jstor.org/stable/3656145>.

Harley, Joseph. 'Consumption and Poverty in the Homes of the English Poor, *c.*1670–1834'. *Social History* 43, no. 1 (2018): pp. 81–104. <https://doi.org/10.1080/03071022.2018.1394001>.

Harrison, Brian. 'The Sunday Trading Riots of 1855'. *Historical Journal* 8, no. 2 (1965): pp. 219–45.

Hart, Keith. 'Informal Income Opportunities and Urban Employment in Ghana'. *Journal of Modern African Studies* 11, no. 1 (1973): pp. 61–89. <https://www.jstor.org/stable/159873>.

Hartlib, Samuel. *Samuel Hartlib His Legacie: Or an Enlargement of the Discourse of Husbandry Used in Brabant and Flaunders; Wherein Are Bequeathed to the Common-Wealth of England More Outlandish and Domestick Experiments and Secrets in Reference to Universall Husbandry* (London, 1651).

Harvey, Charles, Edmund M. Green, and Penelope J. Corfield. 'Continuity, Change, and Specialization within Metropolitan London: The Economy of Westminster, 1750–1820'. *Economic History Review* 52, no. 3 (1999): pp. 469–93. <http://www.jstor.org/stable/2599141>.

Hayes, Megan. *The London Milk Trail: The Story of Welsh Dairies in the City* (Llanrwst: Gwasg Carreg Gwalch, 2015).

Heglund, N. C., P. A. Willems, M. Penta, and G. A. Cavagna. 'Energy-Saving Gait Mechanics with Head-Supported Loads'. *Nature* 375, no. 6526 (1995): pp. 52–4. <https://doi.org/10.1038/375052a0>.

Henderson, Tony. *Disorderly Women in Eighteenth-Century London: Prostitution and Control in the Metropolis 1730–1830* (Harlow: Pearson Education, 1999).

Hetherington, Jill. 'Dairy-Farming in Islington in the Early Nineteenth Century—the Career of Richard Laycock'. *Transactions of the London & Middlesex Archaeological Society* 38 (1987): pp. 169–85.

Heuvel, Danielle van den. 'Gender in the Streets of the Premodern City'. *Journal of Urban History* 45, no. 4 (2019): pp. 693–710. <https://doi.org/10.1177/0096144218768493>.

Heuvel, Danielle van den. 'Selling in the Shadows: Peddlers and Hawkers in Early Modern Europe'. In *Working on Labor: Essays in Honor of Jan Lucassen*, edited by Marcel van der Linden and Leo Lucassen (Leiden: Brill, 2012), pp. 125–51.

Higgs, Edward. 'Domestic Servants and Households in Victorian England'. *Social History* 8, no. 2 (1983): pp. 201–10. <http://www.jstor.org/stable/4285250>.

Higgs, Edward, and Amanda Wilkinson. 'Women, Occupations and Work in the Victorian Censuses Revisited'. *History Workshop Journal* 81 (2016): pp. 17–38. <https://doi.org/10.1093/hwj/dbw001>.

Hill, Bridget. *Servants: English Domestics in the Eighteenth Century* (Oxford: Oxford University Press, 1996).

Hill, Bridget. *Women Alone: Spinsters in England 1660–1850* (New Haven: Yale University Press, 2001).

Hindle, Steve. *On the Parish? The Micro-Politics of Poor Relief in Rural England c.1550–1750* (Oxford: Oxford University Press, 2004).

Hindley, Charles. *A History of the Cries of London, Ancient and Modern* (London: Reeves and Turner, 1881).

Hinds, Allen B., ed. *Calendar of State Papers Relating to English Affairs in the Archives of Venice: Volume 15, 1617–1619* (London, 1909). <https://www.british-history.ac.uk/cal-state-papers/venice/vol15>.

Hitchcock, David, and Julia McClure, eds. *The Routledge History of Poverty, c.1450–1800* (Abingdon: Routledge, 2021).

Hitchcock, Tim. *Down and Out in Eighteenth-Century London* (London: Hambledon and London, 2004).

Hitchcock, Timothy V., ed., *Richard Hutton's Complaints Book: The Notebook of the Steward of the Quaker Workhouse at Clerkenwell, 1711–1737* (London, 1987). <https://www.british-history.ac.uk/london-record-soc/vol24>.

Hitchcock, Tim, and Robert Shoemaker. *London Lives: Poverty, Crime and the Making of a Modern City, 1690–1800* (Cambridge: Cambridge University Press, 2015).

Hitchcock, Tim, and Heather Shore. 'Introduction'. In *The Streets of London: From the Great Fire to the Great Stink*, edited by Tim Hitchcock and Heather Shore (London: Rivers Oram Press, 2003), pp. 1–9.

Hitchcock, Tim, and Heather Shore, eds. *The Streets of London: From the Great Fire to the Great Stink* (London: Rivers Oram Press, 2003).

Horrell, Sara, and Jane Humphries. 'Women's Labour Force Participation and the Transition to the Male-Breadwinner Family, 1790–1865'. *Economic History Review* 48, no. 1 (1995): pp. 89–117. <https://doi.org/10.2307/2597872>.

Houghton, John. *Husbandry and Trade Improv'd: Being a Collection of Many Valuable Materials Relating to Corn, Cattle, Coals, Hops, Wool, &c.* 4 vols (London, 1728).

Hubbard, Eleanor. *City Women: Money, Sex and the Social Order in Early Modern London* (Oxford: Oxford University Press, 2012).

Hummel, Calla. 'Disobedient Markets: Street Vendors, Enforcement, and State Intervention in Collective Action'. *Comparative Political Studies* 50, no. 11 (2017): pp. 1524–55. <https://doi.org/10.1177/0010414016679177>.

Humphries, Jane. *Childhood and Child Labour in the British Industrial Revolution* (Cambridge: Cambridge University Press, 2010).

Hunt, Arnold. *The Art of Hearing: English Preachers and Their Audiences, 1590–1640* (Cambridge: Cambridge University Press, 2010).

Ingold, Tim. 'Culture on the Ground: The World Perceived Through the Feet'. *Journal of Material Culture* 9, no. 3 (2004): pp. 315–40. <https://doi.org/10.1177/1359183504046896>.

Innes, Joanna. 'Managing the Metropolis: London's Social Problems and Their Control, *c.*1660–1830'. *Proceedings of the British Academy* 107 (2001): pp. 53–79.

International Labour Office, 'Employment, Incomes and Equality: A Strategy for Increasing Productive Employment in Kenya' (Geneva, 1972).

International Labour Organization. 'ILO Monitor: COVID-19 and the World of Work', April 2020. <https://www.ilo.org/global/topics/coronavirus/impacts-and-responses/WCMS_767028/lang--en/index.htm>.

Inwood, Stephen. 'Policing London's Morals: The Metropolitan Police and Popular Culture, 1829–1850'. *London Journal* 15, no. 2 (1990): pp. 129–46. <https://doi.org/10.1179/ldn.1990.15.2.129>.

Ismay, Penelope. *Trust Among Strangers: Friendly Societies in Modern Britain* (Cambridge: Cambridge University Press, 2018).

Jackson, Lee. *Dirty Old London: The Victorian Fight Against Filth* (New Haven: Yale University Press, 2014).

Jankiewicz, Stephen. 'A Dangerous Class: The Street Sellers of Nineteenth-Century London'. *Journal of Social History* 46, no. 2 (2012): pp. 391–415. <https://doi.org/10.1093/jsh/shs096>.

Jeffreys, J. B. *Retail Trading in Britain 1850–1950* (Cambridge: Cambridge University Press, 1954).

Jenner, Mark. 'Circulation and Disorder: London Streets and Hackney Coaches, *c.*1640–*c.*1740'. In *The Streets of London: From the Great Fire to the Great Stink*, edited by Tim Hitchcock and Heather Shore (London: Rivers Oram Press, 2003), pp. 40–53.

Jenner, Mark. 'The Politics of London Air: John Evelyn's Fumifugium and the Restoration'. *Historical Journal* 38, no. 3 (1995): pp. 535–51. <https://doi.org/10.1017/S0018246X00019968>.

Jenner, Mark S. R., and Paul Griffiths. 'Introduction'. In *Londinopolis: Essays in the Cultural and Social History of Early Modern London*, edited by Paul Griffiths and Mark S. R. Jenner (Manchester: Manchester University Press, 2000), pp. 1–23.

Jennings, Paul. *The Local: A History of the English Pub* (Stroud: Tempus, 2007).

Jensen, Oskar Cox. *The Ballad-Singer in Georgian and Victorian London* (Cambridge: Cambridge University Press, 2021).

Jones, Peter T. A. 'Redressing Reform Narratives: Victorian London's Street Markets and the Informal Supply Lines of Urban Modernity'. *London Journal* 41, no. 1 (2016): pp. 60–81. <https://doi.org/10.1179/1749632215Y.0000000013>.

Jonson, Ben. *Epicœne, or The Silent Woman* (London, 1620).

Kalm, Pehr. *Kalm's Account of His Visit to England on His Way to America in 1748*. Translated by Joseph Lucas (London: Macmillan, 1892).

Karlin, Daniel. *Street Songs: Writers and Urban Songs and Cries, 1800–1925* (Oxford: Oxford University Press, 2018).

Kay, Alison C. 'Retailing, Respectability and the Independent Woman in Nineteenth-Century London'. In *Women, Business and Finance in Nineteenth Century Europe*, edited by Robert Beachy, Béatrice Craig, and Alastair Owens (Oxford: Berg, 2006), pp. 152–66.

Kelley, Victoria. *Cheap Street: London's Street Markets and the Cultures of Informality, c.1850–1939* (Manchester: Manchester University Press, 2019).

Kelley, Victoria. 'London's Street Markets: The Shifting Interiors of Informal Architecture'. *London Journal* 45, no. 2 (2020): pp. 189–210. <https://doi.org/1 0.1080/03058034.2019.1703432>.

Kent, D. A. 'Ubiquitous but Invisible: Female Domestic Servants in Mid-Eighteenth Century London'. *History Workshop Journal* 28, no. 1 (1989): pp. 111–28. <https:// doi.org/10.1093/hwj/28.1.111>.

King, Peter. 'The Summary Courts and Social Relations in Eighteenth-Century England'. *Past & Present*, no. 183 (2004): pp. 125–72. <http://www.jstor.org/ stable/3600862>.

Knight, Charles. 'Street Noises'. In *London*, edited by Charles Knight (London: Charles Knight and Co., 1841), vol. 1: pp. 129–44.

Korda, Natasha. 'Gender at Work in the Cries of London'. In *Oral Traditions and Gender in Early Modern Literary Texts*, edited by Mary Ellen Lamb and Karen Bamford (Aldershot: Ashgate, 2008), pp. 117–35.

Korda, Natasha. *Labors Lost: Women's Work and the Early Modern English Stage* (Philadelphia: University of Pennsylvania Press, 2011).

Koslofsky, Craig. *Evening's Empire: A History of the Night in Early Modern Europe* (Cambridge: Cambridge University Press, 2011).

Kostof, Spiro. *The City Assembled: The Elements of Urban Form Through History* (London: Thames and Hudson, 1992).

Kreutzfeldt, Jacob. 'Street Cries and the Urban Refrain: A Methodological Investigation of Street Cries'. *SoundEffects* 2, no. 1 (2012): pp. 61–80.

Laitinen, Riita, and Thomas S. Cohen. 'Cultural History of Early Modern European Streets—An Introduction'. In *Cultural History of Early Modern European Streets*, edited by Riita Laitinen and Thomas V. Cohen (Leiden: Brill, 2009), pp. 1–10.

Lane, Joan. *Apprenticeship in England, 1600–1914* (London: UCL Press, 1996).

Laslett, Peter, ed. *Earliest Classics: John Graunt and Gregory King* (Farnborough: Gregg, 1973).

Lees, Lynn Hollen. *Exiles of Erin: Irish Migrants in Victorian London* (Manchester: Manchester University Press, 1979).

Levenc, Alysa. 'Parish Apprenticeship and the Old Poor Law in London'. *Economic History Review* 63, no. 4 (2010): pp. 915–41. <https://doi.org/10.1111/j.1468-0289. 2009.00485.x>.

Lewis, M. J. T. 'The Origins of the Wheelbarrow'. *Technology and Culture* 35, no. 3 (1994): pp. 453–75. <https://doi.org/10.2307/3106255>.

Linares, Lissette Aliaga. 'The Paradoxes of Informalizing Street Trade in the Latin American City', *International Journal of Sociology and Social Policy* 38, nos 7/8 (2018): pp. 651–72. <https://doi.org/10.1108/IJSSP-09-2017-0119>.

Linebaugh, P. 'The Ordinary of Newgate and His Account'. In *Crime in England 1550–1800*, edited by J. S. Cockburn (London: Methuen, 1977), pp. 246–69.

Lloyd, Paul S. 'Dietary Advice and Fruit-Eating in Late Tudor and Early Stuart England'. *Journal of the History of Medicine and Allied Sciences* 67, no. 4 (2012): pp. 553–86. <https://www.jstor.org/stable/24632080>.

Lloyd, Ray, Bridget Parr, Simeon Davies, and Carlton Cooke. 'No "Free Ride" for African Women: A Comparison of Head-Loading Versus Back-Loading Among Xhosa Women'. *South African Journal of Science* 106, nos 3/4 (2010): pp. 1–5.

London County Council Public Control Committee. *London Markets: Special Report of the Public Control Committee Relative to Existing Markets and Market Rights and as to the Expediency of Establishing New Markets In or Near the Administrative County of London* (London: London County Council, 1893).

London County Council Public Control Department. *Street Markets: Report of the Chief Officer of the Public Control Department as to the Street Markets in the County of London* (London: London County Council, 1901).

London School of Economics. *The New Survey of London Life & Labour. Volume 3: Survey of Social Conditions (1) The Eastern Area* (London: P. S. King and Son, 1932).

Lucas, C. Duncan. 'Coster-Land in London'. In *Living London*, edited by George R. Sims (London: Cassell and Company, 1902), vol. 1: pp. 74–9.

Lupton, Donald. *London and the Country Carbonadoed and Quartred into Severall Characters* (London, 1632).

McEwan, Joanne. 'The Lodging Exchange: Space, Authority and Knowledge in Eighteenth-Century London'. In *Accommodating Poverty: The Housing and Living Arrangements of the English Poor, c.1600–1850*, edited by Joanne McEwan and Pamela Sharpe (Basingstoke: Palgrave Macmillan, 2011), pp. 50–68.

McGrath, Patrick V. 'The Marketing of Food, Fodder and Livestock in the London Area in the Seventeenth Century with Some Reference to the Sources of Supply' (MA, University of London, 1948).

McIntosh, Marjorie Keniston. *Working Women in English Society, 1300–1620* (Cambridge: Cambridge University Press, 2005).

McKellar, Elizabeth. *The Birth of Modern London: The Development and Design of the City 1660–1720* (Manchester: Manchester University Press, 1999).

McManus, John P. 'The Trade and Market in Fish in the London Area During the Early Sixteenth Century, 1485–1563' (MA, University of London, 1952).

McWilliam, Rohan. 'Fancy Repositories: The Arcades of London's West End in the Nineteenth Century'. *London Journal* 44, no. 2 (2019): pp. 93–112. <https://doi.org/10.1080/03058034.2019.1581482>.

McWilliam, Rohan. *London's West End: Creating the Pleasure District, 1800–1914* (Oxford: Oxford University Press, 2020).

Maloiy, G. M. O., N. C. Heglund, L. M. Prager, G. A. Cavagna, and C. R. Taylor. 'Energetic Cost of Carrying Loads: Have African Women Discovered an Economic Way?' *Nature* 319, no. 6055 (1986): pp. 668–9. <https://doi.org/ 10.1038/319668a0>.

Malvery, Olive Christian. 'Gilding the Gutter—My Experiences of Coster Life'. In *The Soul Market, with Which Is Included 'The Heart of Things'* (London: Hutchinson and Co., 1907), pp. 134–50.

Maniates, Maria Rika, and Richard Freedman. 'Street Cries'. *Grove Music Online. Oxford Music Online* (Oxford: Oxford University Press, 2001). <https://doi. org/10.1093/gmo/9781561592630.article.26931>.

Mansell, Charmian. 'The Variety of Women's Experiences as Servants in England (1548–1649): Evidence from Church Court Depositions'. *Continuity and Change* 33, no. 3 (2018): pp. 315–38. <https://doi.org/10.1017/S0268416018000267>.

Marsh, Christopher. *Music and Society in Early Modern England* (Cambridge: Cambridge University Press, 2013).

Massie, Joseph. *An Essay on the Many Advantages Accruing to the Community, from the Superior Neatness, Conveniencies, Decorations and Embellishments of Great and Capital Cities. Particularly Apply'd to the City and Suburbs of London, Renowned Capital of the British Empire* (London, 1754).

Matheson, Julia. 'Common Ground: Horticulture and the Cultivation of Open Space in the East End of London, 1840–1900' (PhD, Open University, 2010).

Matthies, Andrea L. 'The Medieval Wheelbarrow'. *Technology and Culture* 32, no. 2 (1991): pp. 356–64. <https://doi.org/10.2307/3105714>.

Mayhew, Henry. *London Labour and the London Poor*. 4 vols (London: Griffin, Bohn and Co., 1861).

Mearns, Andrew. *The Bitter Cry of Outcast London: An Inquiry into the Condition of the Abject Poor* (London, 1883).

Mehta, Kiran. 'Summary Justice in Eighteenth- and Nineteenth-Century Southwark (London)'. *Crime, histoire & sociétés/Crime, History & Societies* 24, no. 1 (2020): pp. 55–90. <https://doi.org/10.4000/chs.2702>.

Meldrum, Tim. *Domestic Service and Gender 1660–1750: Life and Work in the London Household* (Harlow: Pearson Education, 2000).

Merritt, J. F. *The Social World of Early Modern Westminster* (Manchester: Manchester University Press, 2005).

Middleton, John. *View of the Agriculture of Middlesex* (London, 1798).

Miller, Jonah. 'The Touch of the State: Stop and Search in England, c. 1660–1750'. *History Workshop Journal* 87 (2019): pp. 52–71. <https://doi.org/10.1093/hwj/ dby034>.

Milliot, Vincent. *Les Cris de Paris ou le peuple travesti: les représentations des petits métiers parisiens (XVIe–XVIIIe siècles)* (Paris: Éditions de la Sorbonne, 2014).

Montenach, Anne. *Espaces et pratiques du commerce alimentaire à Lyon au XVIIe siècle* (Grenoble: Presses universitaires de Grenoble, 2009).

Morrison, Kathryn A. *English Shops and Shopping: An Architectural History* (New Haven: Yale University Press, 2003).

Muldrew, Craig. *Food, Energy and the Creation of Industriousness: Work and Material Culture in Agrarian England, 1550–1780* (Cambridge: Cambridge University Press, 2011).

Münch, Ole. 'Henry Mayhew and the Street Traders of Victorian London—A Cultural Exchange with Material Consequences'. *London Journal* 43, no. 1 (2018): pp. 53–71. <https://doi.org/10.1080/03058034.2017.1333761>.

Nead, Lynda. *Victorian Babylon: People, Streets and Images in Nineteenth-Century London* (London: Yale University Press, 2005).

Nevola, Fabrizio. *Street Life in Renaissance Italy* (New Haven: Yale University Press, 2020).

Nord, Deborah Epstein. 'The City as Theater: From Georgian to Early Victorian London'. *Victorian Studies* 31, no. 2 (1988): pp. 159–88. <https://www.jstor.org/stable/3827968>.

Nord, Deborah Epstein. 'The Social Explorer as Anthropologist: Victorian Travellers among the Urban Poor'. In *Visions of the Modern City: Essays in History, Art and Literature*, edited by William Sharpe and Leonard Wallock (Baltimore: Johns Hopkins University Press, 1987), pp. 122–34.

Nord, Deborah Epstein. *Walking the Victorian Streets: Women, Representation and the City* (Ithaca, NY: Cornell University Press, 1995).

O'Dea, William T. *The Social History of Lighting* (London: Routledge and Kegan Paul, 1958).

Ogborn, Miles. *Spaces of Modernity: London's Geographies, 1680–1780* (New York: Guildford Press, 1998).

One of the Crowd. 'Covent Garden Market'. In *Toilers in London* (London: Diprose and Bateman, 1883), pp. 72–7.

One of the Crowd. 'Watercress Sellers'. In *Toilers in London* (London: Diprose and Bateman, 1883), pp. 33–8.

One of the Crowd. 'Working Dogs'. In *Toilers in London* (London: Diprose and Bateman, 1883), pp. 116–22.

Paley, Ruth, ed. *Justice in Eighteenth-Century Hackney: The Justicing Notebook of Henry Norris and the Hackney Petty Sessions Book* (London, 1991). <https://www.british-history.ac.uk/london-record-soc/vol28>.

Panayi, Panikos. *Fish and Chips: A History* (London: Reaktion, 2014).

Parasecoli, Fabio. 'Eating on the Go in Italy: Between *cibo di strada* and Street Food'. *Food, Culture & Society* 24, no. 1 (2021): pp. 112–26. <https://doi.org/10.1080/15528014.2020.1859901>.

Parham, Susan. *Market Place: Food Quarters, Design and Urban Renewal in London* (Newcastle upon Tyne: Cambridge Scholars Publishing, 2012).

Parker, Kenneth L. *The English Sabbath: A Study of Doctrine and Discipline from the Reformation to the Civil War* (Cambridge: Cambridge University Press, 1988).

Pennell, Sara. *The Birth of the English Kitchen, 1600–1850* (London: Bloomsbury, 2016).

Pennell, Sara. ' "Great Quantities of Gooseberry Pye and Baked Clod of Beef": Victualling and Eating Out in Early Modern London'. In *Londinopolis: Essays in the Cultural and Social History of Early Modern London*, edited by Paul Griffiths and Mark S. R. Jenner (Manchester: Manchester University Press, 2000), pp. 228–49.

Pennington, David. 'Taking It to the Streets: Hucksters and Huckstering in Early Modern Southampton, circa 1550–1652'. *Sixteenth Century Journal* 39, no. 3 (2008): pp. 657–79. <https://doi.org/10.2307/20478999>.

Pepys, Samuel. *The Diary of Samuel Pepys*, edited by Robert Latham and William Matthews. 11 vols (London: Bell, 1970).

Picker, John M. 'Aural Anxieties and the Advent of Modernity'. In *The Victorian World*, edited by Martin Hewitt (London: Routledge, 2012), pp. 603–18.

Picker, John M. 'The Soundproof Study: Victorian Professionals, Work Space, and Urban Noise'. *Victorian Studies* 42, no. 3 (1999/2000): pp. 427–53.

Picker, John M. *Victorian Soundscapes* (Oxford: Oxford University Press, 2003).

Pickering, Danby, ed. *The Statutes at Large, From the Thirty-Second Year of K. Hen. VIII. To the Seventh Year of K. Edw. VI. Inclusive* (Cambridge, 1763).

Pinchbeck, Ivy. *Women Workers and the Industrial Revolution 1750–1850* (London: Frank Cass and Co., 1969).

Porter, Roy. *London: A Social History* (London: Penguin, 1996).

Porter, Stephen. *The Great Fire of London* (Godalming: Bramley Books, 1998).

Power, Michael. 'Shadwell: The Development of a London Suburban Community in the Seventeenth Century'. *London Journal* 4, no. 1 (1978): pp. 29–46. <https://doi.org/10.1179/ldn.1978.4.1.29>.

Price, Chris, ed. *Music from the Canterbury Catch Club* (Canterbury: Canterbury Christ Church University, 2015).

Quilley, Geoff. 'The Analysis of Deceit: Sandby's Satires Against Hogarth'. In *Paul Sandby: Picturing Britain*, edited by John Bonehill and Stephen Daniels (London: Royal Academy of Arts, 2009), pp. 39–47.

Raines, Robert. *Marcellus Laroon* (London: Routledge and Kegan Paul for the Paul Mellon Foundation for British Art, 1966).

Raithby, John, ed. *Statutes of the Realm: Volume 5, 1628–80* (London, 1819). <https://www.british-history.ac.uk/statutes-realm/vol5>.

Raithby, John, ed. *Statutes of the Realm: Volume 7, 1695–1701* (London, 1820). <https://www.british-history.ac.uk/statutes-realm/vol7>.

Rappaport, Erika Diane. *Shopping for Pleasure: Women in the Making of London's West End* (Princeton: Princeton University Press, 2000).

Rasmussen, Anthony W. 'Sales and Survival within the Contested Acoustic Territories of Mexico City's Historic Centre'. *Ethnomusicology Forum* 26, no. 3 (2017): pp. 307–30. <https://doi.org/10.1080/17411912.2018.1423574>.

Reddaway, T. F. *The Rebuilding of London after the Great Fire* (London: E. Arnold, 1951).

Reeves, Maud Pember. *Round About a Pound a Week* (London: G. Bell and Sons, 1913).

Reinke-Williams, Tim. *Women, Work and Sociability in Early Modern London* (Basingstoke: Palgrave Macmillan, 2014).

Rendell, Jane. 'Displaying Sexuality: Gendered Identities and the Early Nineteenth-Century Street'. In *Images of the Street: Planning, Identity and Control in Public Space*, edited by Nicholas R. Fyfe (London: Routledge, 1998), pp. 74–90.

Reynolds, Elaine A. *Before the Bobbies: The Night Watch and Police Reform in Metropolitan London, 1720–1830* (Stanford, CA: Stanford University Press, 1998).

Rich, Rachel. *Bourgeois Consumption: Food, Space and Identity in London and Paris, 1850–1914* (Manchester: Manchester University Press, 2011).

Richardson, R. C. *Household Servants in Early Modern England* (Manchester: Manchester University Press, 2010).

Riello, Giorgio. 'The Material Culture of Walking: Spaces of Methodologies in the Long Eighteenth Century'. In *Everyday Objects: Medieval and Early Modern Material Culture and Its Meanings*, edited by Tara Hamling and Catherine Richardson (Farnham: Ashgate, 2010), pp. 40–55.

Ritson, Joseph, ed. *A Digest of the Proceedings of the Court Leet of the Manor and Liberty of the Savoy, Parcel of the Duchy of Lancaster, in the County of Middlesex; From the Year 1682 to the Present Time* (London, 1789).

Roche, Sophie von la. *Sophie in London 1786, Being the Diary of Sophie v. La Roche*. Translated by Clare Williams (London: Jonathan Cape, 1933).

Roever, Sally, and Caroline Skinner. 'Street Vendors and Cities'. *Environment and Urbanization* 28, no. 2 (2016): pp. 359–74. <https://doi.org/10.1177/0956247816653898>.

Rosales, Rocío. *Fruteros: Street Vending, Illegality, and Ethnic Community in Los Angeles* (Oakland, CA: University of California Press, 2020).

Ross, Ellen. *Love & Toil: Motherhood in Outcast London, 1870–1918* (Oxford: Oxford University Press, 1993).

Sacks, David Harris. *The Widening Gate: Bristol and the Atlantic Economy, 1450–1750* (Berkeley: University of California Press, 1991).

Sala, George Augustus. 'The Cries of London'. *English Illustrated* 10 (October 1892–3): pp. 125–35.

Sala, George Augustus. *Gaslight and Daylight, with Some London Scenes They Shine Upon* (London: Tinsley Brothers, 1872).

Sala, George Augustus. 'Locomotion in London'. *Gentleman's Magazine*, 12 (June 1874): pp. 453–65.

Saunders, Ann, ed. *The Royal Exchange* (London: London Topographical Society, 1997).

Schafer, R. Murray. *The Soundscape: Our Sonic Environment and the Tuning of the World* (Rochester, VT: Destiny Books, 1977).

Schmiechen, James, and Kenneth Carls. *The British Market Hall: A Social and Architectural History* (New Haven: Yale University Press, 1999).

Schofield, John, ed. *The London Surveys of Ralph Treswell* (London: London Topographical Society, 1987).

Schwarz, L. D. *London in the Age of Industrialisation: Entrepreneurs, Labour Force and Living Conditions, 1700–1850* (Cambridge: Cambridge University Press, 1992).

Schwarz, Leonard. 'English Servants and Their Employers During the Eighteenth and Nineteenth Centuries'. *Economic History Review* 52, no. 2 (1999): pp. 236–56. <http://www.jstor.org/stable/2599938>.

Scola, Roger. *Feeding the Victorian City: The Food Supply of Manchester, 1770–1870*, edited by W. A. Armstrong and Pauline Scola (Manchester: Manchester University Press, 1992).

Sennett, Richard. *Flesh and Stone: The Body and the City in Western Civilization* (London: Faber & Faber, 1994).

Serjeantson, D., and C. M. Woolgar. 'Fish Consumption in Medieval England'. In *Food in Medieval England: Diet and Nutrition*, edited by C. M. Woolgar, D. Serjeantson, and T. Waldron (Oxford: Oxford University Press, 2006), pp. 102–30.

Shammas, Carole. *The Pre-Industrial Consumer in England and America* (Oxford: Clarendon Press, 1990).

Sharma, Jayeeta. 'Food Cries, Historical City Sounds, and the Twentieth Century Silencing of Street Vendors'. *Food, Culture & Society* 24, no. 1 (2021): pp. 16–30. <https://doi.org/10.1080/15528014.2020.1859923>.

Shaw, Gareth. 'The Role of Retailing in the Urban Economy'. In *The Structure of Nineteenth Century Cities*, edited by James H. Johnson and Colin G. Pooley (Beckenham: Croom Helm, 1982), pp. 171–94.

Shaw, Gareth, and M. T. Wild. 'Retail Patterns in the Victorian City'. *Transactions of the Institute of British Geographers* 4, no. 2 (1979): pp. 278–91. <https://doi.org/10.2307/622039>.

Shaw, George Bernard. *Pygmalion: A Romance in Five Acts* (Harmondsworth: Penguin, 1941).

Shepard, Alexandra. *Accounting for Oneself: Worth, Status and the Social Order in Early Modern England* (Oxford: Oxford University Press, 2015).

Shepard, Alexandra. 'Crediting Women in the Early Modern English Economy'. *History Workshop Journal* 79, no. 1 (2015): pp. 1–24. <https://doi.org/10.1093/hwj/dbv002>.

Shepard, Alexandra. 'Poverty, Labour and the Language of Social Description in Early Modern England'. *Past & Present* 201, no. 1 (2008): pp. 51–95. <https://doi.org/10.1093/pastj/gtn004>.

Shepard, Alexandra, and Judith Spicksley. 'Worth, Age, and Social Status in Early Modern England'. *Economic History Review* 64, no. 2 (2011): pp. 493–530. <https://doi.org/10.1111/j.1468-0289.2010.00533.x>.

Sheppard, F. H. W. *Local Government in St. Marylebone, 1688–1835: A Study of the Vestry and the Turnpike Trust* (London: Athlone Press, 1958).

Sheppard, F. H. W., ed. *Survey of London: Volume 35, The Theatre Royal, Drury Lane, and the Royal Opera House, Covent Garden* (London, 1970). <http://www.british-history.ac.uk/survey-london/vol35>.

Shesgreen, Sean. *Images of the Outcast: The Urban Poor in the Cries of London* (Manchester: Manchester University Press, 2002).

Shesgreen, Sean. 'William Hogarth's "Enraged Musician" and the Cries of London'. In *Hogarth: Representing Nature's Machines*, edited by David Bindman, Frédéric Ogée, and Peter Wagner (Manchester: Manchester University Press, 2001), pp. 125–45.

Shoemaker, Robert. 'Gendered Spaces: Patterns of Mobility and Perceptions of London's Geography, 1660–1750'. In *Imagining Early Modern London: Perceptions and Portrayals of the City from Stow to Strype, 1598–1720*, edited by J. F. Merritt (Cambridge: Cambridge University Press, 2001), pp. 144–65.

Shoemaker, Robert B. 'Reforming the City: The Reformation of Manners Campaign in London, 1590–1738'. In *Stilling the Grumbling Hive: The Response to Social and Economic Problems in England, 1689–1750*, edited by Lee Davison, Tim Hitchcock, Tim Keirn, and Robert B. Shoemaker (Stroud: Sutton, 1992), pp. 99–120.

Shoemaker, Robert B. 'Public Spaces, Private Disputes? Fights and Insults on London's Streets, 1660–1800'. In *The Streets of London: From the Great Fire to the Great Stink*, edited by Tim Hitchcock and Heather Shore (London: Rivers Oram Press, 2003), pp. 54–68.

Simonton, Deborah. 'Apprenticeship: Training and Gender in Eighteenth-Century England'. In *Markets and Manufacture in Early Industrial Europe*, edited by Maxine Berg (London: Routledge, 1991), pp. 227–58.

Simonton, Deborah. 'Widows and Wenches: Single Women in Eighteenth-Century Urban Economies'. In *Female Agency in the Urban Economy: Gender in European Towns, 1640–1830*, edited by Deborah Simonton and Anne Montenach (New York: Routledge, 2013), pp. 93–115.

Simpson, Claude M. *The British Broadside Ballad and Its Music* (New Brunswick, NJ: Rutgers University Press, 1966).

Sims, George R. *How the Poor Live* (London: Chatto and Windus, 1883).

Sims, George R. 'Kerbstone London'. In *Living London*, edited by George R. Sims (London: Cassell and Company, 1902), vol. 1: pp. 378–84.

Skelton, Leona J. *Sanitation in Urban Britain, 1560–1700* (Abingdon: Routledge, 2016).

Smith, Bruce. *The Acoustic World of Early Modern England* (Chicago: University of Chicago Press, 1999).

Smith, Bruce. 'What Means This Noise?' In *'Noyses, Sounds, and Sweet Aires': Music in Early Modern England*, edited by Jessie Ann Owens (Washington, DC: Folger Shakespeare Library, 2006), pp. 20–31.

Smith, Colin. 'The Wholesale and Retail Markets of London, 1660–1840'. *Economic History Review* 55, no. 1 (2002): pp. 31–50. <https://doi.org/10.1111/1468-0289.00213>.

Smith, Colin Stephen. 'The Market Place and the Market's Place in London, c.1660–1840' (PhD, University College London, 1999).

Smith, Drew. *Oyster: A World History* (Stroud: History Press, 2010).

Smith, John Thomas. *The Cries of London: Exhibiting Several of the Itinerant Traders of Antient and Modern Times* (London: John Bowyer Nicholas and Son, 1839).

Smollett, Tobias. *The Expedition of Humphrey Clinker*, edited by Lewis M. Knapp (Oxford: Oxford University Press, 1984).

Snell, K. D. M. *Annals of the Labouring Poor: Social Change and Agrarian England, 1660–1900* (Cambridge: Cambridge University Press, 1985).

Society of Arts, 'Proceedings of the Society: Food Committee'. *Journal of the Society of Arts* 16, no. 788 (1867): pp. 91–102. <https://www.jstor.org/stable/41323861>.

Society of Arts, 'Proceedings of the Society: Food Committee'. *Journal of the Society of Arts* 16, no. 790 (1868): pp. 121–6. <https://www.jstor.org/stable/41334681>.

Society of Arts. 'Traction on Roads'. *Journal of the Society of Arts* 23, no. 1179 (1875): 689–722. <https://www.jstor.org/stable/41335074>.

Spence, Craig. *Accidents and Violent Death in Early Modern London* (Woodbridge: Boydell Press, 2016).

Spence, Craig. *London in the 1690s: A Social Atlas* (London: Centre for Metropolitan History, Institute of Historical Research, 2000).

Sponza, Lucio. 'Italian "Penny Ice-Men" in Victorian London'. In *Food in the Migrant Experience*, edited by Anne J. Kershen (Aldershot: Ashgate, 2002), pp. 17–41.

Spranger, John. *A Proposal or Plan for An Act of Parliament for the Better Paving, Lighting and Cleansing the Streets, Lanes, Courts, Alleys, and Other Open Passages, and for Removing of Nusances as Well within the Several Parishes of the City and Liberty of Westminster, as of St Mary Le Bone, St Giles's in the Fields, St George the Martyr, St George Bloomsbury, That Part of St Andrew Holborn Which Lies in the County of Middlesex, the Several Liberties of the Rolls and Savoy, and That Part of the Duchy of Lancaster Which Lies in the County of Middlesex* (London, 1754).

Spufford, Margaret. *The Great Reclothing of Rural England: Petty Chapmen and Their Wares in the Seventeenth Century* (London: Hambledon Press, 1984).

Statistical Society of London, 'Police of the Metropolis'. *Journal of the Statistical Society of London* 1, no. 2 (1838): pp. 96–103. <https://doi.org/10.2307/2338065>.

Statistical Society of London, 'Report to the Council of the Statistical Society of London from a Committee of Its Fellows Appointed to Make an Investigation into the State of the Poorer Classes in St. George's in the East'. *Journal of the Statistical Society of London* 11, no. 3 (1848): pp. 193–249. <https://doi.org/10.2307/2337956>.

Stedman Jones, Gareth. 'The "Cockney" and the Nation, 1780–1988'. In *Metropolis London: Histories and Representations since 1800*, edited by David Feldman and Gareth Stedman Jones (London: Routledge, 1989), pp. 272–324.

Stedman Jones, Gareth. *Outcast London: A Study in the Relationship Between Classes in Victorian Society* (Oxford: Clarendon Press, 1971).

Stenton, Alison. 'Spatial Stories: Movement in the City and Cultural Geography'. In *Walking the Streets of Eighteenth-Century London: John Gay's Trivia (1716)*, edited by Clare Brant and Susan E. Whyman (Oxford: Oxford University Press, 2007), pp. 62–73.

Stephenson, Judy Z. ' "Real" Wages? Contractors, Workers, and Pay in London Building Trades, 1650–1800'. *Economic History Review* 71, no. 1 (2018): pp. 106–32. <https://doi.org/10.1111/ehr.12491>.

Stern, W. M. 'Fish Marketing in London in the First Half of the Eighteenth Century'. In *Trade, Government and Economy in Pre-Industrial England: Essays Presented to F. J. Fisher*, edited by D. C. Coleman and A. H. John (London: Weidenfeld and Nicolson, 1976), pp. 68–77.

Stern, W. M. *The Porters of London* (London: Longmans, Green and Co., 1960).

Stern, Walter M. 'The Baroness's Market: The History of a Noble Failure'. *Guildhall Miscellany* 2, no. 8 (1966): pp. 353–66.

Sterne, Jonathan. *The Audible Past: Cultural Origins of Sound Reproduction* (Durham, NC: Duke University Press, 2003).

Sterne, Jonathan. 'Sonic Imaginations'. In *The Sound Studies Reader*, edited by Jonathan Sterne (Abingdon: Routledge, 2012), pp. 1–17.

Stobart, Jon. *Sugar and Spice: Grocers and Groceries in Provincial England, 1650–1830* (Oxford: Oxford University Press, 2012).

Stow, John. *A Survey of London. Reprinted from the Text of 1603*, edited by Charles Lethbridge Kingsford. 2 vols (Oxford: Clarendon Press, 1908).

Styles, John. *The Dress of the People: Everyday Fashion in Eighteenth-Century England* (New Haven: Yale University Press, 2007).

Swift, Jonathan. 'A Description of a City Shower'. In *Jonathan Swift: The Complete Poems*, edited by Pat Rogers (Harmondsworth: Penguin, 1983), pp. 113–14.

Swift, Jonathan. *Journal to Stella*, edited by Harold Williams. 2 vols (Oxford: Clarendon Press, 1948).

Taithe, Bernard. *The Essential Mayhew: Representing and Communicating the Poor* (London: Rivers Oram Press, 1996).

Taverner, Charles Robert. 'Selling Food in the Streets of London, c.1600–1750' (PhD, Birkbeck, University of London, 2019).

Taverner, Charlie. 'Consider the Oyster Seller: Street Hawkers and Gendered Stereotypes in Early Modern London'. *History Workshop Journal* 88 (2019): pp. 1–23. <https://doi.org/10.1093/hwj/dbz032>.

Taverner, Charlie. 'Moral Marketplaces: Regulating the Food Markets of Late Elizabethan and Early Stuart London'. *Urban History* 48, no. 4 (2021): pp. 608–24. <https://doi.org/10.1017/S0963926820000450>.

Taylor, Millie. 'Lionel Bart: British Vernacular Musical Theatre'. In *The Oxford Handbook of the British Musical*, edited by Robert Gordon and Olaf Jubin (Oxford: Oxford University Press, 2017), pp. 483–506.

Thick, Malcolm. *The Neat House Gardens: Early Market Gardening Around London* (Totnes: Prospect Books, 1998).

Thirsk, Joan. *Food in Early Modern England: Phases, Fads, Fashions 1500–1760* (London: Hambledon Continuum, 2007).

Thomas, Keith. 'Numeracy in Early Modern England'. *Transactions of the Royal Historical Society* 37 (1987): pp. 103–32. <https://doi.org/10.2307/3679153>.

Thompson, Emily. *The Soundscape of Modernity: Architectural Acoustics and the Cultural of Listening in America, 1900–1933* (Cambridge, MA: MIT Press, 2002).

Thomson, John, and Adolphe Smith. *Street Life in London* (London: Sampson Low, Marston, Searle, and Rivington, 1877).

Tinker, Irene. *Street Foods: Urban Food and Employment in Developing Countries* (Oxford: Oxford University Press, 1997).

Torode, Angeliki. 'Trends in Fruit Consumption'. In *Our Changing Fare: Two Hundred Years of British Food Habits*, edited by T. C. Barker, J. C. McKenzie, and John Yudkin (London: Macgibbon and Kee, 1966), pp. 115–34.

Truax, Barry. *Acoustic Communication* (Norwood, NJ: Ablex Publishing, 1984).

Trusler, John. *The London Adviser and Guide: Containing Every Instruction and Information Useful and Necessary to Persons Living in London and Coming to Reside There: In Order to Enable Them to Enjoy Security and Tranquillity, and Conduct Their Domestic Affairs with Prudence and Economy* (London: 1768).

Tuer, Andrew M. *Old London Street Cries and the Cries of To-Day* (London: Field and Tuer, Leadenhall Press, 1885).

Turnbull, George. 'Lighting'. In *London in the Nineteenth Century*, edited by Walter Besant (London: Adam and Charles Black, 1909), pp. 317–26.

Turvey, Ralph. 'Horse Traction in Victorian London'. *Journal of Transport History* 26, no. 2 (2005): pp. 38–59. <https://doi.org/10.7227/TJTH.26.2.3>.

Turvey, Ralph. 'Street Mud, Dust and Noise'. *London Journal* 21, no. 2 (1996): pp. 131–48. <https://doi.org/10.1179/ldn.1996.21.2.131>.

Val, Dorothy de. *In Search of Song: The Life and Times of Lucy Broadwood* (Farnham: Ashgate, 2011).

Vickery, Amanda. 'An Englishman's Home Is His Castle? Thresholds, Boundaries and Privacies in the Eighteenth-Century London House'. *Past & Present* 199, no. 1 (2008): pp. 147–73. <https://doi.org/10.1093/pastj/gtn006>.

Vickery, Amanda. 'Golden Age to Separate Spheres? A Review of the Categories and Chronology of English Women's History'. *Historical Journal* 36, no. 2 (1993): pp. 383–414. <http://www.jstor.org/stable/2639654>.

Waddell, Brodie. *God, Duty and Community in English Economic Life, 1660–1720* (Woodbridge: Boydell and Brewer, 2012).

Walkowitz, Judith R. 'Going Public: Shopping, Street Harassment, and Streetwalking in Late Victorian London'. *Representations* 62 (1998): pp. 1–30.

Walkowitz, Judith R. *Nights Out: Life in Cosmopolitan London* (New Haven: Yale University Press, 2012).

Walkowitz, Judith R. *Prostitution and Victorian Society: Women, Class, and the State* (Cambridge: Cambridge University Press, 1980).

Wallis, Patrick. 'Consumption, Retailing, and Medicine in Early-Modern London'. *Economic History Review* 61, no. 1 (2008): pp. 26–53. <http://www.jstor.org/stable/40057555>.

Walsh, Claire. 'Shop Design and the Display of Goods in Eighteenth-Century London'. *Journal of Design History* 8, no. 3 (1995): pp. 157–76. <https://www.jstor.org/stable/1316030>.

Walsh, Claire. 'Stalls, Bulks, Shops and Long-Term Change in Seventeenth- and Eighteenth-Century England'. In *The Landscape of Consumption: Shopping Streets and Cultures in Western Europe, 1600–1900*, edited by Jan Hein Furnée and Clé Lesger (Basingstoke: Palgrave Macmillan, 2014), pp. 37–56.

Walton, John K. *Fish and Chips and the British Working Class, 1870–1940* (London: Leicester University Press, 1992).

Walvin, James. *Fruits of Empire: Exotic Produce and British Taste, 1660–1800* (Basingstoke: Macmillan, 1997).

Ward, Ned. *The London Spy Compleat, In Eighteen Parts* (London: Casanova Society, 1924).

Warde, Alan, and Lydia Martens. *Eating Out: Social Differentiation, Consumption and Pleasure* (Cambridge: Cambridge University Press, 2000).

Watt, Paul. 'Street Music in London in the Nineteenth Century: "Evidence" from Charles Dickens, Charles Babbage and Lucy Broadwood'. *Nineteenth-Century Music Review* 15, no. 1 (2018): pp. 9–22. <https://doi.org/10.1017/S1479409817000040>.

Watt, Tessa. *Cheap Print and Popular Piety 1550–1640* (Cambridge: Cambridge University Press, 1994).

Webber, Ronald. *Covent Garden: Mud-Salad Market* (London: J. M. Dent and Sons, 1969).

Webber, Ronald. *Market Gardening: The History of Commercial Flower, Fruit and Vegetable Growing* (Newton Abbot: David and Charles, 1972).

Weir, Robin. 'Penny Licks and Hokey Pokey, Ice Cream Before the Cone'. In *Oxford Symposium on Food and Cookery 1991: Public Eating: Proceedings*, edited by Harlan Walker (London: Prospect Books, 1991), pp. 295–300.

White, Eileen, ed. *Feeding a City: York: The Provision of Food from Roman Times to the Beginning of the Twentieth Century* (Totnes: Prospect Books, 2000).

White, Jerry. *A Great and Monstrous Thing: London in the Eighteenth Century* (Cambridge, MA: Harvard University Press, 2013).

White, Jerry. *London in the Nineteenth Century: A Human Awful Wonder of God* (London: Vintage, 2008).

White, Jerry. *London in the Twentieth Century: A City and Its People* (London: Vintage, 2008).

Whittle, Jane, and Mark Hailwood. 'The Gender Division of Labour in Early Modern England'. *Economic History Review* 73, no. 1 (2020): pp. 3–32. <https://doi.org/10.1111/ehr.12821>.

Whitworth, Charles. *A Plan for the More Easy and Speedy Execution of the Laws Relating to the New Paving, Cleansing and Lighting the Streets of Westminster* (London, 1762).

Williams, Juliet, Lucy E. Broadwood, and A. G. Gilchrist. 'London Street Cries'. *Journal of the Folk-Song Society* 6, no. 22 (1919): pp. 55–70. <https://www.jstor.org/stable/4434063>.

Wilson, Beckles. 'Midnight London'. In *Living London*, edited by George R. Sims (London: Cassell and Company, 1902), vol. 1: pp. 125–31.

Wilson, Elizabeth. *The Sphinx in the City: Urban Life, the Control of Disorder, and Women* (London: Virago, 1991).

Wilson, Eric. 'Plagues, Fairs, and Street Cries: Sounding Out Society and Space in Early Modern London'. *Modern Language Studies* 25, no. 3 (1995): pp. 1–42. <https://doi.org/10.2307/3195370>.

Winter, James. *London's Teeming Streets, 1830–1914* (Abingdon: Routledge, 1993).

Wohl, Anthony S. *Endangered Lives: Public Health in Victorian Britain* (London: J. M. Dent and Sons, 1983).

Wohl, Anthony S. *The Eternal Slum: Housing and Social Policy in Victorian London* (New Brunswick, NJ: Transaction, 2002).

Womack, Elizabeth Coggin. 'Walking as Labour in Henry Mayhew's London'. In *Walking Histories, 1800–1914*, edited by Chad Bryant, Arthur Burns, and Paul Readman (London: Palgrave Macmillan, 2016), pp. 115–37.

Woolgar, C. M. 'Meat and Dairy Products in Late Medieval England'. In *Food in Medieval England: Diet and Nutrition*, edited by C. M. Woolgar, D. Serjeantson, and T. Waldron (Oxford: Oxford University Press, 2006), pp. 88–101.

Woolley, Hannah. *The Cook's Guide: Or, Rare Receipts for Cookery* (London, 1664).

Wrigley, E. A. 'Urban Growth in Early Modern England: Food, Fuel and Transport'. *Past & Present* 225, no. 1 (2014): pp. 79–112. <https://doi.org/10.1093/pastj/gtu032>.

You, Xuesheng. 'Women's Labour Force Participation in Nineteenth-Century England and Wales: Evidence from the 1881 Census Enumerators' Books'. *Economic History Review* 73, no. 1 (2020): pp. 106–33. <https://doi.org/10.1111/ehr.12876>.

Index